Tokyo
Before Tokyo

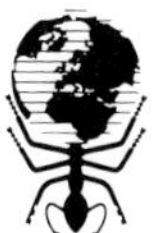

Tokyo Before Tokyo

Power and Magic in the Shogun's City of Edo

Timon Screech

REAKTION BOOKS

Published by Reaktion Books Ltd
Unit 32, Waterside
44–48 Wharf Road
London N1 7UX, UK
www.reaktionbooks.co.uk

First published 2020
First paperback edition published 2024
Copyright © Timon Screech 2020

The publishers would like to thank The Great Britain Sasakawa
Foundation for its support in the publication of this work

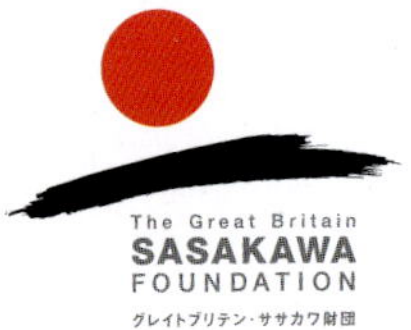

Printed and bound in India by Replika Press Pvt. Ltd

A catalogue record for this book is available from the British Library

ISBN 978 1 78914 955 5

Contents

Introduction **7**

One The Ideal City **25**

Two The Centre of the Shogun's Realm **51**

Three Edo as Sacred Space **89**

Four Reading Edo Castle **129**

Five The City's Poetic Presence **161**

Six A Trip to the Yoshiwara **185**

Epilogue From Edo to Tokyo **211**

References **218**
Selected Sources and Further Reading **228**
General Bibliography **231**
Acknowledgements **236**
Photo Acknowledgements **237**
Index **239**

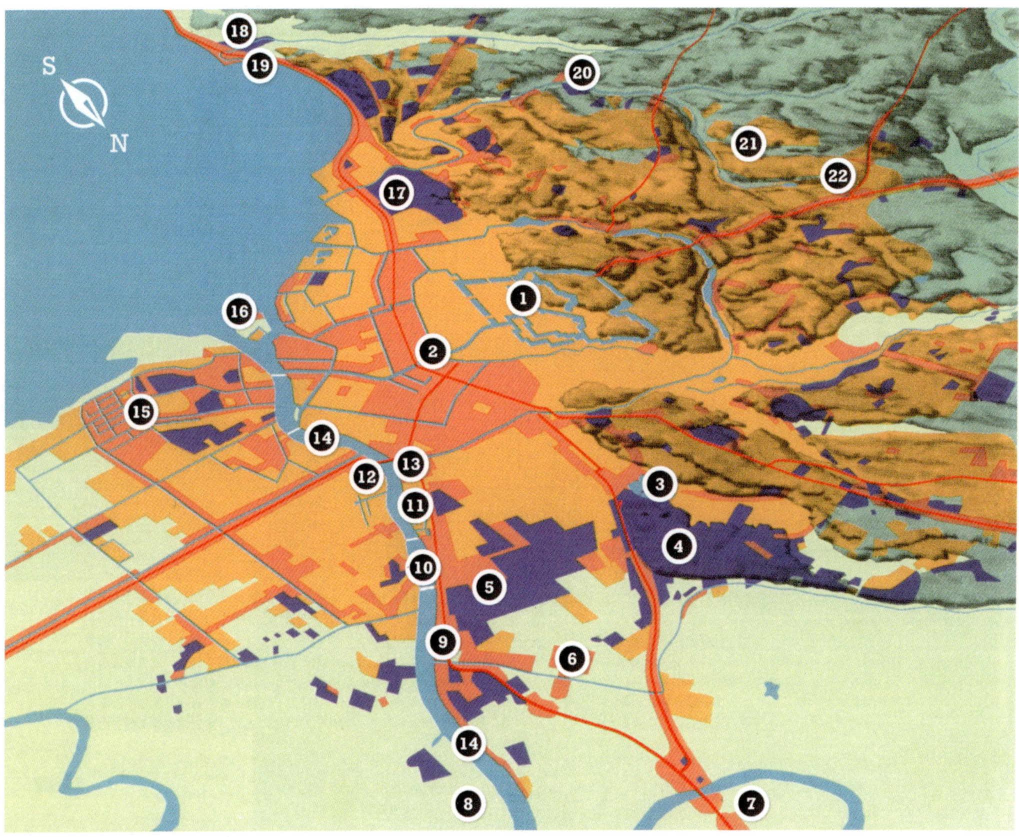

1 Edo, c. 1850. Conjectural view of the shogunal city at its greatest extent. Orange for military (samurai) districts, red for commoners, and purple for religious institutions.

1 Edo Castle
2 Nihon-bashi
3 Shinobazu Pond
4 Kan'ei-ji
5 Sensō-ji ('Asakusa Kannon')
6 Yoshiwara
7 Senju
8 Mokubo-ji
9 Matsuchi-yama
10 Azuma-bashi
11 Kuramae
12 Ryōgoku-bashi
13 Yanagi-bashi
14 Great River (the Sumida)
15 Gohyaku Rakan-ji
16 Tsukada-jima
17 Zōjō-ji
18 Shinagawa
19 Kaian-ji
20 Meguro
21 Yamanote
22 Shinjuku

Introduction

This book is about Tokyo before it became known by that name. Before it became the modern capital of Japan. Until 1868 the city was known as Edo (pronounced to rhyme with 'meadow'). The city of Edo always stood in counterpoise to the more ancient capital of Kyoto – indeed, *kyōto* (properly written with a long first 'o') meant simply 'the capital'. The ancient capital was defined as the place of residence for a shadowy religious-cum-cultural figure known as the *dairi*, literally 'the palace'. In early times his ancestors had ruled Japan under the title of *tennō*, or 'heavenly sovereign'. But the heavenly sovereigns lost power to the military class in the twelfth century, with a concomitant downgrading of their title. The dairi are thus the ancestors of the modern emperors of Japan, who in 1868 reconfigured themselves as monarchs on European constitutional lines. Japan became a modern nation state and the dairi relocated to Edo, which therefore became the capital. Since it lies in the east (*tō*), it was named Tokyo (properly, Tōkyō, the 'eastern capital'). *Kyōto* was then turned into a proper name. Those later processes are discussed in the Epilogue; this book is about Edo. It is the story of Tokyo before Tokyo.

The small town of Edo had existed since time immemorial, and prehistoric artefacts have been found in the area. But it was only in

1590 that Edo became important, when it came under control of the Tokugawa family. This great warrior clan had risen from nothing during the previous decades. They won a huge battle in 1600 and in 1603 were able to persuade the dairi to nominate them to the defunct post of shogun, or chief military figure of the state. Shoguns had to be appointed by the dairi, and they controlled and ran a realm over which the latter had notional ultimate sway, if without actual power; in practice, the dairi's hand was forced, and once they had secured it, shoguns handed on the title hereditarily. Over history there had been three dynasties of shogun. The Tokugawa would be the last.

In the pages that follow, we will assess Edo, its urban planning, its culture and its life. But this is not a chronology, nor a methodical overview of Edo's huge diversity and 250-year history. It is a selection of vignettes that are especially telling about how the city worked and how it was experienced. Part of this story is about the way in which Edo positioned itself against the capital, as we will call it (leaving 'Kyoto' to refer to the city in the modern period). The two metropoles were, and are, almost exactly 500 kilometres apart on an East–West axis. Today, guidebooks refer to Kyoto as 'Japan's ancient imperial capital', and in a way it is. But in our period, 1590–1868, the capital was under warrior control every bit as much as Edo was. The dairi was no 'emperor' as we understand the word today. The twin centres of rule and suasion were in actuality both Tokugawa domains.

☙

Japan is an archipelago and an extremely long one. It extends from about 41 degrees to 31 degrees north and covers some 20 degrees of longitude from east to west. Positioned over a map of Europe, the Japanese islands stretch northeast to southwest from about Bucharest to the middle of the Sahara Desert; plotted over the USA, they cover from Boston to the southeast corner of Texas. Japan is also mountainous, with a topography akin to Switzerland. Nowhere in Europe or North America has such a density of peaks and also such a dearth of open spaces to accommodate centres of human habitation. Over the course of history, Japan's few flatlands had been built on. But the area around Edo had not. It lies in the extensive Plains of Musashi, but settlements had remained mostly scattered villages. Being on the coast, the region was home to fishing communities, its position meaning it was also protected from storms: Edo means 'door to the bay'. Yet Edo did not grow. It played no role as a significant centre of any kind and was nothing compared to the great cities of early times – not just the capital, but Nara and Osaka too. In 1590 Edo was a backwater.

It lagged for a reason. Edo was – as Tokyo still is – highly prone to earthquakes. Tremors led to the collapse of buildings, but also, and much worse, the spread of fires as braziers and stoves toppled over. It made no sense to construct buildings of importance here. Earthquakes create tsunamis, and Edo's 'door' was only a partial guard against them. Much of Japan is volcanic, and earthquakes are common in many places. But Edo, specifically, is one of the least seismically stable places on earth.

Apart from the rigours of nature, Japan was repeatedly wracked by civil wars. Edo acquired a castle, like numerous other locations in the country, but only late, in 1457, to be precise. Its seaboard location made Edo potentially strategic, if only as a lookout post. Near the bay and above the generally marshy ground was an outcrop, and the castle was built here. It was far from impregnable, and when besieged in 1524 by Hōjō Ujitsuna, it quickly fell. Below its walls, fishing communities carried on using the sea.

The wide River Sumida meanders along the edge of the Plains of Musashi and empties into the bay here, so Edo had fresh water, too. It happened that a Buddhist temple lay upstream of Edo – on raised land, so protected from floods – with a surrounding hamlet called Asakusa ('shallow grass'). Monks at the temple claimed that their icon was capable of working wonders. The place was a site of local pilgrimage, though the name of the temple indicates it was a lowly affair: Asakusa-dera. The word *tera* or *dera* denotes a Buddhist institution, but it is rare for temples to take simple geographical names. Most have elegant designations derived from theological concepts. The Asakusa-dera, however, would play a key role in Edo's eventual rise.

Edo grew hugely after declaration of the Tokugawa, or Edo, shogunate in 1603. In the course of the seventeenth century, barracks, mansions, religious buildings and sites of popular residence and diversion proliferated. By about 1720 Edo was the world's biggest metropolis, at fully one million inhabitants. Keeping order, bringing in food, removing effluence and maintaining sanitary conditions were massive and continuous struggles. Perhaps the legacy of this is still to be seen in Japanese society. But the physical presence of Edo is almost entirely gone. Not more than a handful of Edo's buildings survive in Tokyo. Most of the castle moats have been filled in. The coastline is utterly altered by reclamation. The base of Edo Castle keep has anomalously endured, along with parts of one or two gates and a few temple halls, but no secular buildings remain. The disasters of the twentieth century do not need reiterating, but long before them, repeated fires had already wiped out the urban fabric again and again. Edo was in a perpetual state of architectural shift. Building was in wood, and timbers had to be replaced anyway. Edo was always like 'grandfather's axe'. But today, in the twenty-first century, Edo, apart from pockets of street layout, is utterly gone. Some historians call Tokyo a 'city of stories'. It has memories, but few objects. This book is not quite so emphatic on this. Here we will fill in the spaces around and between stories, if not quite with concrete structures, then at least with life and experience on the ground. We will unearth, sometimes literally, the forces that shaped the shogun's city and governed its spatial logic. These were twofold and are in the subtitle of this book: power, that is, the enforcement of military security; and magic, or the harnessing of invisible forces. From high to low, Edo residents lived between these two necessities. The shogunate had no idea, in 1603, that it would last for 250 years.

If we are short of built material fabric for this history, we are not lacking in other data. Edo's mobile culture survives quite well, in paintings, prints and printed books (illus. 2). These can be very useful as they are full of urban views. There are written records too. Such texts form major resources for this book. There are diaries and commonplace books (*zuihitsu*), and also comic haiku called *senryū*, which treat the

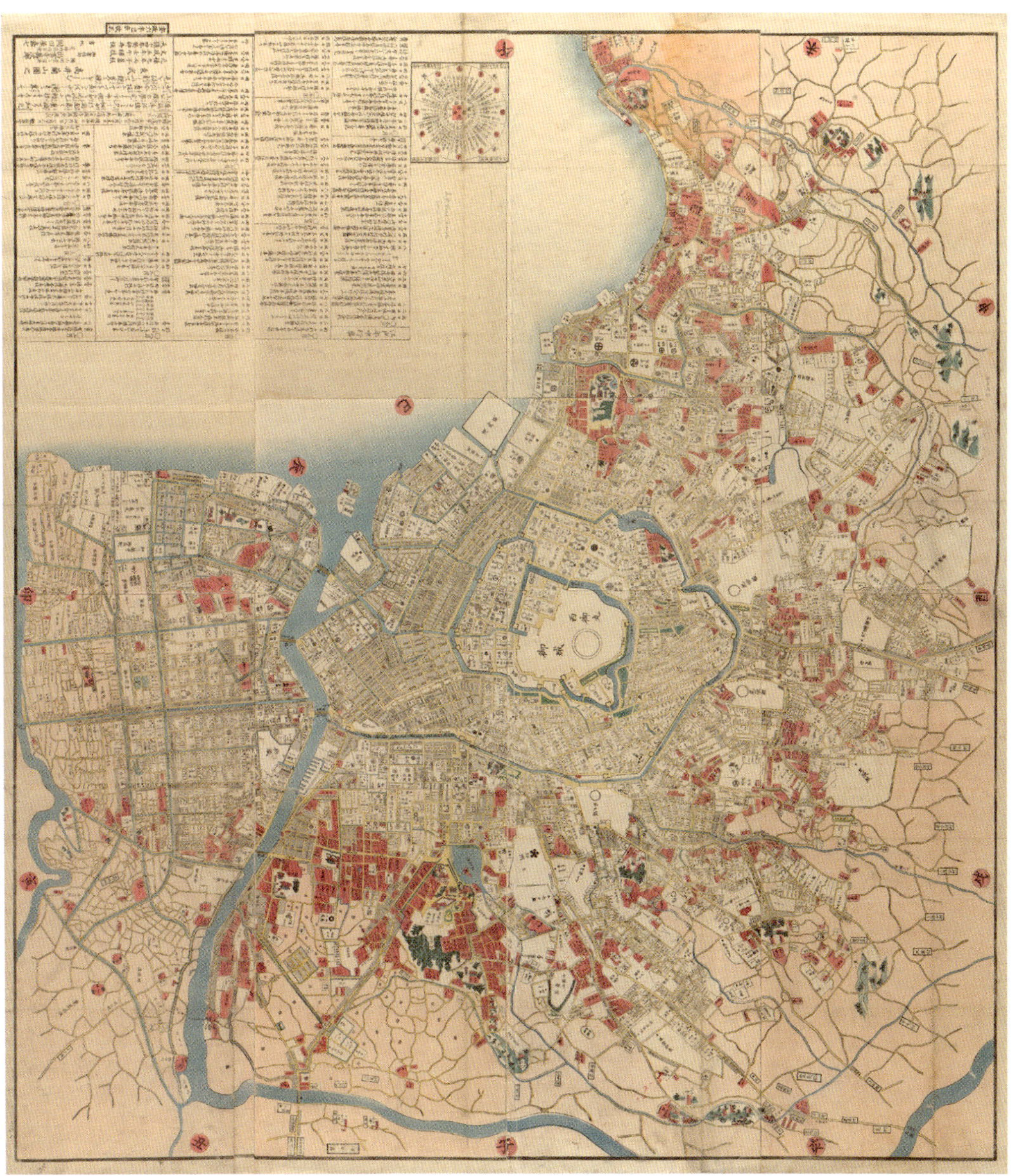

2 Takai Ranzan, map of Edo, 1849 (revised 1861), 117 x 131 cm. One of the most complete printed maps of Edo ever produced. Such works were popularly available, but had to show the castle and other sites of power with due deference, meaning that here they are left blank. The map is rotated, taken from approximately the same angle as illus. 1, with west upwards.

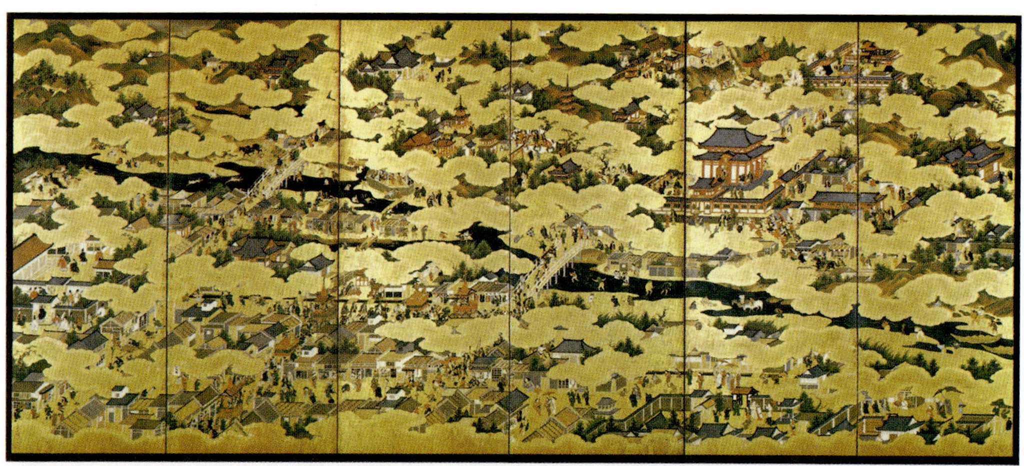
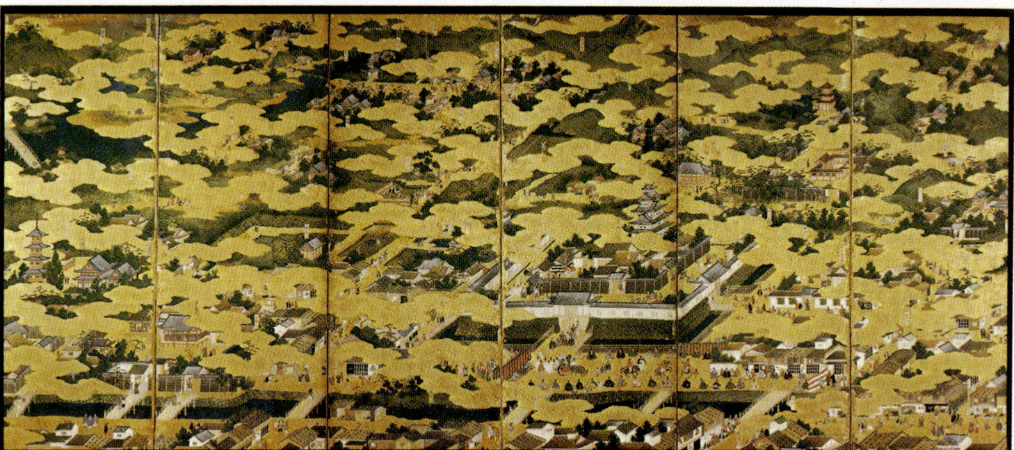

3 Unknown artist, *Scenes in and around the Capital* (*Rakūchū Rakugai-zu*), c. 1660, pair of six-panel screens (*byōbu*), colour and gold on paper, 227 x 152 cm each. Gorgeous paired screens of the capital (Kyoto) became popular in the 16th century, and continued to be made during the Edo Period. The large building to the right is the Great Buddha Hall, matched on the left by Nijō-jo, the shogunal castle. The right-hand screen is above, and the left below.

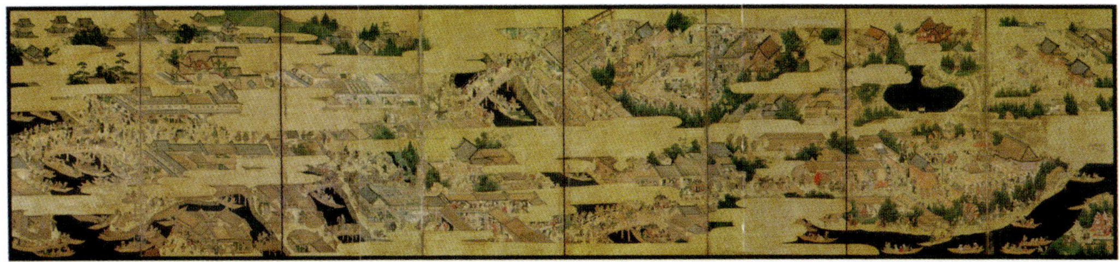

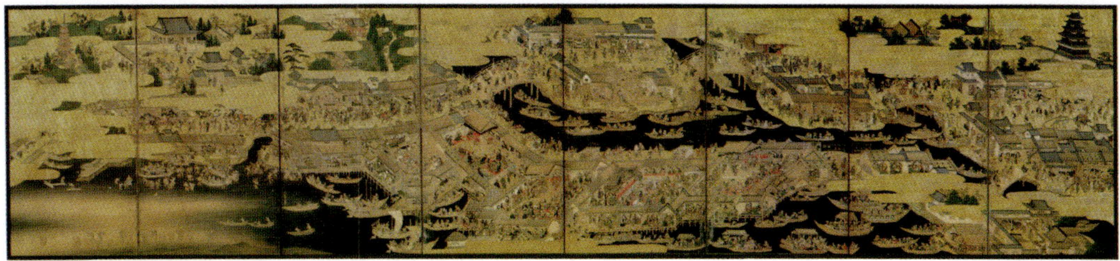

foibles of civic life. Pictures are perhaps more valuable still, though they must be viewed judiciously, being artistic constructions, not factual delineations of the city.

During the longest period of civil wars, which lasted the entire sixteenth century, artists had developed a genre of panoramic renditions of the contested and often burned-out capital. These were painted for maximum impact on large folding screens (*byōbu*). Screens come in pairs, generally with six leaves on either side, each leaf approximately the size of a person. They are imposing, all the more so for often being covered in gold leaf prior to painting. The first one depicting the capital is recorded in 1506, when a courtier excitedly records hearing of this.[1] Extant examples date to somewhat later (illus. 3). From about 1630, one generation into Tokugawa rule, analogous screens of Edo began to be made. Two will be of special use to us in retrieving an understanding of Edo. Both are known today by their current locations, one in the Idemitsu Museum, the other in the National Museum of Japanese History, known as the Rekihaku (illus. 4 and 5). They are crucial documents, though there is little consensus about either. The Idemitsu screens are unusually long, but also curiously lower than commonly found. Edo's great river, the Sumida, runs mostly along the bottom,

4 Unknown artist, *Views of Edo*, early 17th century, pair of eight-panel folding screens, ink, colours and gold on paper, 107.5 × 49.0 cm each. Screens of Edo were seldom made, as it was indelicate to show the shogunal seat so openly. This pair may be the earliest extant. Longer and lower than most screens, the layout replicates that of screens showing the capital, with the main temples to the right and the castle to the left.

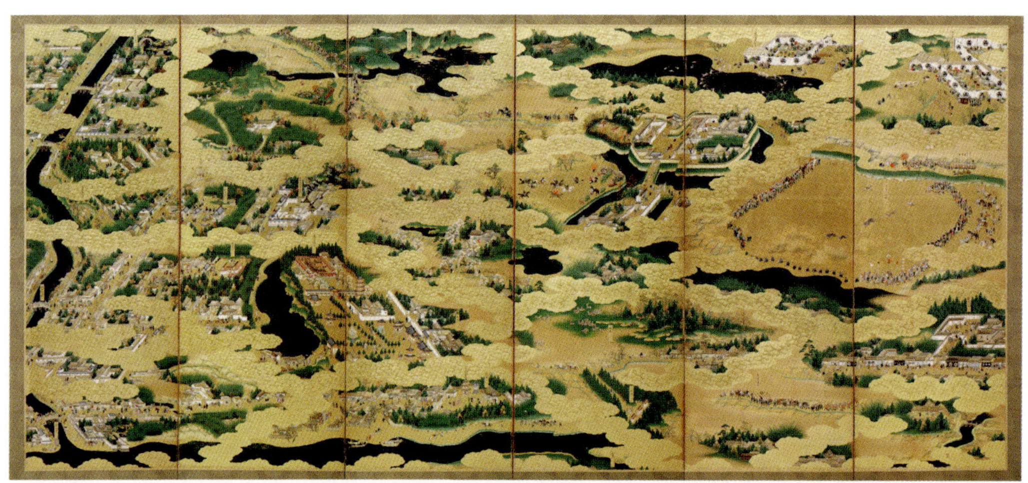

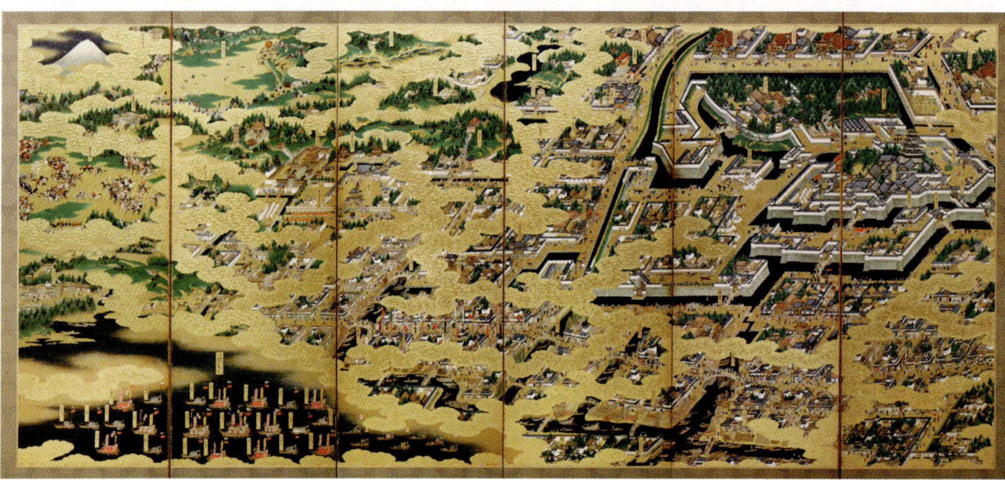

5 Unknown artist, *Views of Edo* (*Edo zu*), 17th century, pair of six-panel folding screens, colour and gold on paper, 366.0 x 162.5 cm each. This magnificent pair must have been made for a very senior official. It includes several portraits of the shogun, Tokugawa Iemitsu, though each time with his face concealed. It may be posthumous, recalling Iemitsu's city, which was lost to the fire in 1657. The right-hand screen is above, and the left below.

and the panorama extends from right to left (as all East Asian art should be read), with Asakusa in Edo's northeast in the top right, and then Edo Bay, in the southwest, at bottom left. This means that Edo Castle sits in the middle, appropriately enough, as Edo's governing centre. It appears in first place on the left screen, rather than in last place on the right, probably as a mark of authority. Peace, plenty, the ability of all people to go about their trades, enjoying the fruits of work, under the shelter of the shogunal regime, seem to be the Idemitsu screens' real theme. The person who commissioned them must have been of high status. Sites of government importance could not be depicted by and for commoners — a matter that erodes the utility of urban paintings and prints, as we shall see.

The date of the Idemitsu screens is contested. The earliest proposals are for about 1630, so well after the Tokugawa were ensconced, peace had come and Edo was beginning to rival the capital in extent and sumptuousness. The date of the screens from the Rekihaku is also contested, though agreed to be later. This is apparent from its inclusion of the figure of the third shogun, Tokugawa Iemitsu, who died in 1651. Naturally, these screens too were made for a person of the highest standing, for otherwise the shogun could certainly not be shown. Most scholars accept that the screens were made retrospectively, after Iemitsu's death. In 1657 a terrible fire destroyed most of Edo. It was perhaps the most devastating of the whole fire-prone city's history. The screens were likely made after that, to hold on to Edo's past under its strong ruler. Iemitsu's sons, who carried the succession into the next century, were not, on the whole, admired. These Rekihaku screens follow the Idemitsu panoramic layout, from Asakusa to the Bay, but are taller, altogether more elegant and elevated in every way. A raised angle of vision looks downwards, while the castle is allocated much more space. Though Iemitsu appears in person, he is always shown concealed, by a hat, umbrella or suchlike.

From a century later, in the 1760s, comes another visual archive. The medium is at the other end of the scale: cheaply produced prints made for common consumption. Edo had a vibrant print culture, with notable subjects including kabuki actors and sex workers – two pillars of the hedonistic environment known as the 'floating worlds' (*ukiyo*). But in the 1760s there suddenly emerged a form of prints showing regular urban landscapes. These were likely to have been aimed at migrant workers or tourists, to be taken away and viewed by regional people unable to visit the shogun's seat. Another viewership would have been Edo residents confined by reason of status or gender and unable to walk the streets freely. These popular urban views do not show sites of power, unless with excruciating levels of deference, but they do attest to a new sense of Edo's place in the world. The comparator is no longer the capital but somewhere further away. Intriguingly, these prints' appearance coincides with the rise of the European cityscape, which stemmed from the popularity of Grand Tours and became widespread in European countries. The wealthy acquired paintings of Rome or Paris done on site, while less affluent, armchair travellers had recourse to prints, mostly published in Augsburg, London and Paris. Examples would have been brought to Japan by Europeans. The Iberians were expelled from Japan definitively in the 1640s, after problems between the shoguns and aggressive Christian missions. Thereafter, the sole Europeans trading into Japan were members of the Dutch East India Company. Their records are also of use in understanding Edo. European prints were cheap at home and made excellent bribes and gifts, and the Company brought many. Such pictures could also have come to Japan via third-party ports, carried by Chinese ships.

One example is worth discussing in a detail. It is not remotely on the artistic level of the Idemitsu or Rekihaku screens but is telling nonetheless. It shows the most visited of European cities, Venice, best captured in the work of Giovanni Antonio Canal, called Canaletto. In 1735 the British Consul arranged for some of his works to be printed in a monochrome set. They were a fraction of the price of a Canaletto painting and so had wider reach. Still expensive, they were then pirated, probably in Germany, in the 1760s, with colour added by hand but at a much lower cost. At least one such found its way to Edo. What is clearly a Canaletto from the consul's set, reprinted, was replicated

6 Antonio Visentini, after Antonio Canal, called Canaletto, 'View from the Church of S Croce to the Holy Discalced Fathers [S Maria di Nazareth]', c. 1735, copperplate etching. This work is untitled and is labelled only in arabic numerals (as No. 2). It must be related to the famous set of twelve images created in 1735 for the British consul to Venice, Joseph Smith, entitled *Prospectus magni canalis venetarum*, but labelled in roman numerals. All were from paintings by Canaletto. Many pirate copies of the Smith set were produced, sometimes hand-coloured, and Toyoharu must have seen one.

7 Utagawa Toyoharu, *The Bell that Rings for 10,000 Leagues in the Dutch Port of Frankai*, c. 1770, multicoloured woodblock print. Toyoharu was uncertain of the location, so he invented a florid title, which is prefaced by the term *uki-e*, 'floating picture', or perspective view. The original is cropped to the left.

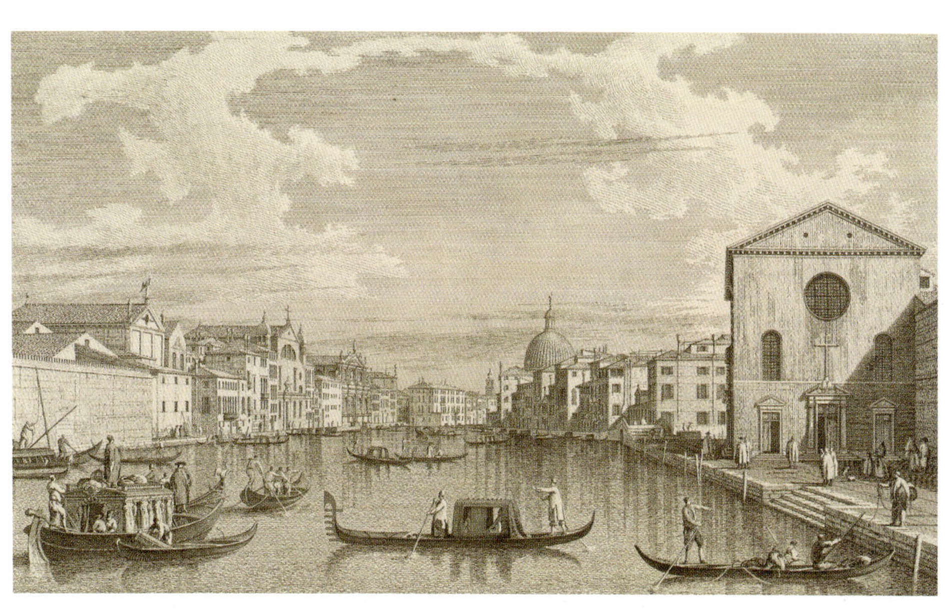

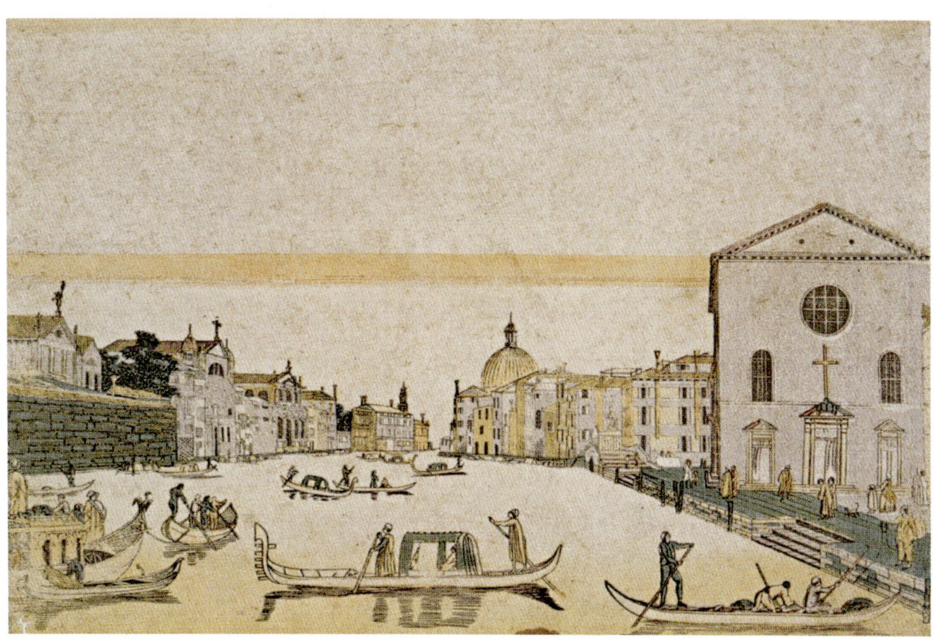

again by the Edo artist Utagawa Toyoharu. The Utagawa school were established makers of 'pictures of the floating worlds', but Toyoharu branched out with some import substitution. European prints were copperplate etchings, whereas in Japan the technology was woodblock, which allowed for colour printing. Toyoharu probably produced his print in about 1770 – that is, it comes at the beginning of the period of urban views made in Japan (illus. 6 and 7). Views of Edo beyond the theatres and bordellos would emerge as a consequence.

❧

At first, Edo was a village, and then a castle town. It then became more, but it was never the capital. Chapter One considers how Edo's unique conceptualization was forged. We assess this via its urban layout. The precedent for grandiose cities was followed to a degree, but also avoided, notably in a refusal to deploy the expected grid. Today Tokyo is often said to be unplanned, and this is attributed to the casual growth of Edo. This opinion is mistaken. Chapter One investigates the models and anti-models behind Edo's apparent sprawl.

The single biggest discrepancy in Edo's layout, though, compared with precursors in Japan or elsewhere in northeast Asia, was its great bridge. This is the subject of Chapter Two. The bridge was not only exceptionally large and impressive, but was designated as the city centre. No previous city in Japan had a centre; there was no concept of a monumental focal point at which a regime could represent itself to those over whom it ruled. European cities had centres as a matter of course, in a tradition stemming from the Roman forum. In this sense Edo was a first. Its central bridge was built in 1603, the very year the shogunate was promulgated, and although documentation is lacking, it was surely erected to emblematize Tokugawa rule.

Chapter Three moves from the concrete city to its abstractions, and investigates magical protection. As Edo metamorphosed, becoming more than a stronghold but less than the capital, one factor hugely influenced the disposition of its various elements. This was geomancy, the 'magic of the earth'. Sometimes known in English by the Chinese term *fengshui*, the Japanese for which is *fūsui*, Edo experts actually called their art *onmyō-dō*, or 'the way of yin and yang'.[2] *Fengshui* means 'wind and water' and refers to the two great forces humanity needs, but cannot tame. Wind and water must be coaxed and rendered meek by mystic calculation. The 'way of yin and yang' alludes to this too, but in a more conceptualized way. Yin (or in Japanese, *on*) is the female principle, while yang (*myō* in Japanese) is the male. They encompass all dualities and antinomies, such as moist/dry, dark/bright, recessive/protrusive. Yin and yang implicate all powers, whether seen or unseen. The 'way of yin and yang' was a discipline to balance opposites whose tension generated all things but which out of tune could be baleful. Equilibrium reaped benefit; mishandling bred chaos. Most fundamentally, Edo was built according to the geomantic principles of yin and yang.

There was a second means of furnishing magical protection, and this is also the topic of Chapter Three. This means was theological, or rather, Buddhological. Edo had its one old temple, but soon added to this were others. The shogunate also ordered the borrowing of sacred sites from across the landscape, mostly from the capital, to be recreated in Edo. Buddhist history was mapped onto Edo's quite recent space. By this, Edo was sacralized and became custodian and successor of the entire history of Japanese faith.

Chapter Four addresses Edo's single greatest and most visible structure, Edo Castle. Though inaccessible to commoners and entirely gone today (save for the base of the keep mentioned earlier), it was once a vast agglomeration of towers and ramparts, residences and audience halls spreading across the skyline. Tokugawa power emanated from here. Edo Castle's shape and internal layout – room after lavishly decorated room – can be reconstructed to a degree. We will read its features to understand the messages it was intended to convey, both inside and out. Helpful in this endeavour is the equivalent space in the capital, which is partially extant as Kyoto's Nijō Castle. Also useful are preparatory paintings made for a reworking of the Edo Castle murals in the early nineteenth century, as well as paintings by the same artists that were not painted directly onto the walls, and so could be detached and saved.

To be fully noble, a Japanese city still needed something more. This was a highly elusive cultural presence, which is the topic of Chapter Five. The prime role of the dairi was to pass on a canon of classical literature, especially a type of court poetry called *waka*. Waka was anthologized, studied and transmitted with great care and admiration in palace circles. A special feature of waka was to be set in real, physical locations. Most sites that had prompted literary outpourings were inevitably near the capital, since courtiers seldom ventured far. Very few writers had gone to the wild east, where Edo would later be. Edo consequently had a thin and denuded feel in terms of cultural history. However, one ancient text was an exception. Anonymous and composed before 900, it was a series of verses with fictionalized narrative contexts, and it did speak of a courtier who went so far. The *Tales of Ise* (*Ise monogatari*) has an unnamed protagonist who grows weary of life at court and wanders off with some companions. From the capital they pass by real places, travel through mountains, including past Mount Fuji, and then come to a large river, which the text identifies as the Sumida. There was nothing here at the time, but seven hundred years later the place was the Tokugawa city and the locus of Japanese power. *Ise* was the sole mention of the Edo area in the whole of the literary canon, but it was a strong one. The *Tales* had long been honoured for their antiquity and the compelling quality of their verses. Some of the poems it contained appeared elsewhere attributed to Ariwara no Narihira, who had died in 880, though it is not clear if *Ise* recounts anyone's factual journey – a distinction of less concern then than it might be for us today. Unlike many classics, which were obscure to any but scholars, *Ise* remained fairly comprehensible. The tales are disparate, but one segment has the man (perhaps Narihira) make a 'Descent to the East' (*Azuma-kudari*), composing as he progresses. To Edo people, it was an astonishing prefiguration of their city and of shogunal rule, and it validated the Edo region, not least as the man went eastwards out of exhaustion from the capital's supposed joys and was impressed by what he found here. This 'descent' became a major theme in Edo period texts and pictures.

Chapter Six looks at something different. For all the formal qualities of Edo, it also had its 'floating worlds', or pleasure districts. As well known today as the word *shōgun* is the word *geisha*. Many Japanese cities had a so-called 'stockade' (*kuruwa*), an officially licensed place of drinking, entertainment and commercial female sex work. Edo's 'stockade' developed into the largest of these and was known by its location, as the Yoshiwara. This meant 'field of reeds', but was soon rewritten with a merrier-sounding homophone, as 'happy fields'. As we shall see, puns were much used in Japanese, not at all regarded as the lowest form of wit (as Dr Johnson said). 'Pictures of the floating worlds' (*ukiyo-e*), made long before European-inspired urban views began, have attracted worldwide attention. They copiously show Edo's restaurants and boudoirs. As sites of sexual exploitation, there is much to condemn in these red-light districts, and the Yoshiwara most of all, but they gave rise to an astonishing array of cultural expressions. Chapter Six will thus engage with the Yoshiwara, and specifically its place within Edo's civic fabric. At some distance outside Edo, the Yoshiwara was built to fit within – or rather without – the discipline and propriety of the shogun's city. We will consider the experience of transit there, and see how 'fixity' gave way to 'floating'.

Lastly, an Epilogue takes us from Edo to Tokyo, in 1868. With the demise of the shoguns, land changed hands. Edo Castle became the Imperial Palace. Warrior compounds were seized and changed to meet the needs of a new type of government. Hotels, courts and railway stations were built. Brick was added to wood. The palanquin and the ferry, by which Edo people had negotiated their city, gave way to the rickshaw and the horse-drawn bus. Edo sank into story, as the shogun's city transitioned into the modern capital of Japan.

⁊

Edo may lack the name recognition of Kyoto or Tokyo, with those two cities today defining 'Japanese culture'. But actually much of what we think of under that label is really the culture of Edo, not the whole archipelago at all. Mount Fuji was the symbol of Edo, only later of

Japan, while only Edo people ate sushi. Multicoloured woodblock prints were almost exclusively made in Edo, while cherry blossoms were the hallmark only of Edo's beauty. A love of natty things was entirely a feature of Edo, little found elsewhere in Japan before modern times.

In about 1800, looking back over two centuries of his city, the shogun's chief minister wrote about this. Matsudaira Sadanobu copied into his commonplace book something he had heard relating to Edo's special culture and also to its cause:

> Someone said that if Edo did not have frequent fires, then people would be more showy and flash. In the capital or in Osaka they do everything with lavish elegance: people hang up paintings in their homes or put out arrangements of flowers. But in Edo, even in the affluent areas, everything is restrained. People only display a single flower in a bamboo tube or a simple pot. The wealthy have fine chess sets, but the box will have paper fixed under the lid to double up as the board. Edo's sense of conciseness comes from continual fires.[3]

Lest it be thought that the elite control our understanding of Edo, in this book, due weight is also given to its common people. Something of how regular residents saw themselves can been seen in a bottom-up articulation. As Sadanobu was compiling his commonplace book, the townsman author Shikitei Sanba wrote a comic novel, illustrated by the floating-world artist Utagawa Toyokuni (illus. 8). The opening page shows the birth of an Edoite, or, as they called themselves, *edokko*, 'children of Edo'. A boy is born to a loving, modest home. As he takes his natal bath, he springs to his feet, scratches one armpit and readies for the struggle ahead; even, perhaps, for his first bout of fisticuffs. Edoites saw themselves thus, as 'rough diamonds' (*otoko-date*), 'a bit hard' actually, in distinction to the effete denizens of the capital. Osaka was a merchant city too, but in Edo the townspeople lived alongside the shogun's entourage. The warrior spirit rubbed off on those below. Perhaps there is an Edo legacy here too, in the respectful diligence

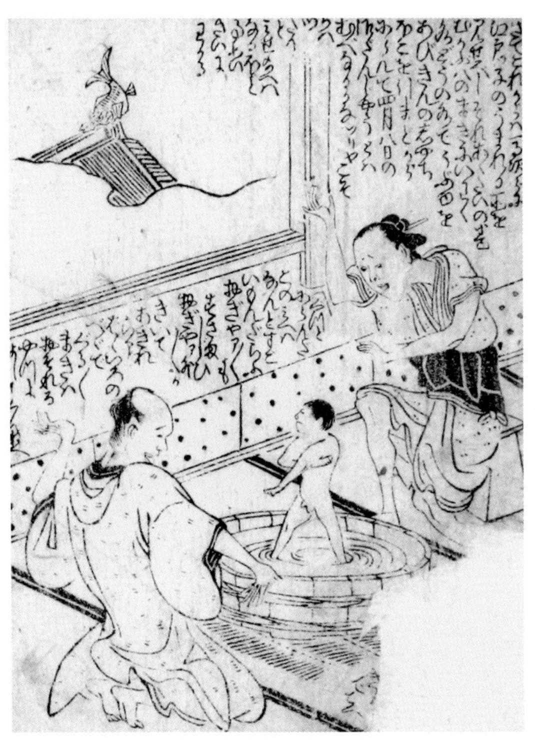

8 Utagawa Toyokuni, illustration from Shikitei Sanba, *Ningen isshin nozoki-karakuri*, monochrome printed book (Edo, 1794). From a popular printed storybook, this page shows the birth of a commoner Edoite, robust in appearance. With the shogunal castle (suitably occluded) outside, he spoils for a fight.

and strong pride of the modern Japanese. Low-born Edo residents said that their city was full of three things: 'shrines to the fox-god, disputes and dog mess' (*inari kenka to inu no fun*). Neighbourhoods were protected by these humble divinities; but then, foxes come and go and are famous for outwitting more pompous animals. 'Disputes' (*kenka*) were inevitable when living cheek-by-jowl in a city that was large and anonymous. But actually, although *kenka* means 'disputes' in modern Japanese, in Edo times it denoted a managed disagreement, one lodged with the authorities, and not a cause for resorting to random violence. Canine excrement was perhaps unpleasant, but it also showed how Edoites fed stray dogs, rather than killing them. Edoites were modest, but nobody's fools, kind and honest to goodness. Toyokuni shows this, while rising outside the window is the finial of Edo Castle, its characteristic upturned fish a prophylactic against fire.

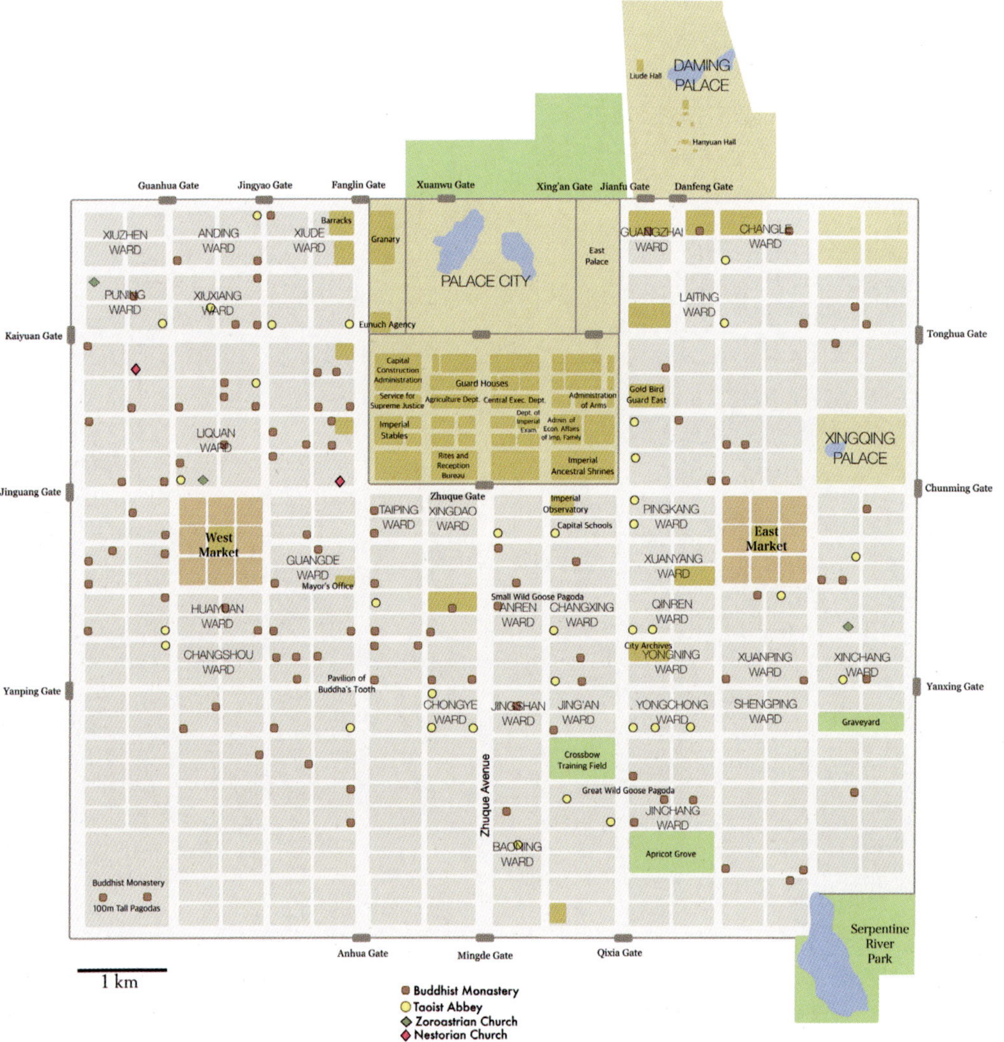

9 City of Chang'an during the Sui and Tang Dynasties, 582–750. Chang'an became the template for many later capitals, as an exact grid with the palace to the north, a temple to the northeast and a great gate in the south. Institutions were mirrored across the central axis.

One
The Ideal City

Since early times, Japan had been part of the wider Chinese cultural world, or what in English is known as the Sinosphere. This was a loose collectivity of ethnic and social groups that used written Chinese and read books in Chinese to understand human life and the universe. 'China' comes from *Zhungguo*, literally meaning the Central States (often mistranslated as Middle Kingdom), and its first large consolidation was under the Han dynasty, before the opening of the Common Era. The Han capital was Chang'an, close to modern Xi'an, and it was the starting point of the Silk Road that led all the way to Lebanon, and thence to Rome. In 25 CE the Han capital was moved to Luoyang, 375 kilometres to the east, estimated symbolically to be the midpoint of the Central States. Marcus Aurelius sent an embassy here in 166, the Roman emperor referred to as Andun, from his third name, Antonius.[1] Chang'an and Luoyang existed in parallel, with the status of capital moving between them. In 493 the rising Northern Wei dynasty moved its capital to Luoyang, while in 557, as the dynasty splintered, the Western Wei established theirs at Chang'an.

Though the capital was not stationary, a clear notion spread through the Sinosphere of how a noble city should look. The realities may or may not have matched the aspirations, or the reputations that grew up around the cities, but Chang'an and then Luoyang, with modifications and misrememberings, fixed the template for ever after (illus. 9).

The primary condition for a proper city was that it must be designed along a grid. Towns and villages were haphazard, higgledy-piggledy, built as the land required. But a city that stood for power and authority, and which well might be the capital, should evince order and stasis in rectilinear, symmetrical form. Streets were laid north–south and east–west along the cardinal vectors, or at least approximating them. In English convention we call the north–south ones 'streets' and east–west ones 'avenues' (the opposite of New York). The palace of the ruler would be set on the northern edge, occupying several blocks. Avenues were numbered southwards from this, One to Ten, while the streets had actual names. A wide thoroughfare ran from the palace to a South Gate, which was the city's only official point of entrance and exit.

The first Japanese city to follow this model definitively was Japan's second capital, completed in 711, by which time the Central States were under the powerful Tang Dynasty. Much of it lies beneath the modern city of Nara, but archaeological work has allowed some reconstructions. It was built to announce a new and more unified Japanese polity, which proclaimed itself within the Sinosphere for the first time. The international word for a 'capital' was suffixed to the name, *jing* in Chinese, pronounced *kyō* in Japanese (hence Kyoto, Tokyo and Beijing).

An open spot was selected and staked out at a pre-existing village called Nara, which was entirely revised and rebuilt. Japan's debut internationally correct conurbation was given an auspicious title, Heijō, literally 'peaceful walls', or, fully, Heijō-kyō.[2] Unlike Chinese cities, Japanese ones did not have actual walls, owing to a scarcity of solid stone (many of Japan's rocks are volcanic) and the likelihood that walls would collapse in earthquakes, doing more harm than good. Heijō-kyō was to be a peaceful enclosure, metaphorically demarcating order in what remained a problematic and contested landscape.

After a couple of generations, Heijō-kyō was abandoned. There are several possible reasons for this.[3] One is the power that metropolitan temples had begun to assert over civil rule. A new gridded metropolis was laid out at a site called Nagaoka ('long hill'). Yet before even Nagaoka-kyō could be fully built, or given an auspicious name, it was abandoned and the capital relocated again. This time the problem seems to have been flooding. The third grid city was completed in 794 and would remain the capital for over a thousand years, until modern times (illus. 10). Japan's third capital was given an auspicious name, Heian-kyō. This was even more redolent than Heijō-kyō, for it coupled the previous capital's name, *Heijō*, with Chang'an, the capital of the glorious and extensive Tang dynasty. Both *hei* and *an* mean 'peace', though in English, Heian-kyō is usually translated as the 'capital of peace and tranquillity'.

Yet the Tang dynasty had fallen by 907. The Central States were at war. As Heian-kyō was being planned, Chang'an came under the control of the Uighur Khaganate. Heian-kyō was thus its parallel and to some extent its successor.

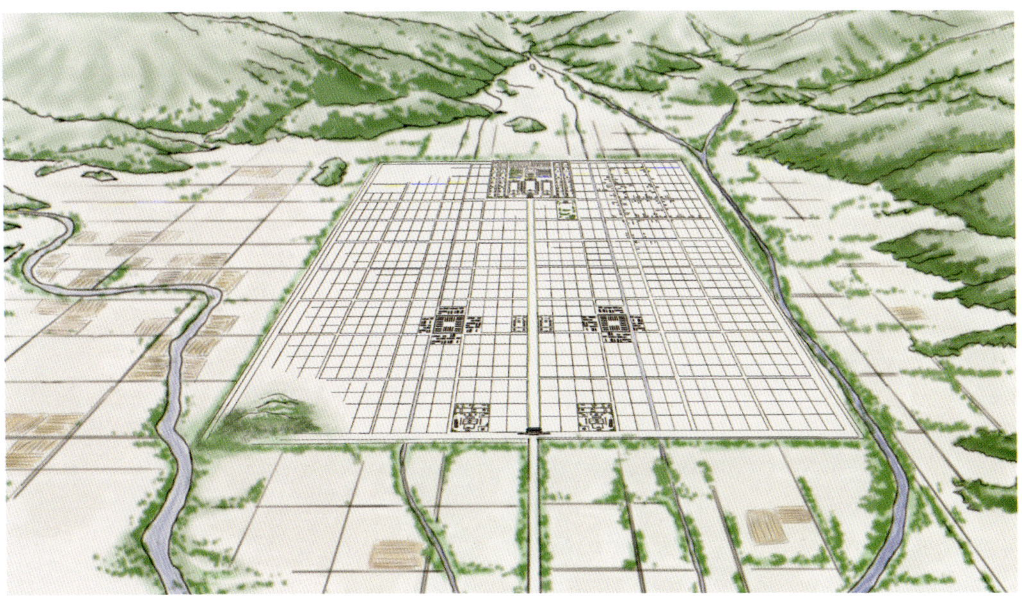

10 The Heian capital, bird's-eye representation from the south, 794, illustration by Yoriko Igari in Matthew Stavros, *Kyoto: An Urban History of Japan's Premodern Capital* (Honolulu, 2014). The Heian capital followed Chang'an, though probably not all its grid was ever filled, with large parts remaining as fields. The protector temple was pushed far beyond the boundaries of the city, to reduce clerical power.

Heian-kyō fulfilled the role of capital of Japan for so long that its became simply known as *kyō*, 'capital'. Conversely, this name was rather brief, so for clarity *to*, meaning 'metropolis', might be appended to give *kyōto*, or 'metropolitan capital'. This was also the continental practice, where formal capital names often fell from use in favour of the generic term 'capital' – *jing,* or *jingdu* in Chinese. There was also an indigenous Japanese word for a capital, *miyako*, and Heian-kyō might be known by this name, too. For most of history, then, Japan's centre of authority was known as *kyō*, *kyōto* or *miyako*, though none was a proper name.

✑

The palace was situated in the north because it was believed that a ruler should face south, with the sun on his face. The palace was the place of control, and by analogy with the human body, the head. The palace gate was the mouth, by which orders were dispatched, and a fine Suzaku-mon, or Gate of the Red Bird, would be built here, the 'red bird' being guardian of the south. The north–south thoroughfare, the Street of the Red Bird, was a spine, and if people referred to the city's north as the head (*kubi*), then the south was its tail (*o*). A great gate, mirroring that of the Red Bird, was set at the city's exit, which might therefore be analogized as its anus. This was the Rajō-mon, where *rajō* means a wall or enclosure, while *mon*, again, is a gate (the title of Kurosawa Akira's famous film *Rashōmon* of 1950 is a variant pronunciation). The Suzaku-mon of Heijō-kyō (Nara, not Kyoto) can be seen again today, reconstructed near its original location (illus. 11).

Animal bodies have a line of symmetry down the middle. What exists on one side is replicated on the other. A great city, and certainly a capital, should be the same. The Avenue of the Red Bird was this line, and buildings or institutions were matched on both sides. If there was an office to the left, there would be one on the right; if an eastern market, there would be a western market; if an eastern temple, a western one too. Admittedly, this was rather theoretical, as sites tended to move, but complete lateral symmetry was an aspiration. The

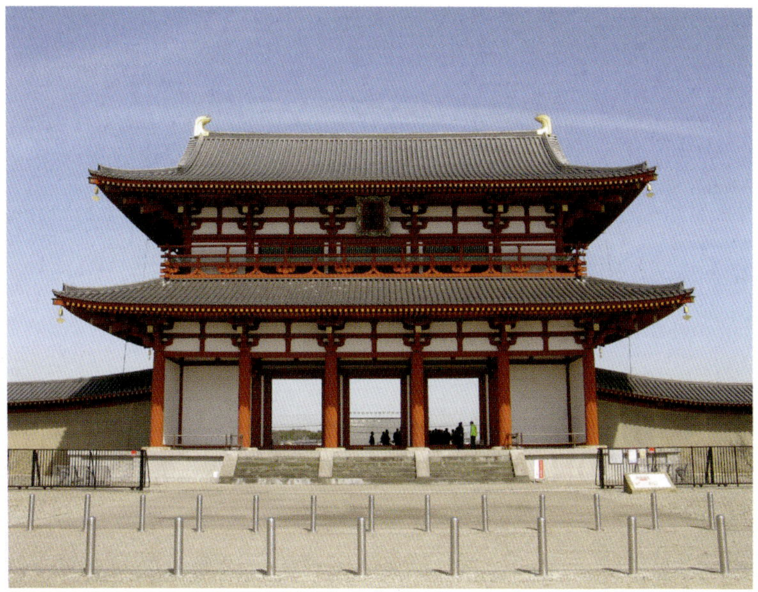

part of the city to the east of the avenue was called the Left Capital (*sakyō*) and the western side the Right Capital. This continues to be the case in Kyoto, though to the confusion of tourists the Left Capital is on the right and the Right Capital is on the left, since the labels are governed by the view from the palace.

Bodies are not entirely symmetrical, for the most vital organ, the heart, is single. The heart is on the left and therefore, in a capital, left took precedence. Anything situated in the Left Capital was superior to its equivalent in the Right. The three great offices of state were the Minister of the Left, then the Minister of the Right, and third, the Minister of the Centre.

This ideal, geometric, corporeal system was given a higher, more abstract level of meaning through another overlay. This came from geomancy, the divination (*mancy*) of the earth (*geo*). The differences between northeast Asian and European geomancy have led to the concept being left untranslated, and the Chinese term, *fengshui*, is also now used in English. *Feng* means wind and *shui* water, seen as the two great creative, but potentially destructive, forces of nature.

Geomancy is the art of propitiating and taming these powerful forces. Architects and engineers across northeast Asia took account of the many directives of geomancy as they worked, and sometimes still do. The Japanese pronunciation of *fengshui* is *fūsui*, but this word was not often deployed. Instead, they said *onmyō-dō*, or the 'way of yin and yang' (C: *yinyang-dao*). It refers not to actual forces, but to generic principles. *On* (C: *yin*) is the female principle, said to encompass characteristics of moistness, darkness and recession. *Myō* (C: *yang*), the male principle, is the contrary, connoting dryness, brightness and protrusion. Harmony lay in their balance. Working out how to achieve this was the art of the geomancer, the yin-yang master or, in Japanese, *onmyō-shi*. Their job was to apply fixed rules to specific cases.

Geomancers referred to the cardinal points via colours. A given direction was affiliated with a guardian force that had this colour. Hence the south was associated with a 'red bird'. The guardian of the north was a 'dark tortoise'. The east was a 'blue dragon', and the west a 'white tiger'. The centre was yellow, fixed, and with no specific protector. The *huangdi* (Chinese emperor) wore yellow clothes for this reason, though such was not the practice in Japan.

The colours had their logic. Red is for the bright southern sun; black for northern darkness; blue for dawn; white the haze of twilight; yellow the overhead sun. For the animal forms, too, there was a rationale: the sun in the south moves swiftly like a bird; the chill north is still like a tortoise; dragon and tiger are respectively creation's finest creatures, but the dragon precedes the tiger as lord of all five elements (earth, air, fire, wind, water), while tigers are confined to the earth.

Geomancy has one overriding concept, above all else. This relates to what is known as *ki* (C: *qi*). It is an invisible force pervading the universe. *Ki* is in constant motion but tends to progress from northeast to southwest. The northeast was known to geomancers as the 'gate of *ki*, or *kimon*'. In Japanese, this was often written with a homophone, *ki* meaning 'demon' – there is no clear explanation for the change, but as *ki* can be capricious, an association with demons seems logical enough. In itself, however, *ki* is neither pure nor impure. It picks up valence from what it passes over. The most crucial requirement of geomancy is therefore to ensure the purity of the northeast, so that entering *ki* comes in limpid form. In a city, the 'gate of *ki*' might be protected by human guards, but it was also guarded by magical means. The specific case of Edo will be considered in Chapter Three. Here we need think only of how matters worked for an ideal city. As at Chang'an, at both Heijō-kyō (Nara) and Heian-kyō (Kyoto) a whole 'outer capital' (*gekyō*) was built, an excrescence on the grid to equip the city with the necessary measures to cleanse *ki*. This northeast zone was home to a temple built on raised land. It was a religious and also physical block. An important icon would be enshrined, and monks charged with caring for it.

Having entered in a pure state, *ki* passes on, so a mechanism was also required for it to cross the city and to leave again smoothly. If blocked, *ki* becomes turbid. Another geomantic requirement, therefore, was to ensure its even transit. This was no simple matter in a grid city without diagonal lines. The matter was resolved by the use not of a road, but a river. Cities were laid out in a manner that allowed a stream to be canalized to run from northeast to southwest. In some cases, it might literally cross the city, bisecting the grid. More often, it flowed north–south down a city's eastern flank, externally, then turned to continue along the southern edge before veering off westward. Heijō-kyō is an example of the former, Hcian-kyō of the latter. The River Kamo, which still runs in modern Kyoto, is so straight it is obviously canalized, though the city has jumped across and the Kamo is now fairly central in Kyoto.

The name of Chang'an was invoked at Heian-kyō, but it was Luoyang's name that was more generally recycled. *Luo yang* means the sunnier, *yang* bank of the river Luo, on which the city had been built. Luoyang was (and is) at the Luo's confluence with the Yellow River (Huang He), named for its muddy waters, though in an appellation that sounded auspicious to Chinese-speakers, and also suggested the centre. Luoyang was said to have been founded in 1036 BCE by the Duke of Zhou, regarded throughout subsequent history as a paragon of virtue and good rule. Being very ancient, Luoyang lacked some of the elements that would define mature geomantic thought, seen better at Chang'an, but it was so foundational that its name (Rakuyō, in Japanese) was also used for Heian-kyō. As well as its formal name and the generic labels of *kyō*, *kyōto* and *miyako*, then, Heian-kyō was sometimes called Rakuyō, though the nuances were poetic rather than political. The first character, *luo* or *raku*, could be used in other combinations too where the capital was invoked. For example, a traveller would say they went 'up to the capital', *jōraku*, literally 'ascending to Raku'. Even today this can be used to mean a trip to Kyoto, though it sounds a little precious. The capital and its surroundings could be called 'in and around Raku' (*rakuchū rakugai*). This terminology was universally applicable and could potentially be used for the capital of any nation, even outside the Sinosphere. A person could *jōraku* to Lisbon or Delhi. Foreign capitals might be referred to by suffixing *raku* to the first part of their names. In principle, one might talk of *Ronraku* (London) or *Washinraku* (Washington) – though, again, it would be pretentious to do this today.

Cities that were not capitals but sufficiently splendid might take the second character of Luoyang, pronounced *yō* in Japanese. Nagasaki was one of Japan's finest conurbations and also its best port, so people routinely added *yō* to a shortened version of its name. For technical linguistic reasons, the result came out not as Sakiyō, as might be expected, but as Kiyō (*ki* being another pronunciation of the character *saki*).

❧

The template for a capital outlined above was good times of peace and order, but in the same degree it was useless in times of war. The failing was only too obvious in perennially bellicose Japan. The universality of the model made location of important buildings predictable to invaders, who could instantly find, and neutralize, sites of power. The wide, straight streets were impossible to defend. Worst of all, to capture the palace, an enemy needed merely to attack from the north. True, the capital would have crack troops stationed there (the 'guards who face north' were an elite brigade), but this was insufficient in times of real urgency.

The first complete Japanese capital, Heijō-kyō, was not in existence long enough to suffer attack, but Heian-kyō (Kyoto) was repeatedly assaulted. During the medieval and post-medieval periods, that is, the twelfth to sixteenth centuries, it became utterly unmanageable. The formal city was erased and its grid entirely lost. Terrified residents broke it up into petty, practical units to make life and property more resistant to capture. Fighting required the erection of internal barriers and the cutting up of streets, until, in due course, every one of the

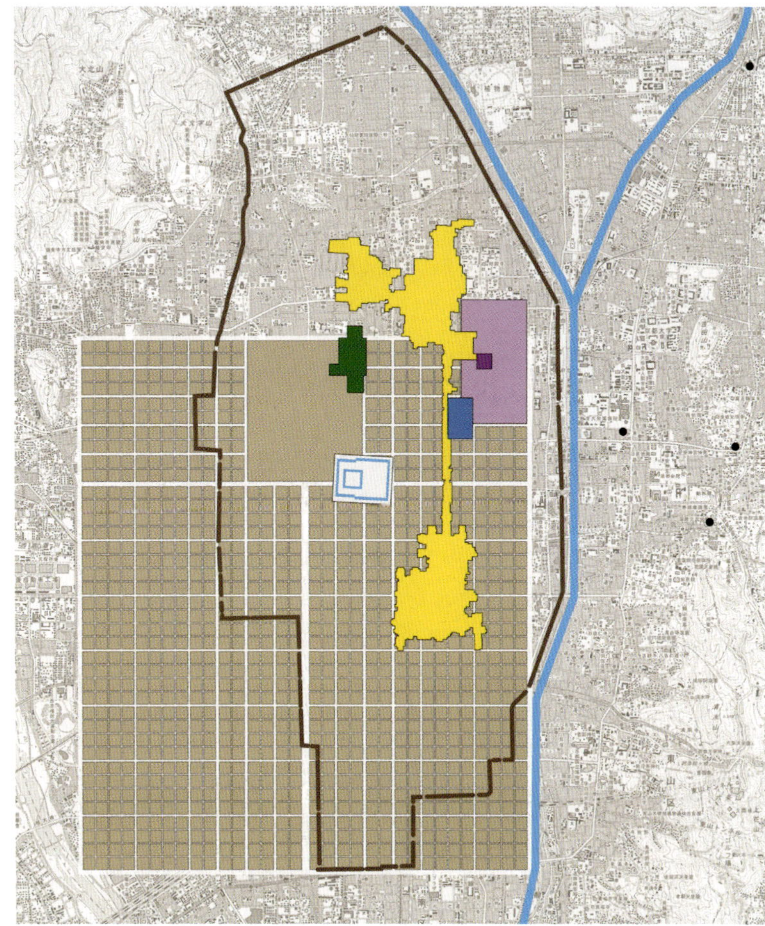

12 The capital over the ages, illustration by Yoriko Igari in Matthew Stavros, *Kyoto: An Urban History of Japan's Premodern Capital* (Honolulu, 2014). Brown: original Heian (completed 794); yellow: 16th century; blue: Nijō Castle, c. 1569–73; green: Hideyoshi's palace; dark brown: Hideyoshi's embankment; blue and white, Tokugawa Nijō Castle. The city was dramatically reduced in the medieval period but was rebuilt under Hideyoshi and by the Tokugawa, whose Nijō Castle became the capital's administrative centre.

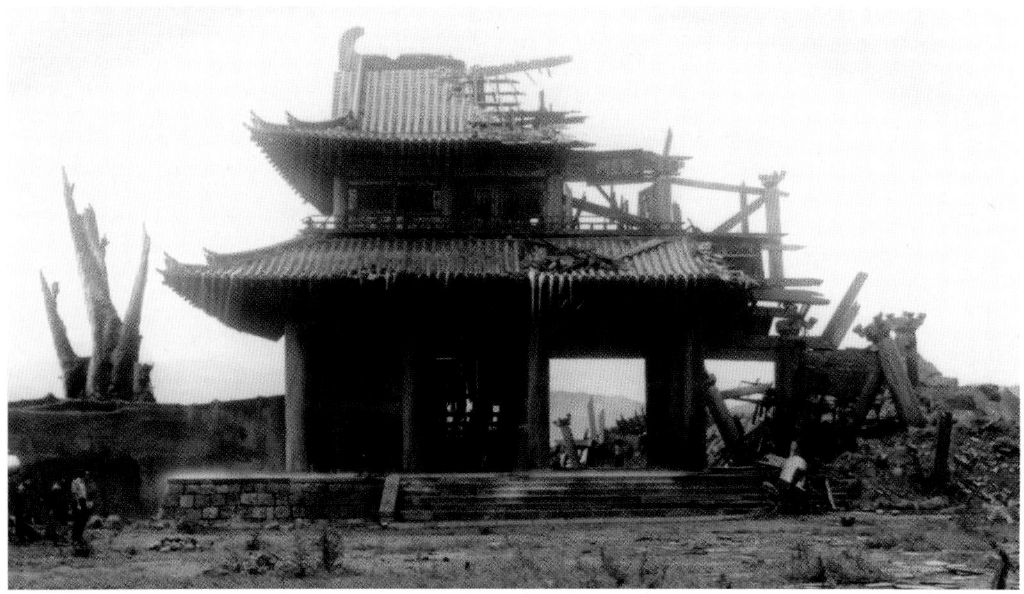

13 Image from *Rashomon*, directed by Kurosawa Akira (1950). The film tells of the gate in medieval times, half-ruined and standing among fields, an abode of brigands and ghosts.

capital's streets and avenues was sundered, not a single remaining one running the full length from east to west or north to south. Heian-kyō's fulsome dimensions had exceeded the requirements of the actual population anyway, and it had always suffered from vacant and unfinished plots. By 1400 the elegant Left and Right capitals had been replaced with zoning more suited to diminishing power, with an Upper Capital (*kamigyō*) around the dairi's residence and a Lower Capital (*shimogyō*) in the central area, both pretty small, and with burned-out buildings, or just fields, between (illus. 12). The palace disappeared, the Rajō-mon as captured in Kurosawa's film, isolated among grasses, haunted by wolves or ghosts (illus. 13).

Heian-kyō stopped being called Heian-kyō, but it did remain the capital – the *kyō, kyōto, miyako* or *raku*. It looked more like a warrior garrison, dozens of which had sprouted throughout the archipelago. Japan entered its longest period of civil war in 1467, and this lasted for a century. True, the capital still had its temples, but these were outside the city – a fact that the sprawl of modern Kyoto makes it hard to recognize. Indeed, Heian-kyō had been built *without* temples, almost all Buddhist institutions being relegated outside the city boundaries to avoid the clerical power that had undermined civil rule in the first capital. Temples, for their part, began equipping themselves with a new category of cleric, called warrior monks (*sōhei*).

This civil war led right up to the Edo period and continued into it. During the sixteenth century, competing warrior strongholds with their surrounding supply bases were known as castle towns (*jōka-machi*). They are the origins of many modern Japanese cities. After countless attacks and counter-attacks, a formidable fighter named Toyotomi Hideyoshi attained pre-eminence in the 1580s. He was able to assert authority in the wider region of the capital. Hideyoshi undertook military and political reforms, expending great effort on cultural hegemony. One of his most significant, and difficult, acts was to force the capital back into at least a semblance of its grid. No one would have thought it possible. Kyoto as seen today is Hideyoshi's reconstruction, its streets and avenues only inexactly placed where those of Heian-kyō had formerly been. The dairi and his court were so thrilled by the return of their idealized capital that they overlooked discrepancies.[4] Hideyoshi rebuilt the palace, too, but he did not allow it back into its original location. Most of the former palace site had been used by earlier warrior groupings, and Hideyoshi reserved it for his own castle. These military forts had migrated over the old compound area but would be consolidated finally as the Tokugawa Nijō Castle, named, like its predecessors, after the location in Second Avenue (*ni* = two; *jō* = avenue). Hideyoshi hailed from peasant stock but arranged to have himself adopted into an ancient court family, thus becoming eligible for what had become the highest position in the offices of state, largely ceremonial: Regent (*kanpaku*). Officially, this role was to advise the dairi, the incumbent being named Ōgimachi-in. Dairis have *-in* suffixed to their names (in ancient times and then again after 1868, the more august suffix *-tennō* was used).

In 1590 Hideyoshi led some of his trusted generals to the east to destroy the Hōjō clan, who had eluded his hegemony. Paramount in Hideyoshi's staff was Tokugawa Ieyasu. He knew the region well, having lived as a child in Sunpu Castle (in modern Shizuoka), at the foot of Mount Fuji. Beyond the mountain was the extended Hōjō territory of Musashi province, their main redoubt being at Odawara Castle. In 1524 the Hōjō had added Edo Castle to their holdings, though this was a minor addition for surveillance of its small harbour. Edo was assaulted just 25 years later, and ruined. The Hōjō did not trouble to rebuild it, though they still controlled the land.

Hideyoshi's attack on the Hōjō eradicated that ancient group. He awarded their holdings to Ieyasu. The real story of Edo begins from this, as Ieyasu entered Musashi. Hideyoshi wanted him out of the way, off in the east, dissipating his energies, while Hideyoshi himself continued to formalize control of the vital central region around the capital and Osaka. Ieyasu embedded himself too, rebuilding and expanding Odawara Castle, as expected. But he did not move his base there. Ieyasu had some interest in international trade, so, owing to its promise as a port, he quite unexpectedly made Edo his home. The bay was not deep, but that was an advantage, for big ships could not approach. Portuguese vessels had begun arriving in Japan in the 1540s and were using Nagasaki, a safe and deep natural harbour, as their mercantile centre. These ships could not trade directly with Edo, but they could not threaten it either. Transhipping to Japanese cargo ships would be required. The history of what is sometimes called Japan's Christian Century, from the 1540s to the 1640s, is beyond the scope of this book, but the Portuguese traders, missionaries and slavers did their bit to prolong the civil wars, by making guns available to warlords who turned to Christ. Still, the Tokugawa's eastern garrison rapidly grew. Edo became a focal point for military families and those who provisioned them.

In the capital region, Hideyoshi accrued titles. In 1573 he expelled the shogunal dynasty of the Ashikaga family, whose seat had been in the capital itself, at Nijō Castle in fact. The office of shogun, already powerless, lapsed. The last incumbent, who had become a monk, would die in 1597. As regent, Hideyoshi did much to settle the splintered lands and bring the dismembered Japanese state back together. Perhaps taking a leaf from the Iberian book, he also invaded Korea, a project that utterly failed. He died in 1598, aged 61, leaving only an infant heir, Hideyori. A council of wardship was formed to look after the boy, one member being Tokugawa Ieyasu. Fighting restarted (it had never really ended) until a colossal battle of 1600 took place at Sekigahara, midway between Edo and the capital. This was one of the most epic encounters in human history. Some 100,000 men clashed. Ieyasu led one alliance, and opposing him were forces loyal to Hideyori. There would have been many more dead had not most of Ieyasu's enemies changed sides part way through (so much for the mythic loyalty unto death of the Japanese samurai). Ieyasu had prepared for this cataclysmic encounter militarily. He had also done so religiously, by offering prayers to the wonder-working image of Kannon in the Asakusa-dera, on the banks of the Sumida just upstream of Edo. Ieyasu's spectacular victory could better be attributed to the image than to turncoating by his enemies. The temple was richly thanked. Ieyasu acquired more castles and lands, ousting enemies and rewarding old or new-found allies. Hideyori, aged seven, had not been directly involved at Sekigahara, and with his councillors and armies remained in the Toyotomi stronghold of Osaka, the most impenetrable castle on earth at the time. Ieyasu had sworn to support the boy, and kept his word. In about 1600 there were thus three centres of Japanese authority: Ieyasu in Edo, Hideyori in Osaka and the dairi in the capital.

Ieyasu was no longer just a warrior among many. To make this clear, observers of the time assumed, he would move to the capital, though whether he would choose to follow Hideyoshi and become regent, or assume the defunct title of shogun, was uncertain. Ieyasu spent three years pondering this question. He resided for much of the time in Fushimi Castle, his stronghold near (but not in) the capital, though Edo remained his main seat. Then, in 1603, Ieyasu made his decision. He asked the dairi, now Ōgimachi-in's son, Go-Yōzei-in, to name him shogun. He kept Edo and Fushimi, but also took Nijō Castle, relocating it and adding this key castle to his roster. But he based his shogunate in Edo.

Respecting Hideyori's power in the central region, and wanting distance from the dairi, Ieyasu returned to Edo. He did take court sinecures but was not interested in a ceremonial title. From 1603 onwards, the Tokugawa would hold the office of shogun for fifteen incumbencies.

So began Japan's third shogunate. Ieyasu was well aware of the history. The first shogunate, under the Minamoto family, had lasted from 1192 to 1333; the second, the Ashikaga shogunate, was from 1338 to 1573. In an interesting parallel with Hideyoshi, who had orchestrated adoption into a court family, permitting him to assume the title of regent, Ieyasu declared himself a descendant of the Minamoto. It was a way of turning the clock back, to the dawn of Japanese military rule.

The Minamoto had eventually migrated to the capital and become more courtiers than warriors. But they had begun their shogunate in Kamakura, not far from Edo. One can speculate that Ieyasu might have considered basing his shogunate in the city too. But Kamakura had severe defects that would have ruled it out: it was dangerously exposed to storm and tsunami and lacked Edo's protective bay; its deep waters were open to European shipping; and it was ringed with hills, good for protection but cramping development as a shogunal powerbase and as a future flourishing peacetime city.

Ieyasu copied a host of Minamoto practices, rituals and nomenclature. But he stuck to Edo, and Kamakura remained nothing more than an imaginary origin for Tokugawa rule. Meanwhile, the capital remained the capital, though it gradually lost out to Edo. As long as Hideyori lived, Osaka remained as a semi-independent political entity. In 1615 Ieyasu would attack Osaka, level its castle and integrate the region into his own holdings. Hideyori was never seen again, presumed lost in the fighting.

☙

As a city, the capital followed, or largely followed, the hallowed spatial requirements and aspired to be a grid. Edo, by contrast, was a web of moats, dug to deter attack and also to drain the marshy land. Yet after 1603 Edo had to become more than just a warrior town. Military preparedness precluded it ever becoming a grid, but Ieyasu and his advisers evidently considered other aggrandizing options. Edo Castle – though not Edo city – was given an auspicious and rather flowery name. When this was coined is uncertain, but the stronghold acquired the designation of Chiyoda-jō, its characters literally meaning 'castle in the rice fields for one thousand generations'. The label acknowledges that Edo was still rural, but now proposes its abundant spaces as fruitful cultivated farmland, well able to support a strong army and, in time, a thriving civilian population. It acknowledges Edo as a warrior town, but if it is the fate of most castles to come and go as they are fought over and destroyed, this is one that will last for even a thousand generations.

Edo was not the capital, or *kyō*, but soon the shogunate began applying the word *to* to their city. It was done at least from the late seventeenth century. *To* is the second character in *kyōto*, which above we translated as 'metropolis', but actually, and somewhat confusingly, *to* can also mean 'capital'. This signification was less commonly used in Japan, but Korean capital cities were so designated (pronounced *do* in Korean). The word *to* thus enabled Edo to make veiled but considerable claims to status. The word was deployed punningly, with *to* used to write the *do* of Edo. In Japanese, the doubling up of meanings so as to make two significant statements at the same time was acknowledged as a high rhetorical device. Court poetry is full of it. A second pun was that one of the many possible pronunciations for the word 'east' was *e* (more often it is read as *higashi* or *azuma*). Accordingly, Edo's name could be adapted from its root meaning of 'door to the bay' to 'eastern metropolis' or even, covertly, 'eastern capital'.

True to the castle town that it fundamentally remained, the city of Edo conglomerated around its castle. Buildings and streets spread outwards in a way that might appear random and unplanned, but in fact were far from so. The expectation that a fine city should be based on a grid was responded to by regularizing most quarters in straight, cardinal streets that met at right angles, but this was done only in a partial way, not citywide. A person walking through their home neighbourhood might experience a grid, but after some distance this would end. It would interlock with the next one discontinuously, like in a patchwork quilt. A lack of overall coherence was therefore deliberate – it *was* the plan.

Having a castle in the centre was desirable for both military and populace as it meant residents could take refuge there, if needed, and that the castle was at lower risk of assault. However, centrality caused problems of a conceptual kind. At issue was the vestigial assumption that rulers should be in the north, looking southwards. For an ordinary person, looking southwards on a superior – or even on their own dwelling – felt improper, even psychologically threatening. A castle in the centre meant that about a third of the city could not be comfortably inhabited because it was improper to look south on it. When the castle's inhabitant was the shogun, and when warfare stabilized into enduring peace, such a state of affairs would not do.

The conundrum was solved by giving the whole northern part of Edo over to the Tokugawa family, their vassals and retainers. Some commoners resided here for service and supply, but they were few. To apportion so much space to so few people was an extravagance, and the extended shogunal household did not truly warrant this expanse. But it resolved the issue of what to do with parts north of the castle. Anyway, prominent people expected capacious compounds.

Edo's population was more than the shogunal entourage, of course. Commoners had lived along the waterfront since ancient times, in fishing families and ancillary communities. Numbers increased under the Hōjō. After 1590 all kinds of people migrated to take advantage of the Tokugawa warrior establishment, and from 1603 of the burgeoning shogunal apparatus. From the 1620s, however, another class of resident came, and they dramatically altered the form and appearance of the city. We need to take a step back.

Two years after becoming shogun in 1603, Ieyasu retired. This secured the succession in what were still dangerous times. Ieyasu took his son, Hidetada (not to be confused with Hideyoshi's son Hideyori), to the capital for Go-Yōzei-in to endorse him as second shogun. Ieyasu went into entirely notional retirement at Sunpu, the castle he knew so well. There he was to die, in 1616, but in one final act Ieyasu attacked Osaka Castle, obliterating the Toyotomi line. This ensured enduring Tokugawa paramountcy, but it was an appalling act of betrayal. The Tokugawa would remain sensitive about it for a long time to come. Throughout the Edo period, people were well advised not to talk about it, or to probe. Osaka was rebuilt, and its castle became a Tokugawa stronghold. The dual hegemony of the Tokugawa in the east and the Toyotomi in the central region was expunged. The Tokugawa nevertheless felt it expedient to leave Osaka Castle uninhabited, never residing there, nor even placing it in the hands of a relative as they did in other places. Instead, they installed a chatelain (*jōdai*). Go-Yōzei-in continued in the capital, but with the Toyotomi eradicated, the Tokugawa further expanded control. It should be remembered the shoguns never possessed more than about 20 per cent of Japan's landmass. True, this included all major cities (Edo, the capital, Osaka, its nearby port of Sakai, and Nagasaki). Most of the country, however – some 80 per cent of it – remained in the control of other families. The number of these regional warrior leaders, called *daimyō* ('great repute'), fluctuated, but there were about three hundred of them, some great, some petty, some of ancient stock, others of recent vintage; some daimyo lands were the size of a middling European nation, others little more than a town. These were passed on hereditarily, and the daimyo expected the practice to continue. The key distinction was between those who had fought with the Tokugawa during their rise to power, and those who had opposed them. Weak enemies were deposed and their lands bestowed on meritorious Tokugawa loyalists. The others accepted overlordship of the Tokugawa in return for confirmation of their status.

The change in Edo's fabric in 1620 came with the shogun Hidetada's decision to allot all daimyo 'bestowed residences' (*hairyō-yashiki*) in Edo. This made them available to assist his rule and also kept them under the shogunal gaze, or as they put it, 'at his lap' (*hizamoto*). Many daimyo had already been given Edo residences to serve as embassies for their region, accommodation for passing officials or artists, and to accommodate the daimyo when he had occasion to visit. Since daimyos married their sons to one another's daughters, ladies were brought to the Edo residence and often stayed there permanently. Daimyo wives lacked much first-hand experience of their own regions and never knew the places their husbands ruled. They were unable to speak their dialect or understand their customs. Daimyo children were necessarily born in Edo, too, so they also became estranged from the places their families ruled. A new daimyo might enter his hereditary lands and castle for the first time only on his father's death. Hidetada thus created an effective deracinating system. Since life in Edo was far more exciting than that offered by regional castles, affording ample conviviality on the right social level, daimyo families did not object.

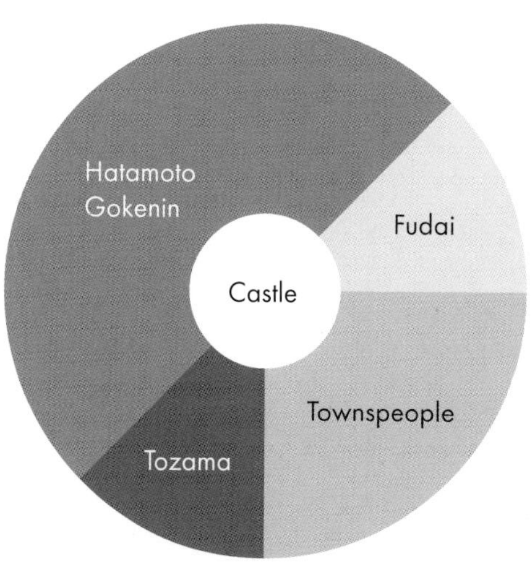

14 Schematic representation of social zoning in Edo. The *fudai* were Tokugawa loyalists, while the *tozama* had formerly been anti-Tokugawa warlords; the *hatamoto* and *gokenin* were shogunal officers and staff. Locations serve geomantic purposes.

It was a dozen years later, in 1635, that Hidetada's son and successor, Iemitsu, the third shogun, made residence a formal requirement for all daimyos against whom the Tokugawa still harboured suspicions, and not just their ladies. Most were already living much of the time in Edo. From 1642 residence became required of all daimyo. Iemitsu, however, realized that absentee daimyo would not foster well-governed regions, so he codified what was called 'alternate attendance' (*sankin kōtai*), with one year of residence in Edo followed by one in the daimyo's castle town. The wives and families were to remain in Edo permanently, part hostage, part socialite. Vast retinues began to cross the country at regular intervals, resulting in a high standard of roads and travel infrastructure, such as post-stations, inns and stables. Moving with the daimyo were advisers, guards and attendants of all stripes, from the high to the low. A daimyo phalanx might take hours to pass. Members acquired Edo's cultural norms, and at the end of their tour of duty they took these home to the hinterlands.[5] Edo itself became a composite, almost a multicultural mix of people from Japan's hills, valleys and islands. Japan is big, and daimyo from the north lived 2,000 kilometres away from those in the south – equivalent to the distance from Stockholm to Venice, or Vancouver to Los Angeles. Edo was the place of meeting and the site of intellectual and political exchange.

Residences of the daimyo were zoned. Plots were apportioned with attention paid to the daimyo's wealth and pedigree, but also trustworthiness. Needless to say, none were located to the north of the castle. Non-loyalists too powerful to annihilate, called 'outer lords' (*tozama*), were placed together. They would bide their time for 250 years and eventually topple the shogunate in the 1860s. The loyalists were called 'continuing generation' (*fudai*) daimyo. The fudai were given land to the northeast of the castle. This was geomantic, for they occupied the point where spiritual forces would enter Edo at the 'gate of *ki*'. As *ki* passed over the compounds of these virtuous people, it would be rendered all the more pure. By contrast, the tozama were placed in the southwest: if passing *ki* were to become sullied by their malevolence it would flow out of Edo, dissipating harmlessly in the countryside (illus. 14).

Three residential directions had thus been defined within Edo's spatial order: north for the shogunal entourage, northeast for the fudai and southwest for the tozama. This covered the key geomantic vectors. Other directions were ritualistically less crucial, or even vacant. The northwest was one. In Edo this area was upland and known as Yamanote ('hillside'). It was breezy and fresh, with a country feel. Yamanote was allocated to specially favoured retainers (*hatamoto*) and additional shogunal staff (*gokenin*), while trusted daimyo were permitted to construct spacious secondary villas and parks (*shimo-yashiki*).

South and southeast of the castle was Edo's old fishing port, now equipped with stone-lined wharves and docks. It was the natural place to locate arriving commoners. The shogun would look southwards onto them, as he should onto the mass of his subjects, who could unproblematically overspill into the geomantically meaningless southeast. Townspeople comprised some 80 per cent of the population, though the areas accorded to them were tight and circumscribed.

It must be remembered that as with other configurations of the ideal city, facts on the ground were never as clear-cut as the theories stipulated. Edo's main geomantic requirements, though, were fully met. Yet there was still the necessity of a passageway for *ki* to flow through the city, like the river that ran the length of the capital. This meant a link between the northeast and southwest had to be created, even at the cost of security. Edo had a river, and this could be enlisted. Once known as the Sumida, and called so today, Edo residents knew it as the Ōgawa ('Great River'). The flow was not exactly in the correct way, and nor could it feasibly be canalized to fit. But the river was close enough, and it did demarcate the city's eastern flank as required, and it also entered the sea properly in the southwest.

The loosely geomantic river was augmented by a second, more precise passageway. This took the form of a road. Since Edo lacked an overall grid, it was not hard to drive through a roadway along the path that *ki* needed to travel. Edo would be given no other thoroughfare. All roads except this one ended somewhere in a T-junction or a hairpin curve, deflected when their respective mini-grid ended and the next one began. Roads coming in from the countryside simply terminated when they hit one of the castle's moats. Unexpected twists and turns did not make for a practical city, so the *ki* highway was a logistical necessity, and it was very much used. But its principal use was geomantic, to traverse the city northeast to southwest, which it did rather more neatly than the Great River. Extraordinarily, however, Edo's single arterial boulevard had no name. The street was crucial for magical and practical reasons, but it was a worrying entity for the shogunate, almost inviting assault. It could be used, but could not be named.

☙

Lavish folding screens (*byōbu*) depicting the capital had been invented about 1500 and gained favour over the ensuing century. Today known as 'scenes in and around the *raku*' (*rakuchū rakugai-zu*), they attest to the continuing aura of the city, even as its classical self faded away (see illus. 3). Folding screens generally come in pairs, with left- and right-hand elements. Being a genre of the civil wars, screens do not use the two halves to show the historic Left and Right capitals, since they were gone. Instead, accepting the city's latter-day dismemberment, the halves show the Lower and Upper capitals. The Lower is on the right, and thus read first. This includes buildings across the Kamo, outside the confines of the original grid. Some of the city's most important medieval institutions were here, especially the temples, since Heian-kyō had allowed very few within the grid. Being outside the city proper, many of these survived the fighting. Included in 'capitalscapes',[6] as these screens have been called, will be the oldest temple of all, the Hōkan-ji ('temple of dharmic visions'), founded in 592 and thus pre-dating the capital itself. Its surrounding halls are gone but its Yasaka Pagoda was there, though this had actually been rebuilt about 1450 so was not very old. Later capital screens bring the city up to date, including the Hōkō-ji ('temple of widening expansion') with its massive Great Buddha Hall, Japan's largest ever temple structure, built by Hideyoshi in 1588. The Lower Capital had no significant secular buildings. The Upper Capital, which would be depicted on the left-hand screen, was different. It included the palace, relocated and much smaller than in former times, with courtiers' mansions close beside. Most prominent of all will be Nijō Castle, a mobile entity until 1603 when it became the shogun's fixed residence in the capital.

At some point – the dating is disputed, though likely the 1630s – the genre of 'scenes in and around the *raku*' was reworked to show not the capital, but Edo. The Idemitsu and Rekihaku screens, today regarded as the finest and earliest examples, were discussed in the Introduction (see illus. 4 and 5). There can be no doubt that an equivalence between the two cities was being demanded.

Screens showing Edo appeared later, and they were never as numerous as those showing the capital, even in the Edo period. This was partly for security reasons. The shogun did not want his city laid out too openly. There was also the matter that viewing things above one's station, even in pictures, was taboo, at least without shows of extreme deference. People who walked through Edo could see important buildings, and the castle's lofty keep was visible far and wide. But they should not stare and must avoid passing judgement. Artists were barely able to depict the castle, or daimyo mansions – unless, of course, the work was destined for the elite's own consumption. Commoners were supposed to experience silencing and blinding sensations, feeling what was termed 'awe' (*osore*). 'Awe' had to be presented in viewing and commenting on the great sites of the capital too, but the matter was much more pressured in Edo. Still, paired gold screens were anyway owned only by the rich, and beyond members of the shogun's entourage, people would have understood it to be improper to commission the subject of Edo's cityscape.

The Edo screens that do exist divide the city in the same manner as screens of the capital, with the temples mostly on the right and the secular powers on the left. The sacred precedes, and protects, the secular. Prestigious gold screens were generally placed behind an important person, to offset them in encounters with underlings. Since important people sat facing south, the right-hand side of a screen pair would be positioned in the east, and the left one in the west. In 'capitalscapes' this put the Lower (southern) part of the city in the east and the Upper (northern) in the west, illogically. Edo screens were actually much more geographically reasonable, since its temples actually were in the east, or rather in the northeast, as will be discussed in the next chapter. Placing them in the top right-hand corner of the right-hand screen put them in the 'gate of *ki*', where they were in reality. Edo Castle was then positioned to match, taking up much of the equivalent upper part of the left-hand screen. Edo Bay is below, and it did indeed open into the sea at the southwest. The water will be shown filled with festive boats, matching the floats of the famous Gion Festival, which are always included processing through the streets in screens depicting the capital. However, Edo views contained something that 'capitalscapes' could not match: the marvel of Mount Fuji, in the top-left corner.

Paired gold screens were used to depict a wide range of topics. Sometimes a pair was a continuous composition across both halves, but there was also the option of discontinuity, with disparate but complementary halves. On occasion, Edo was depicted paired with the capital. Squeezing the older city into just half its normal area while arrogating the resulting space to Edo was a brazen gesture, but perhaps this is why it was done. Edo–capital screen pairs put the shogunal city to the right and the capital to the left. Again, this was rational, since Edo is east of the capital. But the alignment also gives Edo the primary role. Edo becomes the necessary precondition of the capital's newly flourishing condition, even of its ability to survive.

∾

A terrible fire destroyed swathes of Edo in 1657 (see illus. 15). This forced a complete rebuilding of large parts of the city, including the castle. Some scholars believe that the Rekihaku screens were made to memorialize what had been lost in the fire. There would be later disasters too. Edo continually changed, and the shogunate changed with it. The Tokugawa entourage was always a military government, but soon it, the daimyo and their staff were only notional warriors.[7] Few could fight or even stand the sight of blood. Battlefield tactics slipped into martial arts, strenuously exercised but not put to the test. Edo's military aspect largely survived in cliché. In 1813, when Edo had seen no military urgency for two centuries, a person visiting from the capital announced to his friends that all the daimyo and lesser lords passing in the streets with their swords and pikes made him think he was back in the civil war. It was not an intelligent response, or at least not the opinion of those who heard him. His Edo friends teasingly called the man *kyōjin*, punning 'person from the capital' (*kyō* + *jin*) with the homophone 'madman' (*kyō* can also mean idiocy). Perhaps we can translate it as 'capital fool'.[8] He was falling for what had become pure choreography – a shogunal act.

In cultural matters too, despite Edo's newness, it made as much sense to visit the shogunal city as it did the capital when in search of sites of accomplished beauty or cultural interest. The capital too had its colossal fire, in 1788, so that when the 'capital fool' passed judgement,

Edo was actually the old city, in material terms. But the cliché went both ways. Just as people from the capital enjoyed imagining that Edo was warlike and frightening, Edo visitors to the capital liked to think of it as rather stick-in-the-mud. As the Edo person named Shiba Kōkan, who invented the 'capital fool' tag, put it, in urban terms, 'the capital drags its feet, while Edo is on the hop.' When this same person returned from a trip to the capital, he reported that 'with its many shrines, and temples, it is worth seeing,' noting that Edo by contrast has 'few shrines and temples worth seeing'.[9] If travellers move in a fixed frame of mind, they seek out only what they want to see. Actually, the capital's three most impressive sites were the Hōkō-ji and its Great Buddha Hall of 1588, the Shōkoku-ji, of 1382 (though all its structures post-dated 1600), and the Hongan-ji, built by Ieyasu. In historical terms Edo had as much.

A literary genre emerged called 'comparisons of the three ports' (*santsu kurabe*); that is, contrasting Edo, Osaka and the capital (which is inland but had river traffic). The point of such writing was to add clever additional observations to the prevailing view, finding witty extra reasons why Edo was military, rough and new; the capital civil, antique and calm; and Osaka with its empty castle and small military presence the 'nation's kitchen' (*tenka no daidokoro*).[10] If the triadic comparison was cumbersome, Osaka could be removed from the equation, leaving Edo and the capital as stark polarities. Any feature of one city had to be invoked in the exact opposite way for the other, under the tried and tested paradigm.

In about 1670, the famous Edo poet Matsuo Bashō composed a verse when he visited the capital. He was a specialist in the non-courtly *haikai* mode. Bashō's visit fell between the great fires of Edo and the capital. He wrote perceptively,

Even in the capital,
'How nostalgic for the capital!'
Sings the cuckoo.[11]

15 The Edo fire of 1657. This was Edo's worst conflagration, known as the Furisode ('flowing sleeves') fire. All the central and eastern part of Edo were lost, including the castle. A bridge was constructed over the Sumida to allow escape in any future emergency.
1 Edo Castle
2 Nihon-bashi
3 Zōjō-ji
4 Kan'ei-ji
5 Sensō-ji ('Asakusa Kannon')

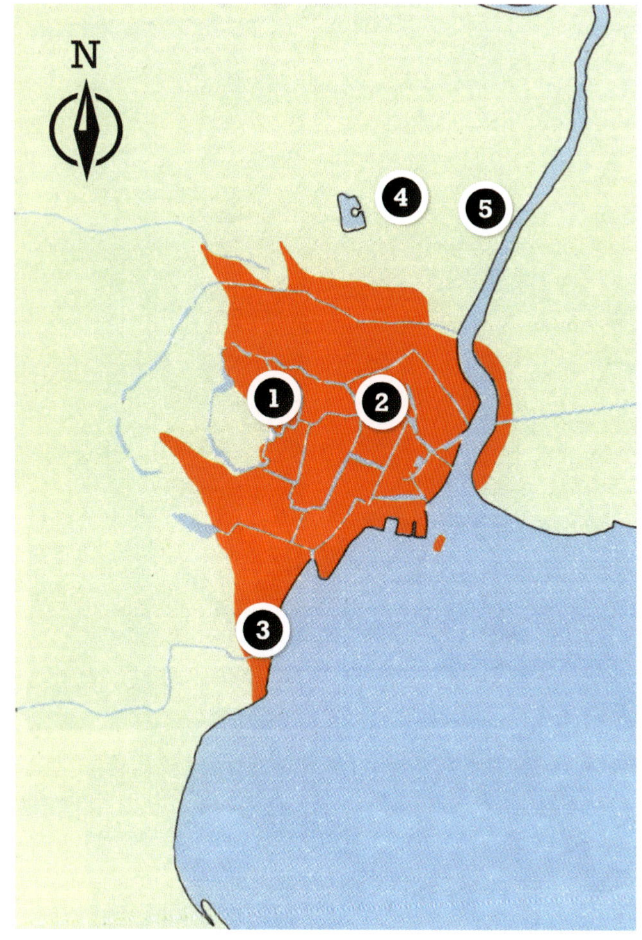

Cuckoos (*hototogisu*) were the fabled bird of the capital region and not to be heard in Edo. Their cry was the happy harbinger of spring. But to Bashō, right there in the middle of it, even surrounded by it, the capital was not there anymore. He was in a new city, and one that looked very like Edo. He had gone all that way only to find that the capital as he imagined it was not really present. The city's finest building, as he well knew, was the shogun's castle, just as it was in Edo. More impertinently, another Edo traveller, Kimuro Bōun, made the same trip about a century later, in 1766, and reported, 'the "flowering capital" is something of two hundred years ago; now it's more like the "flowering countryside"; it's merely provincial.'[12]

While Edo's conflagration of 1657 is always cited as a key moment in its history, the fire that erased the capital in 1788 does not fit its self-created mythology. It soon lapsed from popular memory – today few Japanese people have heard of it (illus. 16). Retention and continuity were supposed to mark the capital. Loss belonged to Edo. These clichés still endure. This book will challenge some of them.

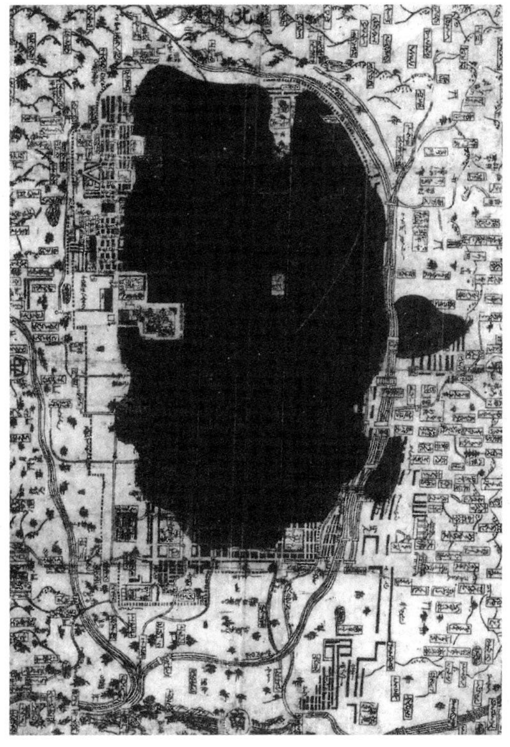

16 The Kyoto fire of 1788, monochrome print, ink on paper. This was the capital's worst fire, and the print shows burned-out parts in black covering almost the entire city. Virtually all buildings were lost, and today just five or six pre-1788 structures remain in central Kyoto.

Two
The Centre of the Shogun's Realm

n 1603 the court agreed to the creation of a new shogunate. It was exactly thirty years since the collapse of the previous one, but nearly a century since any shogun had actually wielded power. This memorable development, which signified reconnection and reconsolidation of the divided Japanese landscape, required commemoration. But how to do so? Japan had little tradition of monuments celebrating historic events. Some commemorative temples existed, but no triumphal arches, statues or inscribed pillars. And yet, for the first time in history, the Tokugawa shogunate did memorialize their nomination in this way. They constructed a vast and visible public edifice, not an arch or a pillar, but a bridge.

From 1600 the Tokugawa were largely in control, though scattered regions resisted their authority. The Toyotomi still held Osaka and its surrounding region. These two powerful families were allied, and peace prevailed between them, despite friction. The older Toyotomi never constructed commemorative monuments as such, but they did engage in public work to consolidate and glorify their rule. Hideyoshi, their patriarch, had built the lavish Hōkō-ji ('temple of widening expansion') in the capital, containing a Great Buddha Hall over 80 metres long and 45 metres high (equal to a dozen modern floors). It was the largest independent structure ever seen in Japan. More unusually, Hideyoshi had erected the capital's first city wall, or rather, embankment (*odoi*) (see illus. 12). It was built of earth since Japan lacks stone suitable for such things. Some 10 metres wide, 3 metres high and over 20 kilometres long, the embankment ringed the city in a previously unseen way.

There were ample precedents for temples, though the size of the Hōkō-ji was particularly stunning. As for the city wall, there were Chinese precedents, and indeed very few Japanese ones. But equally, there were Western examples. European cities were routinely walled at this time. Hideyoshi's embankment was a bricolage taken from several cultural environments, mostly foreign. It was built to meet the protective needs of the capital in a time of ongoing war, but was a way of doing so in outward-looking terms. The Sinosphere was being joined by other iconographical practices as Japan entered into global norms of asserting political authority.

More telling still, and more relevant to this chapter, is another of Hideyoshi's works. Again, it was not built to commemorate any specific moment, as the Tokugawa project would be; it celebrated the Toyotomi in a novel, if generalized, way. The unprecedented structure spoke of power and peace. In 1590 Hideyoshi erected the capital's first permanent bridge over the River Kamo. This joined the grid of the capital, which Hideyoshi had partially restored, to the newer, cross-river districts. The bridge was built at Third Avenue, one block south of what had once been the dairi's palace and was now the location of Hideyoshi's Nijō (Second Avenue) Castle. The structure was accordingly named Third Avenue Bridge or, more often, Great Third Avenue Bridge (Sanjō-[ō] hashi). A plaque was prominently affixed to it reading,

The Third Avenue Bridge of Rakuyō [Luoyang, or the capital] will support human traffic for generations to come. With solid foundations sunk five *jin* [approx. 3.8 m] into the ground, its 63 pillars of hewn stone are like supports to hold aloft our solar realm [*nichi-iki*, i.e. Japan]. It was opened on the First Day of xthe First Month of the eighteenth year of Tenshō [1590].[1]

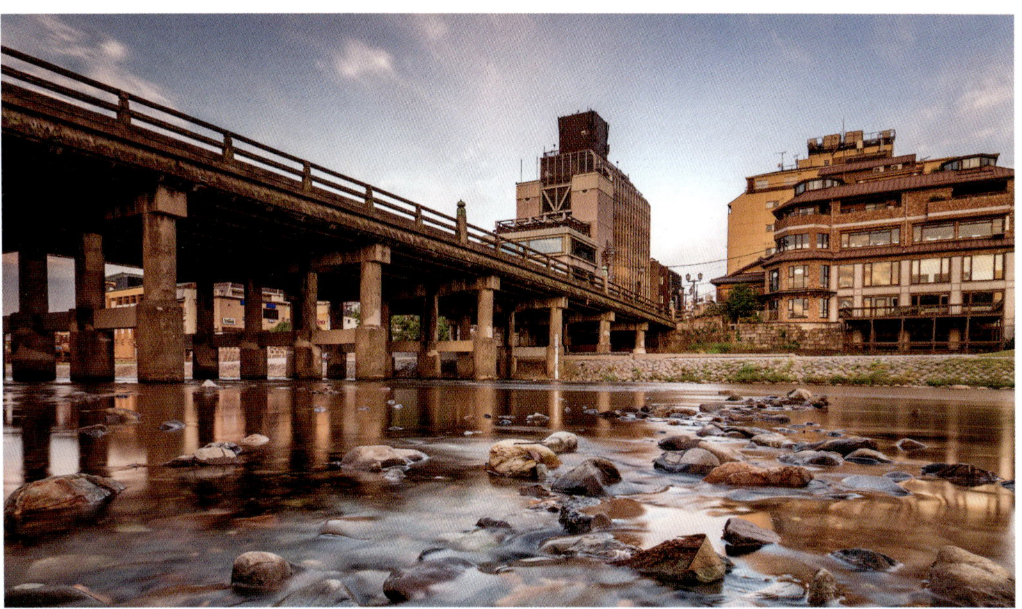

17 Sanjō Ōhashi bridge, Kyoto. The original bridge was built in 1590, and the ferroconcrete structure of 1950 retains some of the original pillars.

The bridge was constructed during the 1580s, to be opened on the first day of the new decade – not that the Japanese used Christian year numbers at the time. Except that some did. Many Europeans were living in Japan, a crucial fact to which we will return. The bridge was indeed well enough built to survive for generations, and some of its pillars continue to hold up its modern replacement (illus. 17).

Historically, the formal means of entering or leaving the capital was at the southern gate, the Rajō-mon. Over time, other access points had appeared, and loss of the grid in the medieval period meant that the Rajō-mon lost all primacy. A more recent point of entry and exit was at Second Avenue, to suit the needs of Nijō Castle. An ad hoc crossing of the river here allowed access to the militarily important east. Hideyoshi ignored this and built his bridge elsewhere. He may not have wanted a robust and permanent crossing too close to his castle. There were practical reasons too, since the land rises at Third Avenue, making it better for a bridgehead, being less likely to flood. Building his new place of access in the east demonstrated that Hideyoshi gave attention to the balance of power in his contemporary world. The south was not germane. He could have rebuilt the Rajō-mon, but he did not. Hideyoshi's new structure was a bridge rather than a gate, to link, rather than separate. He also built it so as to join up with the highway that led to the eastern regions, called the Tōkaidō ('east sea road').

☙

During Hideyoshi's time in power, and from some decades before it, a new ingredient in Japanese culture was the infusion of European norms. Portuguese and then Spaniards freely operated throughout the land, with their shipping calling into many ports. Hideyoshi was welcoming, though not consistently so. The Iberians came as missionaries and traders, and both groups would have expounded on the glory of their cities, whether Lisbon, Madrid or (since southern Italy was under Spanish control) Naples. Many members of the clergy had seen the Eternal City, with its monuments of past and present. Pope Sixtus V, known for extensive commemorative building, was in office as Hideyoshi's bridge went up. The first Japanese embassy to Rome departed in 1582, passing Lisbon, Madrid, Venice and many other fine cities before arriving in 1585.[2] The Japanese delegates happened to be present for the death of Pope Gregory XIII and the accession of Sixtus. They were lavishly provided with gifts, and one was of special significance. This was the period's most important book illustrating European and colonial cities, a compilation of coloured prints by Georg Braun and Frans Hogenberg entitled *Civitates orbis terrarum* (Cities of the World). The vast publishing project was still under way, so the Japanese could only take home the first volume (illus. 18).[3] Hideyoshi interviewed the entourage on its return in 1590. He may have seen the book, or even been given it. At any rate, an unnamed Japanese potentate did see it, and admired the work enough to commission a stunning gold screen pair showing 28 selected cities copied from Braun and Hogenberg's views (illus. 19).[4] European cities had palaces and religious buildings, just like Japan, and also walls and bridges, as Japan's capital has recently been given. But they also contained specifically commemorative structures, and in plenty. The notion was

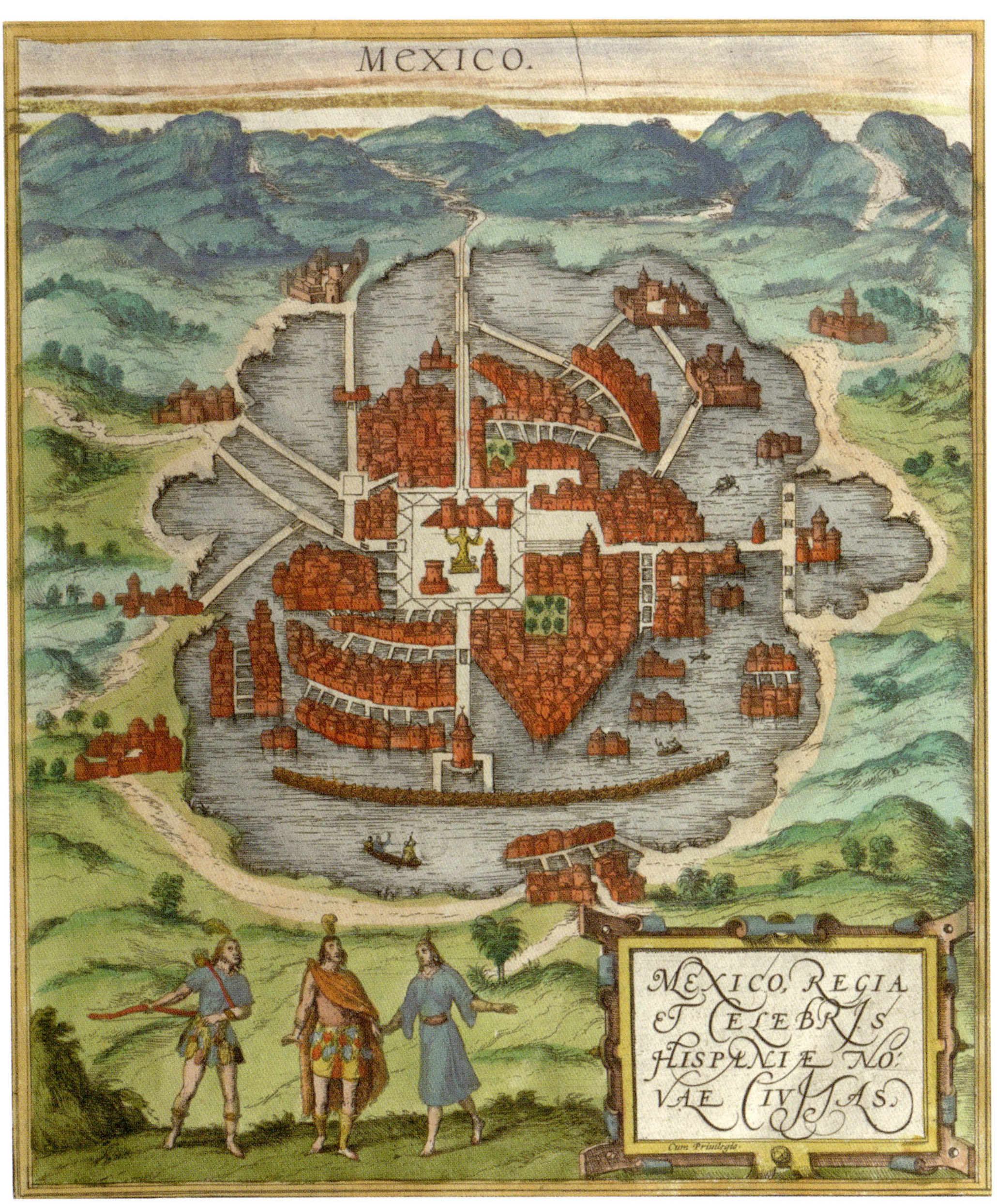

18 Franz Hogenberg, after Antoine du Pinet, Mexico City (formally Tenochtitlán), in Georg Braun and Franz Hogenberg, *Civitates orbis terrarum* (1572). Volume I of this famous compendium was taken home by the first Japanese embassy to Europe in 1587.

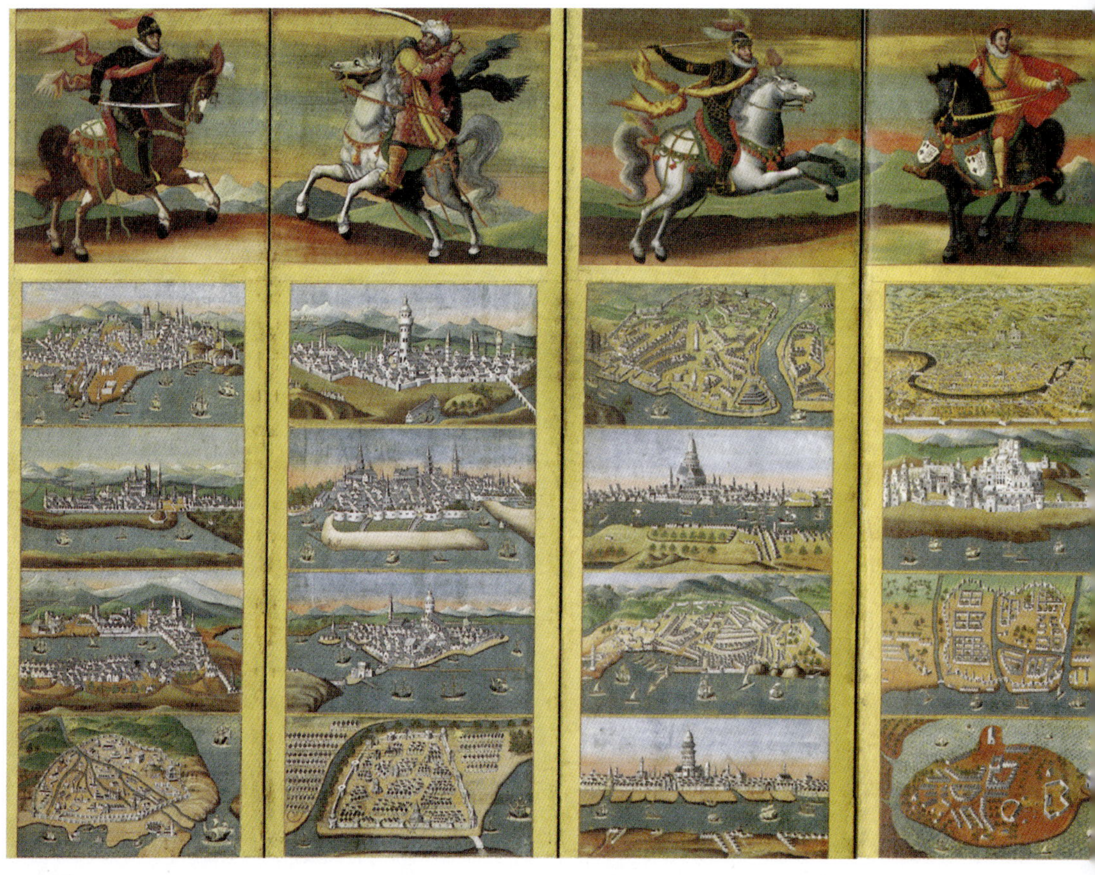

surely put across that historical events could, and should, be recorded in permanent, public and monumental ways. If Hideyoshi was aware of this only at the end of his life, Ieyasu, seven years his junior but much longer-lived, took the initiative further. Ieyasu intended the edifice that is the focus of this chapter to announce who and what the Tokugawa were, and the date this was achieved, 1603. He also wanted to show *where* they were, for his monument was not erected in the capital but in his own, rather remote city. Far from the ancient cultural centres, this monument would begin the shogunate's move to dispel long-standing jibes about the barbaric east, and to provide not just a focal point for Edo but a new centre for the entire 'solar realm'.

19 Unknown artist, *Map with Twenty-eight City Views*, c. 1600, screen (half of pair), gold and colour on paper. The artist, probably Jesuit-trained, transposes views from Braun and Hogenberg onto a gold screen, adding warriors (from another source) along the top. Screens come in pairs, and this composition is paired with a world map (not reproduced here).

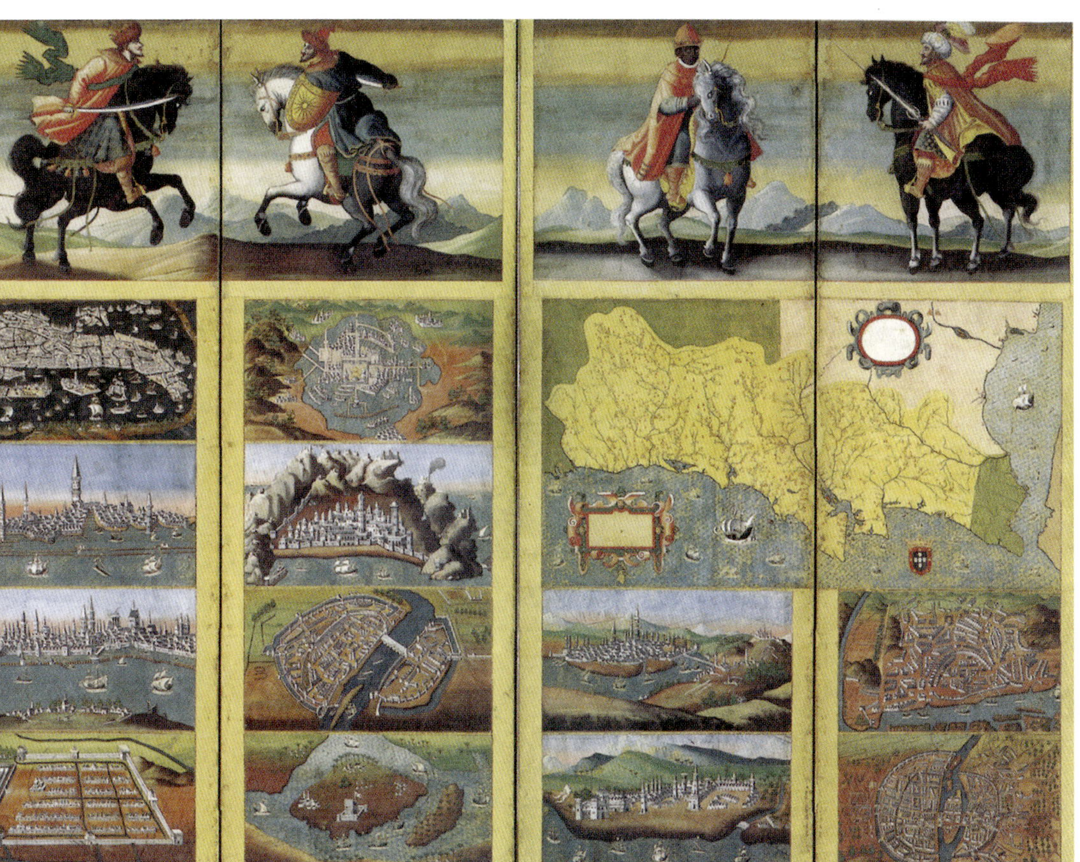

In 1603 Edo was still swampy and ill-defined. Drainage work had been carried out in places and the waterfronts strengthened. Housing was roughly zoned, temples laid out and the colossal Edo Castle had been built over old foundations. But Edo retained a generally unimpressive feel, and the built environment was rather paltry. A large public statement would certainly stand out. As Edo turned from military encampment to shogunal city, with aspirations of being a site of peace and plenty, the monument should speak of present and future hope and the benevolence the shogunate would always show its subjects throughout the land.

No documentation survives to allow us to know motivations behind the building of the great bridge in Edo, but we can make inferences on the evidence of what is there and from our wider understanding of bridges. Hideyoshi had built a bridge in the capital, but the impulse behind Ieyasu's equivalent can be construed as utterly different. It was also far more visible than Hideyoshi's bridge, since it was not built on the city's fringe to link the city with a world beyond, but was put up within the city and declared its central point, and the node that bound Edo together and render it internally whole.

Edo had many moats, dug to protect and drain, and these were negotiated by ferries. Bridges would have negated the defensive purpose. Before 1603 none had been built, and none as large as this would be for some half a century after, either. In commemorating themselves with such a structure, the Tokugawa had to be careful not to undermine internal security, but a bridge gave connectedness, facilitating linkage and coming together, and thus peace.

East Asia's first city centre and its first public commemoration must have had some external input. This is likely to have been European. The Europeans who sought most access to seats of Japanese power, far from the trading ports, were priests. The Japanese called them *bateren*, from *padre*, but the priests' own name for themselves was *pontifex*, Latin for 'bridge builder'. The missionaries would have explained to their Japanese converts that the Pope was the *pontifex maximus*. The priests might also have offered the thought that Christianity's most famous expression of the whole and peaceful city appears in Psalm 122, which calls Jerusalem 'builded as a city that is at unity in itself' (*quae conjuncta est sibi*), 'For there are the thrones of judgement'; the psalmist enjoins, 'Peace be within thy walls, and plenteousness within thy palaces.' From 1603 sectioned-up Edo also became a unity, a place of rule and site of prosperity.

The bridge was not built across the Great River (the Sumida), which was at Edo's flank and would have led outside the city, but across Edo's most central moat. The span was vast, at nearly 50 metres long. It was impressive and elegant, with ornamental iron bollards at both ends. Its curvature rose much higher than Hideyoshi's Great Third Avenue Bridge so as to allow masted boats to pass beneath.

Standing on the apex, a person had a wide view over the growing but mostly single-storey city. Even more remarkable than the length and height, users felt, was the width. It should be remembered that for most people, this was the only bridge they ever crossed, other perhaps than a plank laid over a country stream. A vast volume of traffic could cross en masse, in both directions at once. It had a spar in the centre, separating the two streams of traffic, which passed in an orderly way, each on its own side. The bridge was used voluminously but with a rare decorousness, as proper for a gift from the regime to the people. The name came from its width, and it was known as Nihon-bashi, 'bridge of two carriageways'. The waterway beneath acquired the name of Nihon-bashi-gawa ('river of the bridge of two carriageways').

Nihon, of course, can also mean something else. Here again, the facts are frustratingly unrecorded, but a homophonic pun must have been envisaged from the start. *Nihon* more often means 'Japan' – so this was also the Bridge of Japan. Edo's interior compactor was an emblem for the whole realm. It commemorated Ieyasu's installation as shogun and declared itself not only as the centre of Edo but as the whole country's focal binding point. The Tōkaidō met Hideyoshi's bridge just outside the capital, but in Edo that same highway was drawn right into the city to meet the bridge. It thus formed part of Edo's sole cross-city boulevard (discussed in Chapter One). Importantly, the point where this road met Ieyasu's bridge was now declared the highway's beginning, not its end. The Tōkaidō was conceptually reversed, no longer running from the capital to the east, but the other way around, with Edo now the originating site. The shogunate maintained five roads, the Gokaidō ('five highways'), across the central Japanese island, with each now deemed to begin from Edo. Distances were measured outwards from Edo, and specifically from Nihon-bashi; they still are in Japan today. The name 'bridge of two carriageways' fell from use, if it had ever been widely used, and the place was formally written with characters meaning Bridge of Japan.

The panoramic screens of Edo referred to above invariably show the bridge, often placing it directly under the castle, in an arrangement that suggests the shogun can look directly over it (illus. 20 and 21).

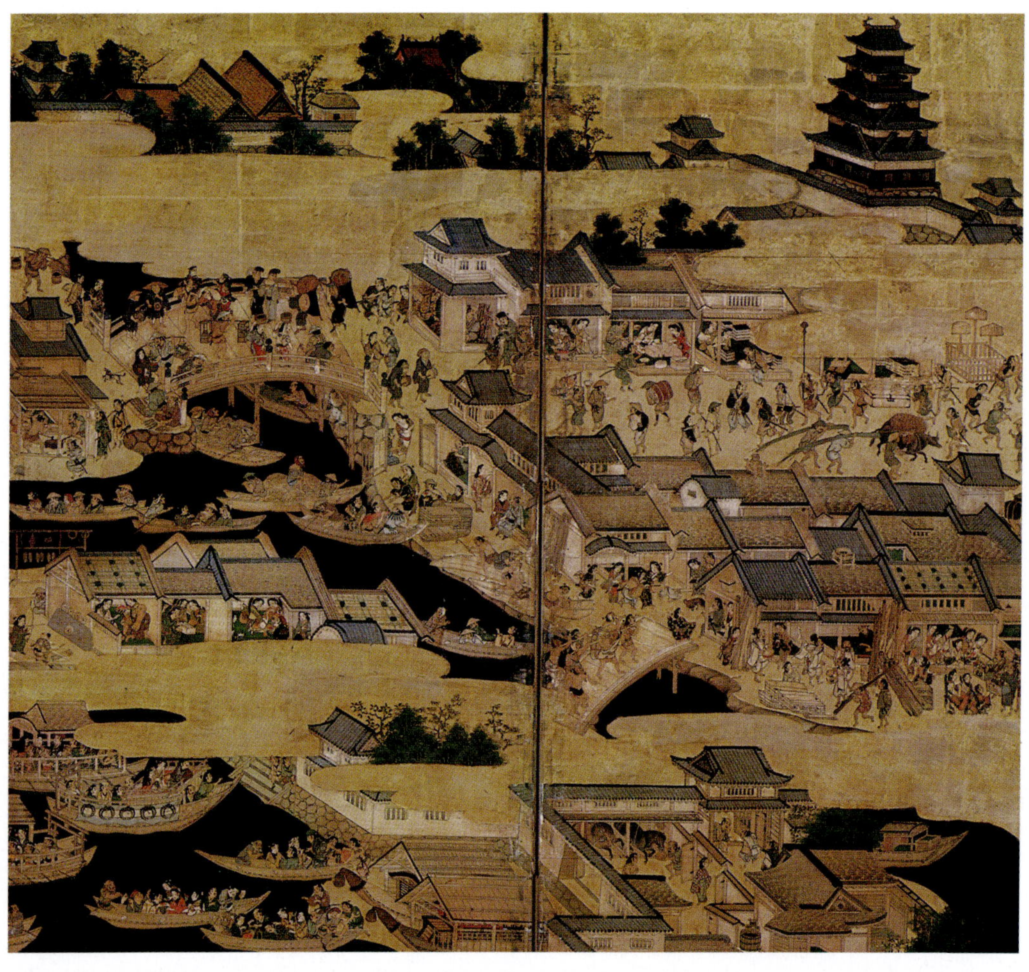

20 Detail of illustration 4, left panel, 'Edo Castle and Nihon-bashi'. The keep of the castle is shown, though the rest is deferentially hidden. Below to the left is teeming Nihon-bashi. The bridge at the lower right was constructed later.

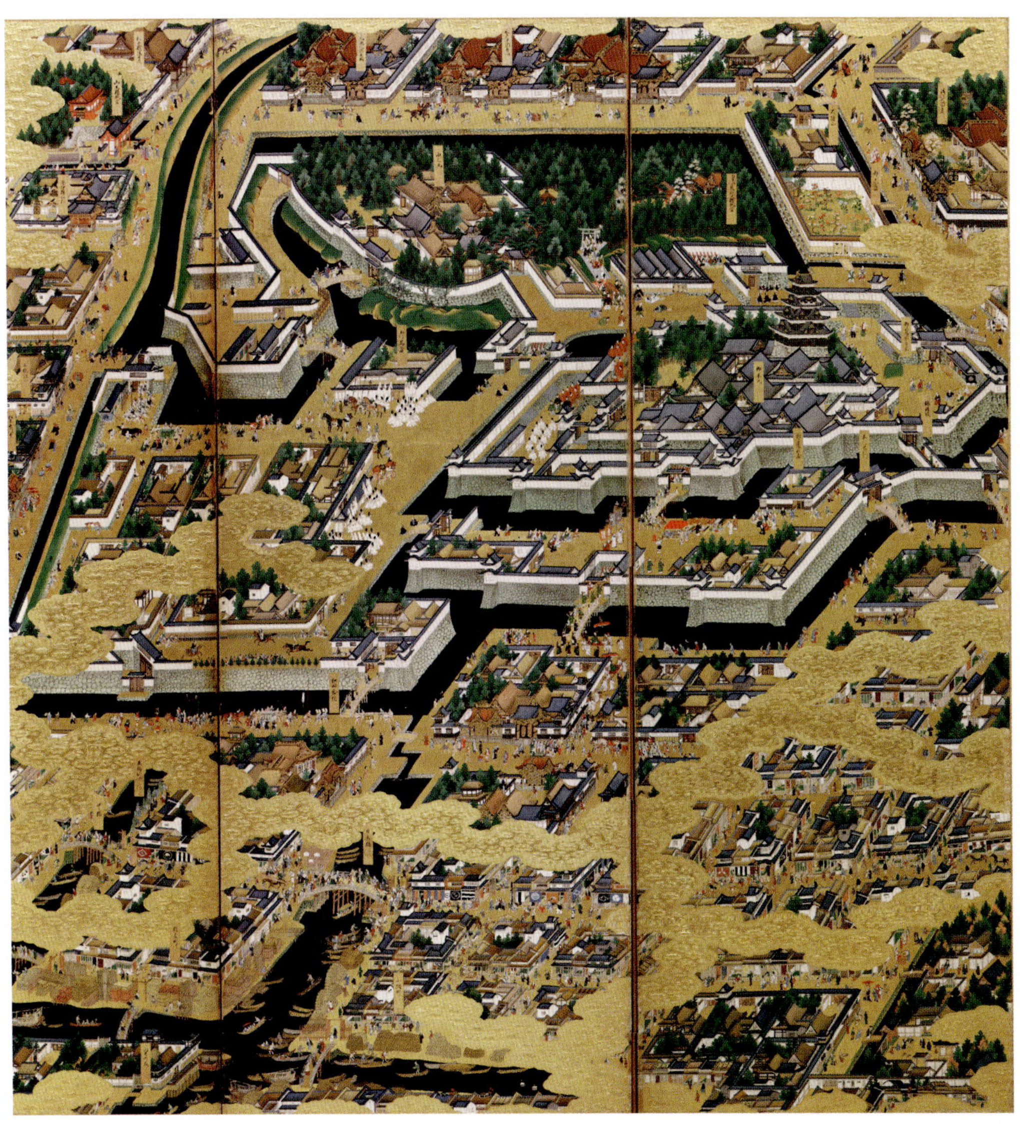

21 Detail of illustration 5, left panel, 'Edo Castle and Nihon-bashi'. Made for a very elite person, this screen shows the castle in considerable detail. Nihon-bashi is to the lower left.

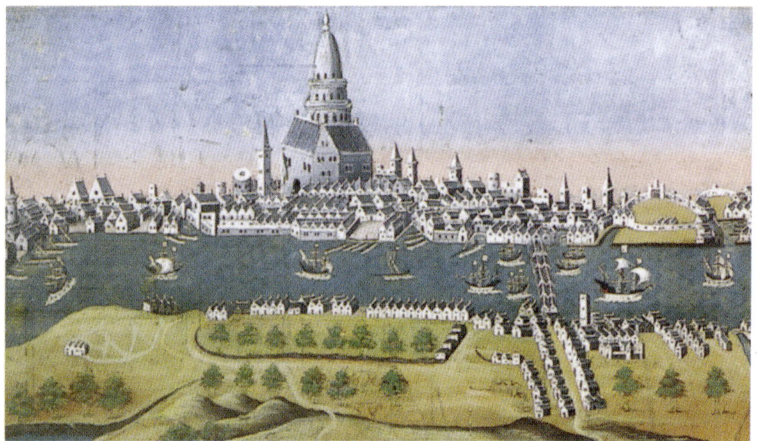

22 Detail of illustration 19, 'London'. The image adds elements to the Braun and Hogenberg original, though still concentrating on Old St Paul's and London Bridge.

Across Europe, cities have centres, but they are not bridges. As Braun and Hogenberg showed, their nodal points of coming together were most often squares, perhaps named after key political moments. Later examples include the place des Victoires in Paris, laid out in 1685, or Trafalgar Square in London of 1844, the latter also the zero point for measuring distances, and named after the existential struggle to preserve the autonomy of the British state. Such civic spaces were available for filling with monuments. Buildings of iconic importance might be gathered around them: palaces, noble residences, perhaps a church. In the case of London, there are colonial embassies and a National Gallery, so proposing British guardianship of European culture, with a church dedicated to St Martin, the patron saint of adventure.

Braun and Hogenberg showed how European cities did indeed have stunning bridges. Notable was London Bridge, its original dating to around the year 55 CE, and the one then standing to 1209. London and its bridge were among the cities included on the gold screen pair decorated with cityscapes from Braun and Hogenberg (illus. 24). Yet all these bridges led *from* the city and on to

23 Rialto Bridge, Venice, Italy, built 1588–91 by Antonio da Ponte with the help of Antonio Contino. Thought almost miraculous when it was built, the Rialto Bridge became the effective centre of Venice.

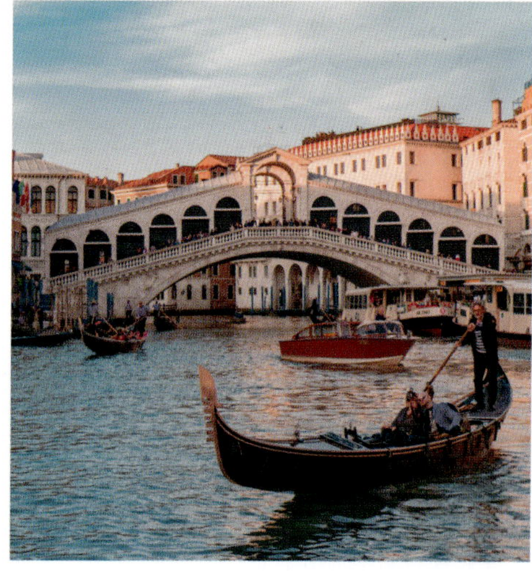

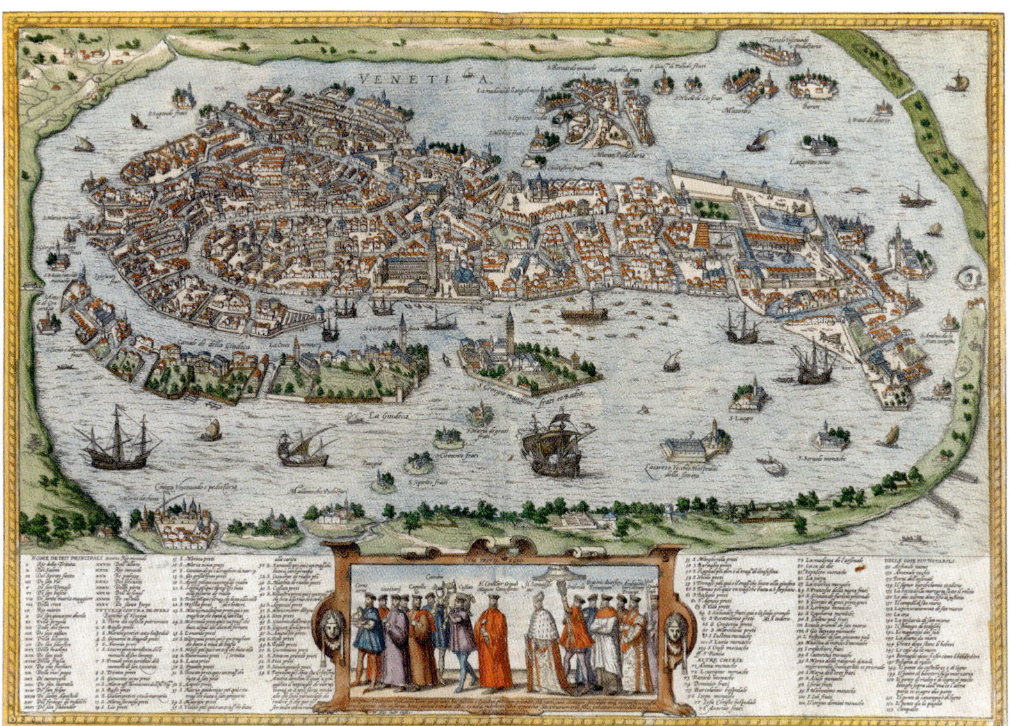

24 Franz Hogenberg, after Joris Hoefnagel, 'Venice', in Georg Braun and Franz Hogenberg, *Civitates orbis terrarum* (1572). Most cities are shown as vistas, but Venice takes the form of a map.

somewhere else, as Hideyoshi's did. Of Europe's cities, only Venice was centred on a bridge. Originally it was built to join the mint to the market – that is, the city's spaces of fiduciary and practical commerce. The golden screen pair also includes Venice, though rendered in the form of a map (illus. 24, see illus. 19). We have already seen how its appearance captured the imagination of Utagawa Toyoharu later in the Edo period (see illus. 7). In 1591 Venice's city council built a new bridge designed by the aptly named Antonio da Ponte, the single span thought miraculous at the time. It remains today as the Rialto Bridge (illus. 23). A civic square was too risky for Edo; a bridge was a more defendable core. But bridges had profound meanings of their own. Being the first things to be destroyed in war, when standing they denote peace. But they also meant more.

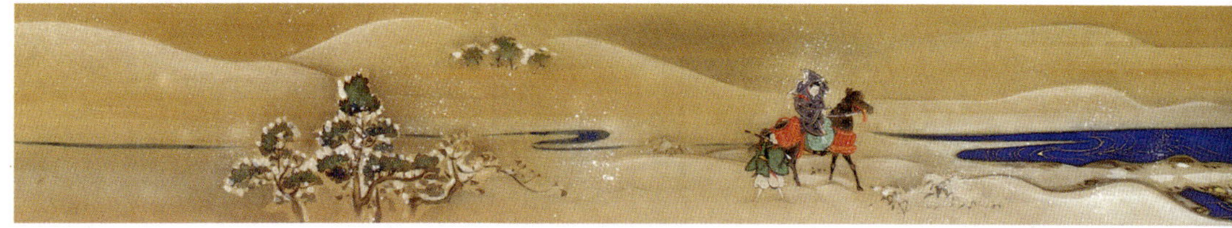

25 Suzuki Kiitsu, 'Sano Crossing', detail from *Poetic Ideas of the Four Seasons*, c. 1830–40, set of four handscrolls, ink and colour on paper. Snow buffets the classical poet Fujiwara no Teika, who raises a sleeve in protection as he prepares to ride over the pontoon bridge at Sano.

There was an international dimension to Ieyasu's monument, but Nihon-bashi also drew on local ideas. Japan is mountainous, and melting snow creates spring torrents. The rainy season and typhoons deposit vast volumes of water. Rather few bridges had ever been built because they were so prone to being washed away. Those that existed were maintained because of utilitarian need, and because of their rarity they played important roles as foci of thought. The two most famous ones, noted since ancient times, were the Sano Crossing (Sano no watari) and Uji Bridge (Uji-bashi). The first was constructed in antiquity and had long since disappeared; Sano was a crossing in memory only. While still there it had figured in one of the most hallowed of court verses, which, as stated above, are often set in real, physical locations. Sites of repeated poetic inspiration were known as 'poetic pillows' (*utamakura*), as if generations of verses reposed on an ever-deepening cushion.[5] Poetic pillows will be discussed in Chapter Four, but Sano and Uji, which numbered among them, are relevant here.

Sano is in remote Kii province, now part of Shingū city, in Wakayama Prefecture. The great poet Fujiwara no Teika had written a verse on the site, anthologized for posterity in 1205:

> To stop my horse
> And shake out my sleeves
> I find nowhere.
> At Sano Crossing
> In snowfall, one evening.[6]

Far from the capital, in the dead of winter, the courtier finds himself pitifully at the mercy of the elements. This sense of woe was an

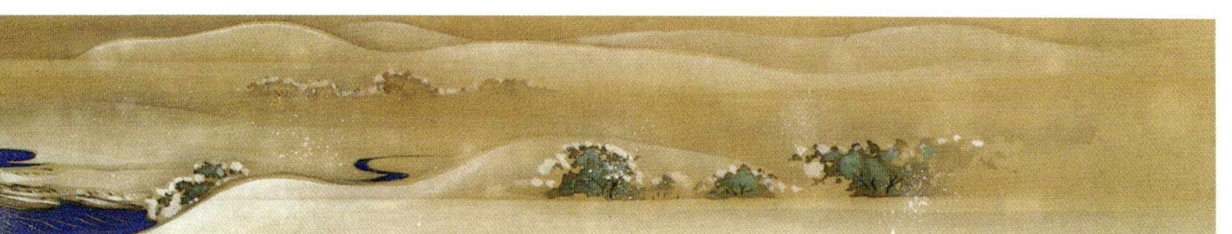

infrequent sentiment for such a powerful man, hence the poignancy of Teika's verse. 'Poetic pillows' were also made the subject of paintings, and by convention Sano was shown as a pontoon bridge, which perhaps it had been, removable when snowmelt made the current too strong. Teika will be depicted holding up a sleeve to ward off falling snow (illus. 25). The crossing swayed and felt dangerous. Invocation of Sano conveyed a sense of tremulousness and insecurity, compounded by the wintry season. Sano offered a connectivity that was somewhat anxious, and not always there (being removed in heavy weather). It was unstable even when in place. By 1603, when Ieyasu built his bridge, the Sano Crossing was gone for good.

Uji Bridge was different. It gave access to the capital from the south, a couple of hours' ride outside the city, so was more central, and was greatly used, especially as the capital's main access gate, the Rajō-mon, led southwards. Uji was far from any mountains so the bridge was less prone to be washed away (though it had still been occasionally). Famously, the span had also been damaged in fighting, at the Battle of Uji Bridge in 1180. On that occasion, defenders had torn up the bridge planks to prevent an enemy army entering and seizing the capital. This was memorably recounted in the much-read war chronicle of about 1325, the *Tales of the Heike* (*Heike monogatari*). Twenty-eight thousand riders descended on the bridge; the first two hundred were the greatest men, but they fell through the holes in the planking, unable to stop in time, and drowned as 'the battle of the bridge raged like fire'.[7] Uji was also much depicted in art as one of the most evoked 'poetic pillows', its symbolic meaning related to the embattled quality of the Japanese realm, built only to be torn apart again (illus. 26). If Sano prompted a personal kind of meditation,

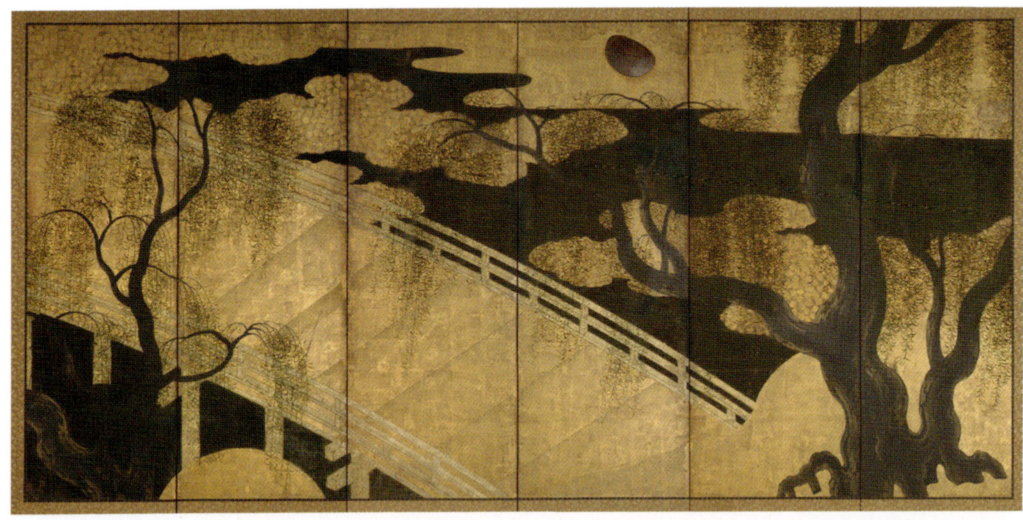

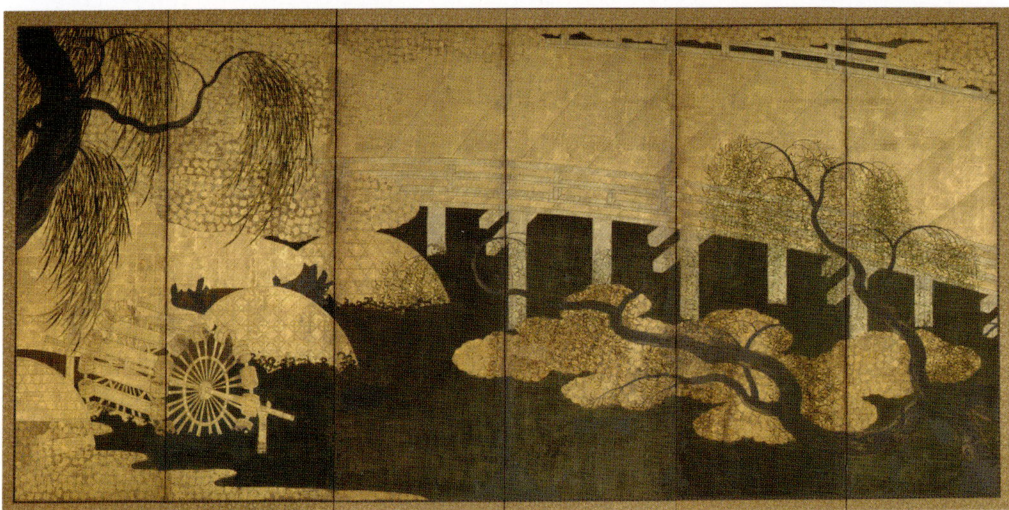

26 Unknown artist, *Willows and Bridge*, early 17th century, pair of six-panel folding screens, ink, colour, copper, gold and gold leaf on paper, 171.8 × 352 cm each. Uji Bridge was a 'poetic pillow' indicative of sadness, and as such was depicted in autumn, under a bright moon. The place invokes the fictional tragic figure of the 'young lady at Uji Bridge'. The upper screen would be positioned to the right, and the lower to the left.

Uji offered scope for statewide cogitation. Both crossings, as literary constructions, connoted the precariousness of interconnection.

Unlike Sano, the toponym Uji offered a pun. Many 'poetic pillows' were evoked not because a poet had truly visited the place, but because the place name was homophonous with the emotional predicament the poet wished to evoke. Written with other characters, *uji* can mean 'sadness', and so this bridge, which connected, also suggested parting. Lament might be heroically masculine, in the doleful loss of brothers-in-arms, or it might be female, owing to another association of the place. In ancient times courtiers built summer houses at Uji to escape the searing heat of the capital. Ladies would reside there, visited by men as their work allowed, and would be called back to the city when autumn approached. Many are the narratives of ladies waiting a recall that never came. A fictional character emerged, known generically as 'the young lady at Uji Bridge' (*Uji no hashi-hime*), eternally abandoned there. One of the best-known verses was again by Teika:

> The desolation of it!
> On a night of waiting,
> With the autumn wind blowing,
> She spreads out half the moon,
> The young lady at Uji Bridge.[8]

In a transferred epithet, Teika elides the loneliness of a single bed with a half-moon. In East Asian verse, autumn moons are invariably shown full, as the harvest moon. Teika breaks this convention to parallel the woman's solitary condition. Paintings of Uji generally have the bridge with a half-moon above. Also included are willows, which often grew by riverbanks but whose tangled branches were said to resemble the unkempt tresses of an abandoned woman.

The above references are secular, but bridges also had significance within Buddhism. To build a bridge was taken as an act of merit. It assisted people, by providing a service that was costly and intricate. But the meaning was more than practical. In China, since ancient times monks had built bridges to demonstrate mercy.[9] In Japanese, the expression 'reaching the opposite bank' (*hitaigan*) meant to attain Buddhist Enlightenment, so a bridge was an apparatus to convey a person, unfailingly and safely, to that further place.

A monk named Dōto is credited with building the first Uji Bridge, perhaps the first bridge in Japan, in 646. The practice of monastic construction continued into Edo times, with immigrant monks playing a major role. A Chinese cleric named Mozi Ruding (J: Mokusu Nyotei), resident in the port of Nagasaki, constructed a bridge in 1634.[10] It was Japan's first double-span stone bridge. Ruding assisted people by showing them advanced technology, but he also announced his evangelistic purposes, and an interconnectedness between Japan and his foreign homeland (illus. 27). Later monks emulated Ruding until Nagasaki had multiple bridges, as it still does, far more than needed, over its central river – fifteen in fact.[11] In 1649 the Dutch East India Company was invited to build one too, in Western style, though they declined.[12]

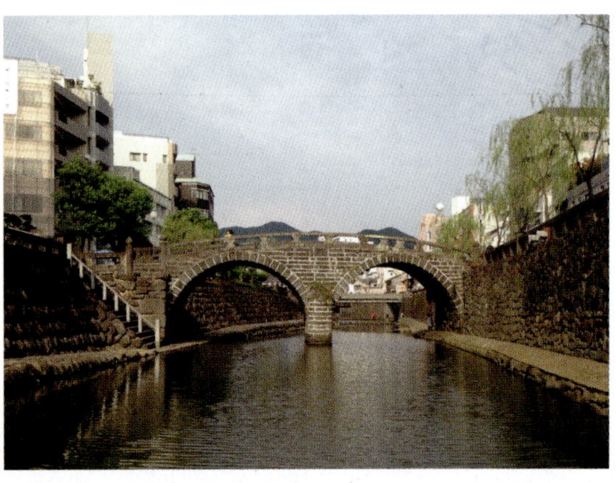

27 Megane-bashi or 'Spectacles' Bridge, Nagasaki, built 1634, rebuilt 1982. The double span is reflected in the water, looking like a pair of glasses. It was built by Chinese monks to assist their adoptive city.

The venerable monk Mokujiki built Edo's only stone bridge, the Drum Bridge (Taiko-bashi) in Meguro, just outside the central area, and although its date of erection is not recorded we know that Mokujiki died in 1695.[13] However, there is also a legend that the Drum Bridge was rebuilt by the monk Saiun, a key figure in Edo popular religion; previously a layman named Kichiza, he had rejected the advances of the woman Oshichi, who in her misplaced love had started one of Edo's worst fires in 1683.[14] Oshichi and Kichiza became the basis for many stories.[15] Kichiza made amends by taking the tonsure and building a bridge. The much-loved bridge is known from a print by Hiroshige (illus. 28).

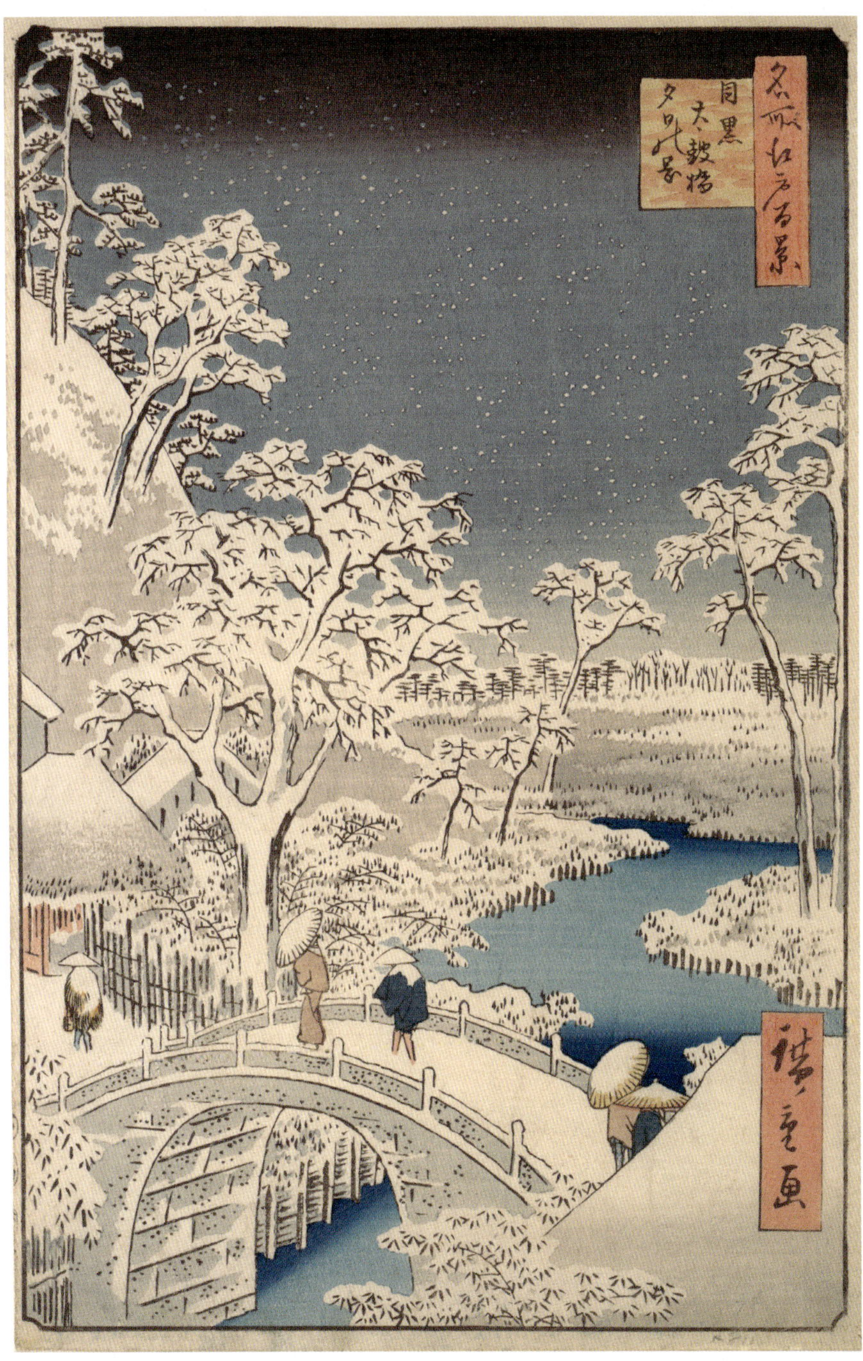

28 Utagawa Hiroshige, 'The Taiko (Drum) Bridge and the Yuhi Mound at Meguro', 1857, from *One Hundred Famous Places in Edo*, multicoloured woodblock print. The single span made a reflection resembling a drum. It was Edo's only stone bridge and a popular site.

Nihon-bashi partook of this wealth of bridge-related imagery, metaphor and story, local and foreign. Its aura was further enhanced by the fact that all roads departed from there. Those who crossed the bridge heading westwards began a fourteen-day walk along the Tōkaidō to the capital. Those who went east joined the Nikkō-dōchū (Nikkō Highway), which led to Ieyasu's splendid mausoleum, four days' walk from Edo. In 1651 the third shogun, Iemitsu, was also buried there (all other shoguns were buried in Edo itself). Edo's central bridge was thus a fulcrum of two great highways, one to the capital, with Japan's historic religious sites, the other to the Tokugawa sanctuaries. To stand on Nihon-bashi was to stand on a spot between the capital and Nikkō, between court and shogunate, with access in either direction.

The Tōkaidō was intensively travelled. It had 53 checkpoints, or stations (*sekisho* or *tsugi*), to strictly control the journey. Fifty-three was no arbitrary number. It specifically invoked the spiritual quest of the boy Sudharna (J: Zenzai-dōji), a 'child of wealth' whose striving for Enlightenment is recounted in the culminating book of the *Garland Sutra* (Skt: *Avatamsaka sutra*; J: *Kegon-kyō*), a primary text of Japanese Buddhism.[16] Sudharna is sent in search of knowledge by the bodhisattva of wisdom, Manjusri (J: Monjū), and in pursuit of this he visits fifty teachers, achieving nothing. His 51st teacher is the future Buddha, Maitreya (J: Miroku bosatsu), who detects an inkling of awakening and sends him back to Manjusri, as his 52nd teacher. Impressed, Manjusri introduces him to Samantabhadra (J: Fugen-bosatsu), the bodhisattva of universal good, who brings Sudharna to Enlightenment. As Samantabhadra tells him:

> By the endless surpassing blessing realised from dedication
> To the practice of good,
> May worldlings submerged in the torrent of passion
> Go to the higher realm of Infinite Light.[17]

This conceptualization of the highway fitted with Edo's status in 1603 as a new city, still largely an encampment, mired in war. After walking the 500 kilometres from Nihon-bashi, passing 53 shogunal inspectors, a person entered the capital to find Japan's most venerable seats of learning.

In the other direction the Nikkō Highway was shorter, at just 23 stations. The number was not significant, but the defining feature of this route was geomantic. It left Edo by the sensitive northeast, or 'gate of *ki*' (*kimon*), passing Asakusa, once outside the city, but now incorporated into Edo.

❧

Every day Nihon-bashi pulsated with people, whose concerns were not necessarily metaphysical. The earliest depictions of the area suggest the atmosphere (see illus. 20 and 21). This was a place where a huge variety of types of people assembled. Bridges channel people into bottlenecks, and the Tokugawa used this funnelling for control, but also to concentrate architectural and spatial statements about their polity. Nihon-bashi gave stunning views – rare in Edo, which lacked the overall grid of formally planned cities. It afforded Edo's only extensive vista, down the Nihon-bashi river directly towards the castle. The bridge had been sited here precisely to present a view on to the seat of authority. It was a castle, after all, so could not but be visible. Nihon-bashi was positioned with the castle to its west, the morning sun brilliantly illuminating its gold-ornamented towers. The castle gate was at its eastern side, meaning the first rays streamed in, radiating the shogun. Later on, another bridge would be built where the Nihon-bashi river entered the castle moat – as is visible in some pictures – but in the original project the view was uninterrupted (illus. 29).

Along both sides of the Nihon-bashi river, running up to the castle, were storehouses. These were for produce from throughout the archipelago and from the wider world. They supplied only the castle, not the city at large. A person looking from the bridge recognized the castle's power to gather and command. Though generally referred to as Edo Castle, its real name, we recall, was Chiyoda-jō, 'castle in

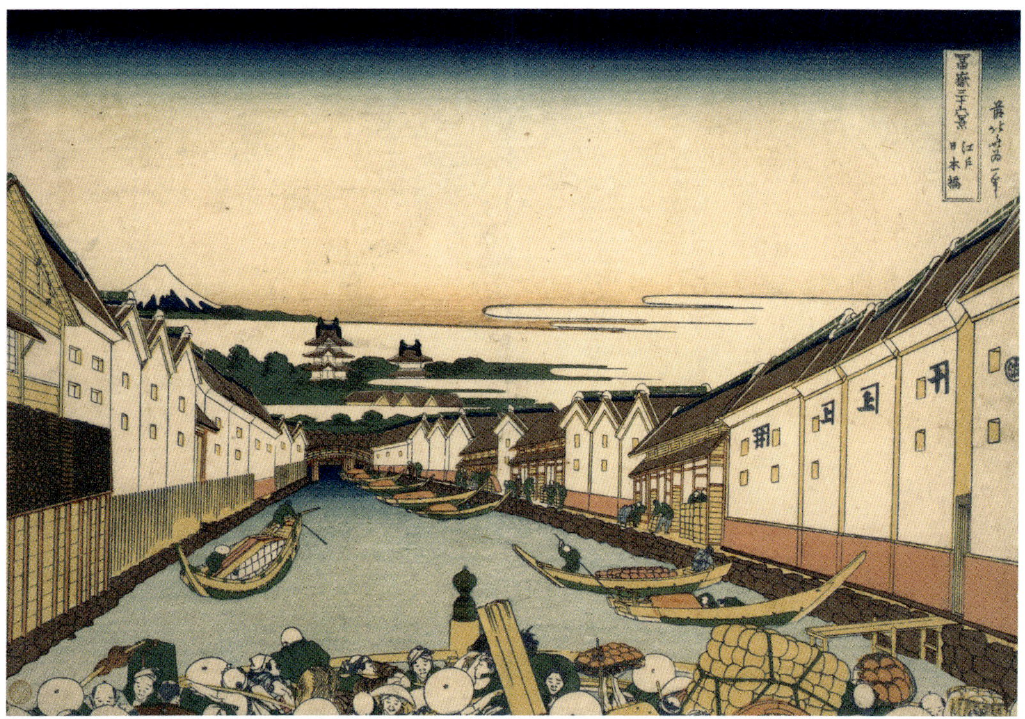

29 Katsushika Hokusai, 'Nihon-bashi in Edo', from the series *Thirty-six Views of Mount Fuji*, c. 1830–32, multicoloured woodblock print. Full perspective would reduce the castle to a speck, so Hokusai positions it in its own separate space, floating above. Only Mount Fuji is higher.

the rice fields for one thousand generations'. Here was the Tokugawa social contract: the regime secured peace, guaranteeing freedom from privation. In return, it intended to endure. In the language of the time, the shogunate 'ordered the world to succour the people' (*keisei saimin*).[18] Order was the primary requirement.

When standing on Nihon-bashi, the castle towered somewhat to the right. It was not aligned to be dead ahead. This was to permit a counterpoising on the left by the conical shape of Mount Fuji. The name is another pun, or rather puns. *Fuji* can mean 'not two', giving the sense that the mountain was peerless. It can also mean 'not death', and thus undying and immortal. Today Fuji is the symbol of Japan as a whole, but it was not so in Edo times. Fuji is far from the capital, and it was thus the symbol of the east, where Edo lay. 'Not two' could indicate that it was unparalleled by anything in the capital. The mountain promised Edo unique permanence.

Bridges have two sides, and Nihon-bashi afforded complementary prospects in the two directions. The eastward view, away from the castle, was another structured iconography. Here was Edo's fish market. Fish was not yet a Japanese staple food, for the capital is inland. But Edo was full of seafood. This market was reputed to gross more than 1,000 *ryō* per day, where 1 *ryō* officially bought 1 *koku* of rice, or enough to feed an adult for a year.[19] Flat-bottomed boats drew up to the bridge, landing vast quantities of fish, these being plentiful and cheap. Pictures show pedlars passing about with panniers (illus. 30). Beyond the fish market were more storehouses, mirroring those on the other side, but these were for commoner use. There was another bridge here too, also a later addition, called Edo-bashi. As people humorously remarked, the market connected Edo and Nihon.[20] But markets are rough and smelly, while buying and selling was unrefined. This demotic landscape was Nihon-bashi's reverse. It was central to the shogun's polity but did not impinge on eyes directed at the castle.

Topographical prints of Edo's notable places became popular in the mid-eighteenth century, far exceeding panoramas on golden screens both in number and availability. They could be bought by anyone – and this necessitated circumspect treatment of elite sites. Any whiff of lese-majesty would bring severe reprimand both to artist and to publisher. It may seem inconsistent that a vista was generated but was also only to be viewed with deference. Indeed it also began to seem inconsistent to the regime. Huge and visible castles were part of the apparatus of civil war. Over time, they embarrassed the shogunate, which wished to withdraw, as all East Asian elites did, into lower visibility. It may even have been a relief when the terrible fire of 1657 took out the main castle keep; it was never rebuilt. In terms of pictures made for commoners, Edo Castle was shown most judiciously. Consider two depictions by the commoner artist Hokusai. One was illustrated above and the other, similarly popular, was a two-page spread of an Edo guidebook (see illus. 29 and 31). The former shows the demotic view. Nothing formal is here, and Hokusai renders the scene open and visible. The second image shows the view towards the castle, though

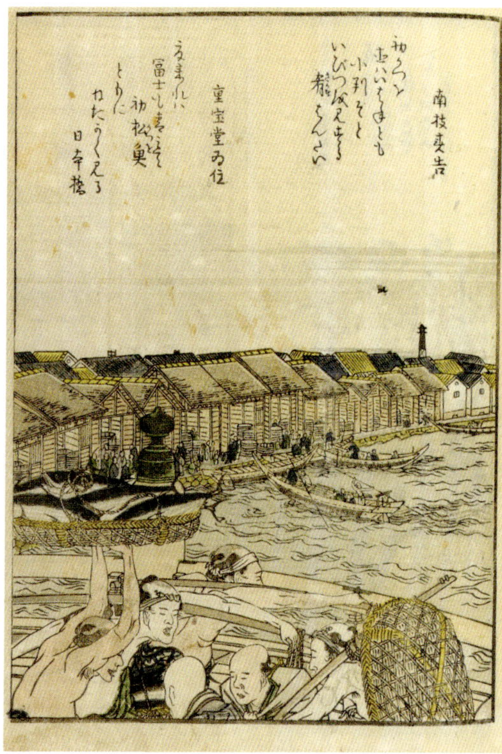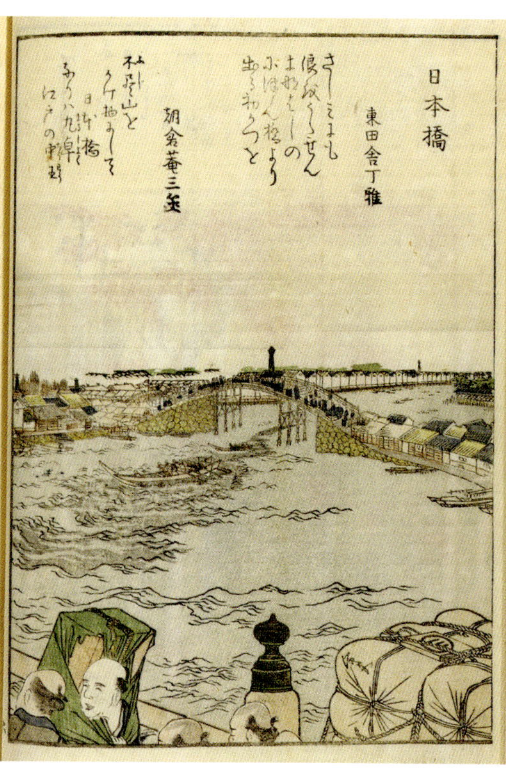

twisted to include the fish market too and including the whole bridge. In this second view the hectic commoners are present and clear to see, but a stately daimyo procession also approaches from the west. The purpose of including it is to conceal it. The retinue is hidden by cloud; only a halberd indicates what it is. Such is how the authorities had to be depicted: shown, because to ignore them was insolent, but not shown, since to stare implied deficiency of 'awe'. Hokusai is scrupulous to obscure the castle too, in clouds and trees. He cannot fail to show it, indeed he *must* show it, since to do otherwise would be to rudely expunge it. He therefore shows it as a site of unreachable difference. Hokusai breaks the castle out of the frame, as a thing uncontainable within the boundaries of an essentially townsperson's picture, and he also puts it top right, taking priority over all else. Hokusai did something similar in another image shown earlier (see illus. 29). Here

30 Katsushika Hokusai, 'Nihon-bashi, Looking Towards Edo-bashi', from *Collection of Famous Places in the Eastern Metropolis* (*Tōto meishō ichiran*), 1800, multi-coloured woodblock print. Looking away from the castle, the view is towards the great river, with the fish market to the left.

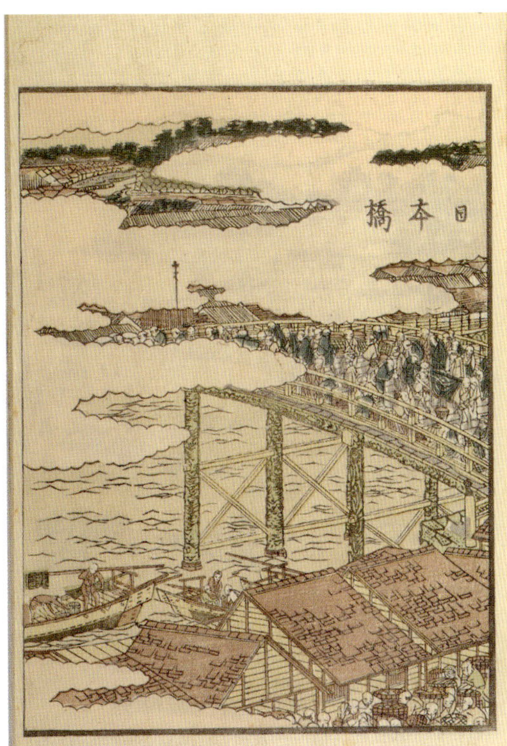
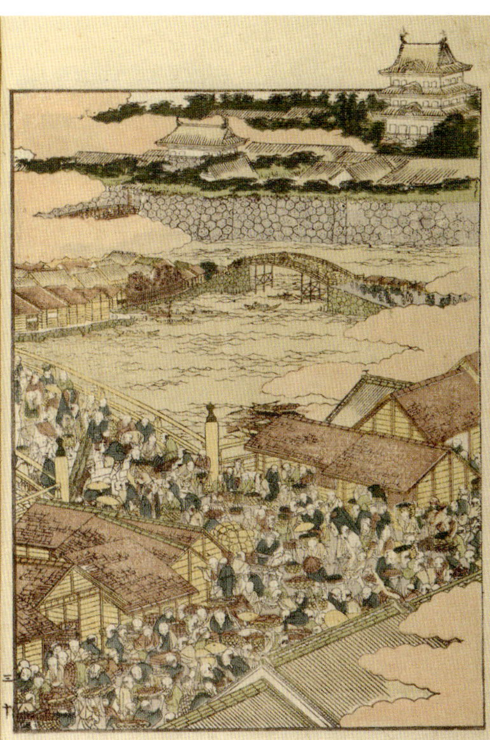

31 Katsushika Hokusai, 'Nihon-bashi', from *Illustrated Book of the Pleasures of the East* (*Ehon azuma asobi*, 1802), colour printed book. The book was published in monochrome in 1799, then reissued with fewer sites, but in colour. The fish market is to the bottom and the castle above, magisterially bursting out of the frame.

Hokusai used perspective to elongate the warehouses, but such an arrangement should properly place the castle at a vanishing point. To show it so reduced would be impertinent, so Hokusai broke it out of the perspectival scheme, with castle floating in the sky, free from a mathematical convention that binds the lower orders. This composition can be further compared with a perspective work by another townsman printmaker, Kitao Masayoshi (illus. 32). Masayoshi actually shows the castle under the bridge, with a rumbling cart and dirty feet above. It was a risky composition.

❧

Nihon-bashi was a site of intense meaning. The shogunate furthered the signification by assembling here institutions that were indicative of its rule. These were displaced, put a street or two back, so that the

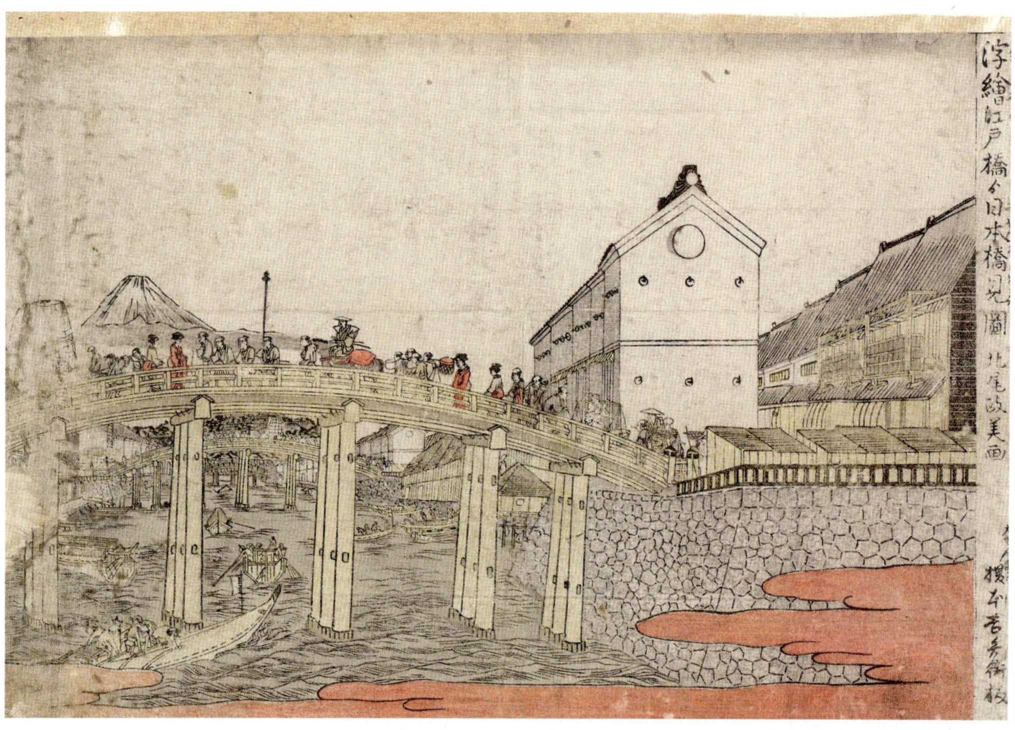

32 Kitao Yoshimasa, 'Nihon Bridge as Seen from Edo Bridge', from the series *Perspective Pictures* (*Uki-e*), multicoloured woodblock print, 1781–9. Careful use of perspective has problematically diminished the sense of the castle's importance.

structures could be known as part of the environment of the bridge but not actually seen, so spared scrutiny by commoners. It was 'awe' meeting city planning. A person on the bridge knew that the shogunate's buildings were situated nearby, but also that, as a commoner, he or she was denied a view of them. This polarity of seeing and not seeing which permeated the shogun's thinking about matters of political significance has been dubbed the 'iconography of absence'.[21]

Ranged between the bridge and the castle, set back from the river, were three sites that can be considered as the concrete embodiment of shogunal domination. All were on the eastern bank, that is, on the Nikkō, 'Tokugawa' side, not on that of the capital. The sites controlled certain matters that were crucial, but also emblematic. They were also features that had eluded all prior Japanese states. The three locations held institutions to regulate value, time and space. First, nearest to the castle, was the mint. As in Venice, this was the paramount office for a functioning commerce, in Japan called the Kinza ('gold monopoly'; not to be confused with the Ginza, 'silver monopoly', in modern Tokyo). Edo's mint actually pre-dated the bridge, having been built in 1601, so Nihon-bashi must have been constructed to align with it. The vast, well-protected structure functioned as a shogunal central bank, and the Bank of Japan still occupies the spot. Japan had a second mint at Ieyasu's retirement castle of Sunpu, though this was closed in 1612 and all production brought to Edo.[22] The block between the Kinza and the water was indicatively named Honryōgai-chō ('true exchange'; *chō* means a city block or district and is suffixed to make urban toponyms). Yet over the course of history, Japanese authorities rarely issued currency. Generally Chinese money was used, or nuggets of pure metal, weighed out. In 1608 foreign currency was banned and the shogunate issued a gold coin, the *koban*, valued at 1 *ryō*.[23] We encountered the *ryō* above, equal to 1 *koku* of rice, but, interestingly, 1 *ryō* was also deemed to equal 1 *real* of colonial Spain. Exchange rates fluctuated over time, but the new Tokugawa currency was integrated into the prime international unit of world trade. One *ryō* was a huge sum, so in 1626 a low-value copper coin was issued too, a *Kan'ei tsūhō* ('Kan'ei piece') named after the era of its production (the Kan'ei era, 1624–44). Perhaps because currency had diffused, open-air money changers are no longer seen in the later Rekihaku screens (see illus. 21). Edo's mint was so crucial that not only was it placed out of view in this picture, but not one picture was ever made of it in the 270 years of its existence. Just its roofline is loosely indicated in Hokusai's perspective print, radiating gold (see illus. 29). But no artist or publisher dared lack 'awe' enough to show its form in detail. We thus have no idea what the buildings looked like.

The second place was similarly occluded and never made the subject of a picture, but was known – and heard – by all. This was Edo's time bell. The block next to Honryōgai-chō ('true exchange') was Hongoku-chō ('true time'). Though generally written with the character *koku,* meaning the unit of rice (*koku/goku*), surely it should be written with the homophone, a unit of time (one temporal koku is about two modern hours). However, this is speculation, as here too, records are missing. Edo had previously lacked any unified time-measuring structure. People used their own time-telling devices or used none. So, not long after Nihon-bashi was built, the shogun, Hidetada, donated a time bell. The shogun, it is said, took down the bell that hung in his castle, donating it to the city. This indicated that the order already exhibited in the administration should now be extended citywide. An officer was charged with ringing the bell, while daily upkeep was secured by a modest tax on the residences deemed to be within earshot.[24]

The bell was the shogun's perpetual gift, and he paid for any repairs. When it was lost to fire, which happened several times (1657, 1666, 1679 and 1711), he offered a replacement. We have no idea of the appearance of the bell-house, but from 1712 its frontage was apparently over 20 metres wide, and the compound 35 metres deep. As for the bell, the last replacement continues to exist, hanging ingloriously near the original site in a park frequented by rough-sleepers, suspended in an unsightly concrete bunker (illus. 33).

Pictorial absence of the bell is total, and literary references scant, though there are some. In 1774 the haikai poet Yosa Buson wrote of it. Buson is today seen as the pillar of haikai after Bashō, and as a young man he visited Edo from the capital to study with Hayano Hajin. 'My master', Buson wrote, 'used to dwell in Edo, in Musashi Province, in a modest dwelling near the celebrated bell tower at [Hon]Koku-chō. The location allowed him to relish city-centre life.' Buson invoked the place because he had

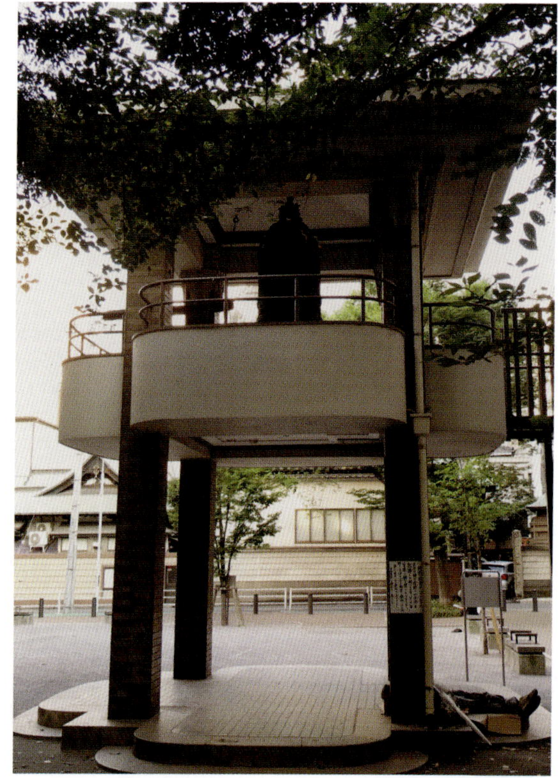

33 The Bell of Kokuchū, 1711 (modern bell tower). The old bell survives, though relocated from its original position and housed in an unsightly ferroconcrete structure.

a matter of 'awe' to impart. He reported that the ringing of the bell had given him artistic awakening:

On frosty nights, my master was awakened by the bell, so he talked to me about haikai. If I ever said something trivial, he affected not to hear. That is how I understood what a remarkable person he was.[25]

The shogun's bell was the recurrent prompt for Buson to receive Hajin's special insights. Hajin often held these midnight talks, and so took the studio name 'Midnight Room' (Yahan-tei), which Buson adopted after Hajin's death.

The bell at Nihon-bashi was the central bell of Edo, but there were eight others dotted about the city (Asakusa, Honjō, Ueno, Shiba, Mejiro, Ichigaya, Akasaka and Yotsuya).[26] They picked up their time from 'True Time', so there was a lag towards the city's fringes. Time evidently lost regulation with distance from the shogunal presence.

Interestingly, when the third shogun made a trip to Osaka in 1634, he noticed that the city lacked a time bell. So Iemitsu commemorated his visit by donating one, along with a bell-house. Here was another commemorative architectural monument. It was the shogun's privilege to confer time, but equally, as he moved about, he could not be without it. The site was known as the 'Hanging Bell' (Tsurigane), and though there is no trace of it today, it survives in an Osaka place name, Tsurigane-chō.[27]

A few houses further on was the third important site of Nihon-bashi. It was often unoccupied and more a symbolic place than a location of much action, though encounters there could be profound. Known as the Nagasaki House (Nagasaki-ya), it was the hostel for European visitors – in effect, for senior members of the United (or Dutch) East India Company. Most were Dutch, though Germans, Swedes and Swiss also visited as Company employees. The VOC, as it was known from its Dutch name, sent visits up from their trading base in Nagasaki and from the late 1630s these became an annual fixture. The purpose was to greet the shogun and his senior officers and to offer gifts. The Nagasaki House was the last addition to the streetscape of Nihon-bashi and was used for only about three weeks each year, during the VOC's 'trip to court' (D: *hofreis*; J: *sanpu*). The ritual ended in the 1790s when the British East India Company drove the Dutch equivalent into insolvency.

The Nagasaki House was described as the 'inn for the red-fur people' (*kōmō-ji no tabijuku*), where 'red fur' (*kōmō*) was the standard term for Europeans.[28] It might sound insulting, but the word was not intended to be so and in fact was regarded as refined, being derived from Chinese usage. Otherwise, Europeans were called *Oranda-jin* (Hollanders), wherever they came from. Not being hampered by the need to display 'awe', many European visitors left useful descriptions of Japan, though their remarks on the Nagasaki House were seldom positive. In 1642, when the building was new, the head of the VOC delegation said it was 'rather bad' and 'like a prison'.[29] In 1776, after more than one rebuilding, an official now thought it 'tolerably neat, though not such as I expected for an embassy from so distant a part of the world'.[30] Other than displaying a general ignorance of Japanese architectural styles, what they perhaps failed to appreciate was the significance of the location. They were within the environs of Nihon-bashi.

The annual arrival of the VOC was something of an occasion for Edo residents. Europeans recorded how swarms of people came to gape at them. One resident wrote, 'the street outside was seldom free of boys who constantly called out and made an uproar as soon as they caught the least glimpse of us, and even went so far as to climb up the walls of the opposite houses in order to see us.' Edifying encounters took place too: he also noted that 'at first we were visited by the learned and great of the country; afterwards even merchants and other people were among our guests.'[31] Nihon-bashi was convenient and was perfect for top officials, who sometimes dropped by incognito, since senior daimyo could not openly consort with merchants, whether foreign or not, and the shogunate did not want personal bonds to be formed. It was a source of pride to the regime that it could summon people from the furthest ends of the world, who would offer gifts, and the

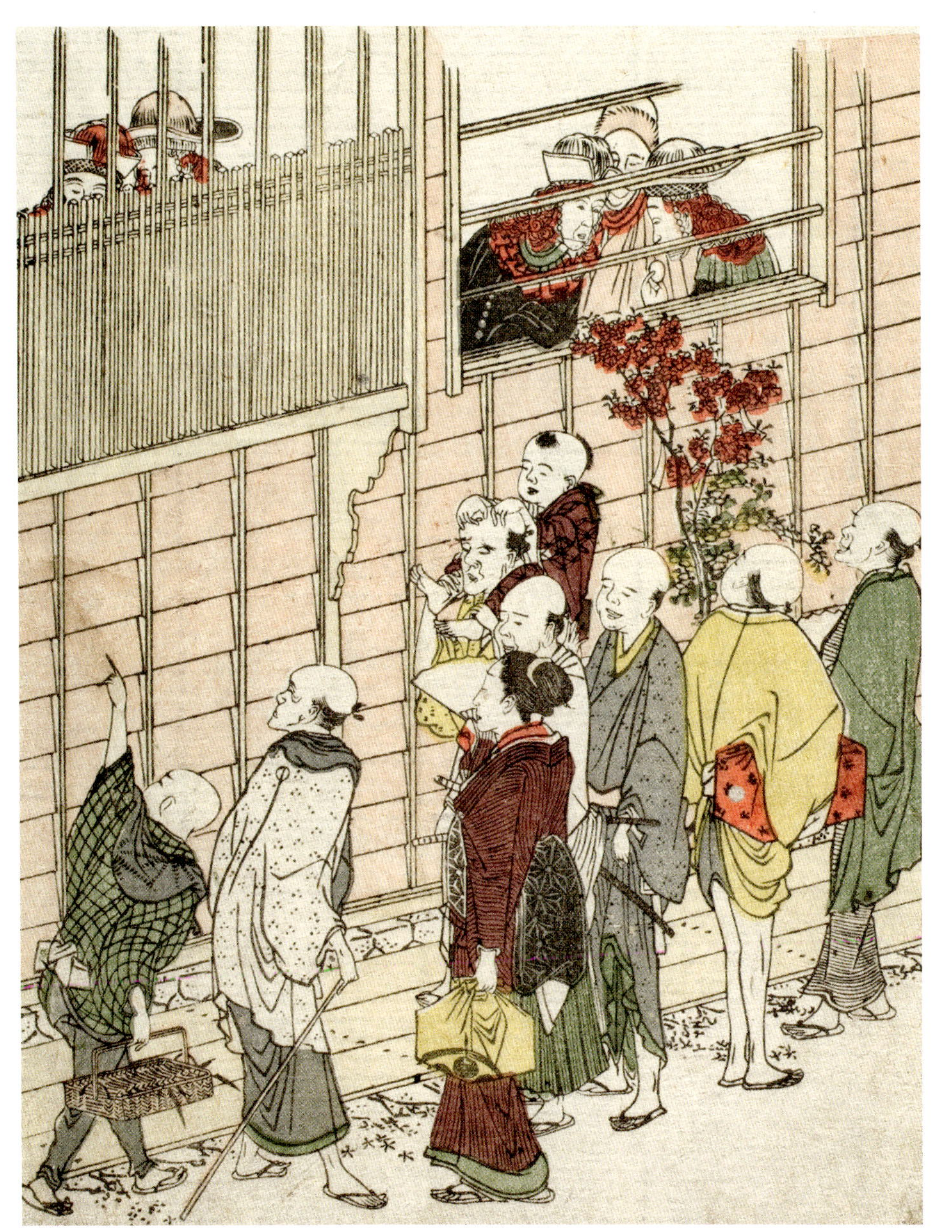

34 Katsushika Hokusai, 'The Nagasaki House', 1802, colour woodblock print from *Ehon azuma asobi* (Illustrated Book of Leisure Time in the East). This was the often-rebuilt residence of the Dutch East India Company in Edo. It was only used for a few weeks per year, and by 1802, with the company bankrupt, it was barely used at all, though Hokusai suggests it remained a famous site in the city.

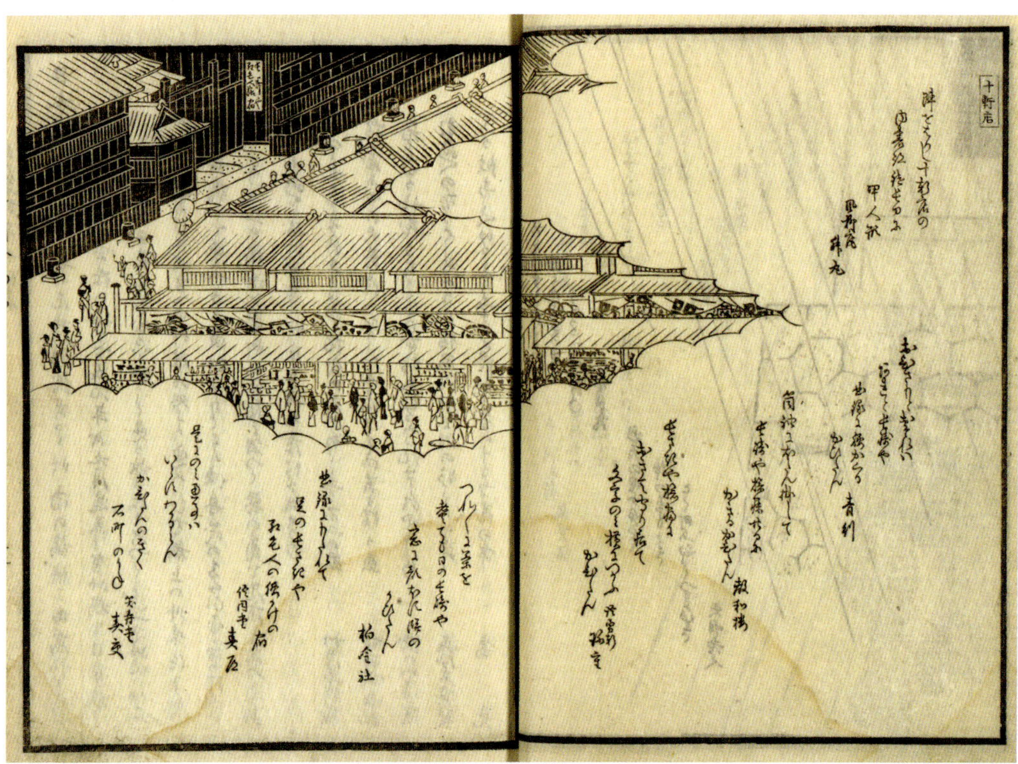

citizenry was supposed to appreciate this. The Europeans were actively shown off to the populace. Pictures showing the Nagasaki House are, of course, few, and in fact there are precisely two; both reproduced here, and made after visits by the voc became rare, so the Nagasaki House was no longer a site of actual government activity (illus. 34 and 35).

In the early Edo period, the voc made its annual trips to Edo in winter. Fires were common at that time of year, and in 1657, the Great Fire of Edo tore through the city just two days after the Dutch had held their audience with the shogun, which was a highly inauspicious thing.[32] The next year a severe fire occurred on the day before the same ritual, destroying the Nagasaki House.[33] It was embarrassing for the shogunate, which had a strong sense of ritual and that vitiation of protocol suggested that heaven was not smiling on the regime. From 1660 the trip to court was moved to the spring, though a fire

35 Utagawa Hiroshige, 'Nagasaki-ya', from Tenmei Rōjin, ed., *Kyōka Edo meisho zue* (Famous Places in Edo Explained in Comic Verses, 1856), monochrome printed book. Nagasaki House is the black building at the top left.

also broke out that year, destroying the Nagasaki House again.[34] Barring disasters, this was a truly lovely time of year, warm and with the cherry blossoms out. The haikai master Bashō wrote of the change in 1678:

> The Dutch chief too
> Bends his knee.
> Springtime for my lord.[35]

The voc came loaded with presents, hence another verse by Bashō:

> The Dutchmen too
> Have come to the blossoms.
> Horses' saddles.[36]

Much Japanese poetry includes a 'seasonal word' (*kigo*). In the first verse above, 'spring' obviously serves. The second seems to have no *kigo*, but in fact it does. By this time the word *oranda* ('Dutch') was associated specifically with spring.[37]

An image of the Dutch at Edo Castle was only attempted once, by the Westernizing artist Shiba Kōkan, almost certainly after the voc had stopped coming in fact (illus. 36). Kōkan rendered the scene in perspective, which gave rise to a problem already seen above. The Castle is not only small but is positioned by the Dutchmen's behinds. This was inappropriate. Kōkan added a gratuitous wall to the right, architecturally implausible but ensuring the castle looms over the foreigners, and not the other way round.

The Nagasaki House and the time bell were so close that the Edo populace sometimes thought of them as a pair. A comic verse (*senryū*) written beside Hiroshige's depiction above refers to this:

> Here at least
> He doesn't need an interpreter.
> Surely he understands it.

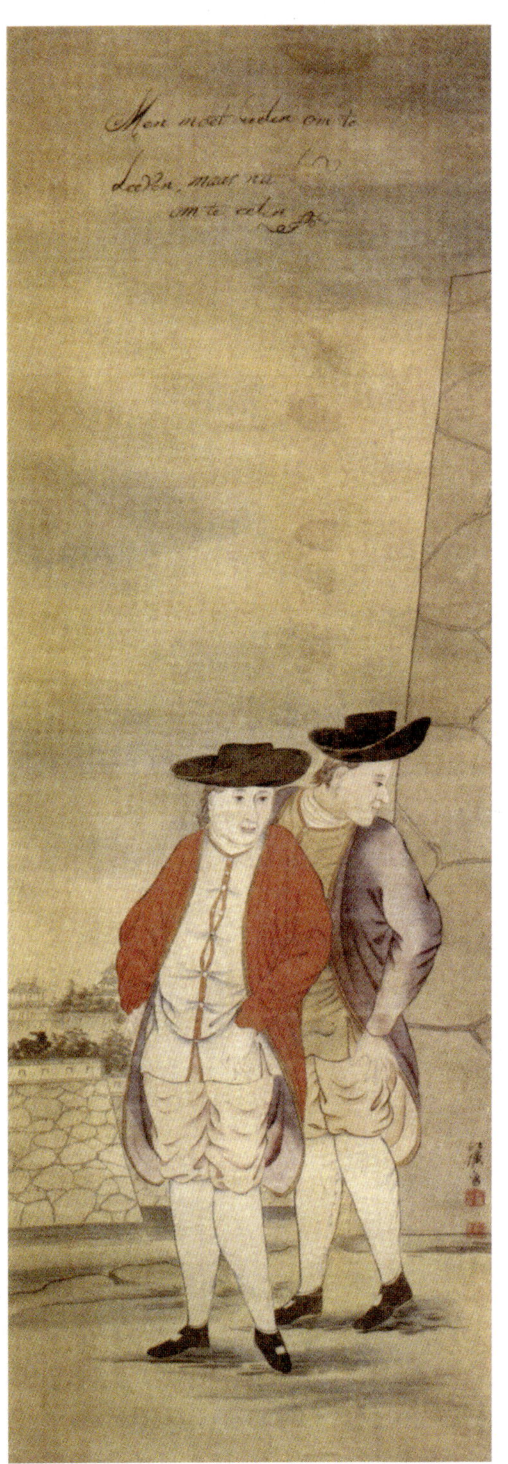

36 Shiba Kōkan, *Dutchmen at Edo Castle*, c. 1785, hanging scroll, colour on silk. Perspective has unfortunately reduced the castle to something small at the level of the Dutchmen's private parts. To avoid the charge of insolence, Kōkan has added a dominating if architecturally meaningless wall to the right. The inscription reads, 'You must eat to live, not live to eat,' a Dutch proverb, but well in keeping with shogunal demands for modesty.

> The Dutch leader hears
> The bell of True Time district.[38]

And another verse, recorded elsewhere,

> The True Time bell
> Even startles
> People in Europe![39]

There are no European comments on the Gold Monopoly, but there are some on the bell – though remarkably few given how often it must have impinged on them. One comment comes from the voc's first springtime visit, in 1660. As stated above, a fire broke out, forcing the men to flee. When they returned next morning their building was gone, with 'the whole area around it, as far as the eye can see, reduced to ruins and ashes', and 'on the spot where the large hour clock hangs – four or five houses away from our lodging – just there alone, twelve people have been burned to death.'[40] Some twenty years later, a German physician employed by the voc, Engelbert Kaempfer, returned home to write a complete book about his visit, *Heutiges Japan* (Japan Today). Sadly, no one wanted to publish it, but the manuscript was found posthumously, taken to England and published there, in 1727, as *History of Japan*. This provided the most trusted information on the shogun's realm for over a century. Kaempfer visited Edo twice, though his only comment on the lodgings was that nearby 'was a wooden clock tower where the time was rung'.[41]

♋

The two views from Nihon-bashi were Edo's great organized vistas. The prime one, towards the castle, however, was mimicked elsewhere. The shogunate must have been aware of this and so permitted it. The replication, or perhaps homage, altered the meaning of the original view and made it an expression for the commoners themselves. It was mercantile, not in the sense of a market given by the shoguns, but the

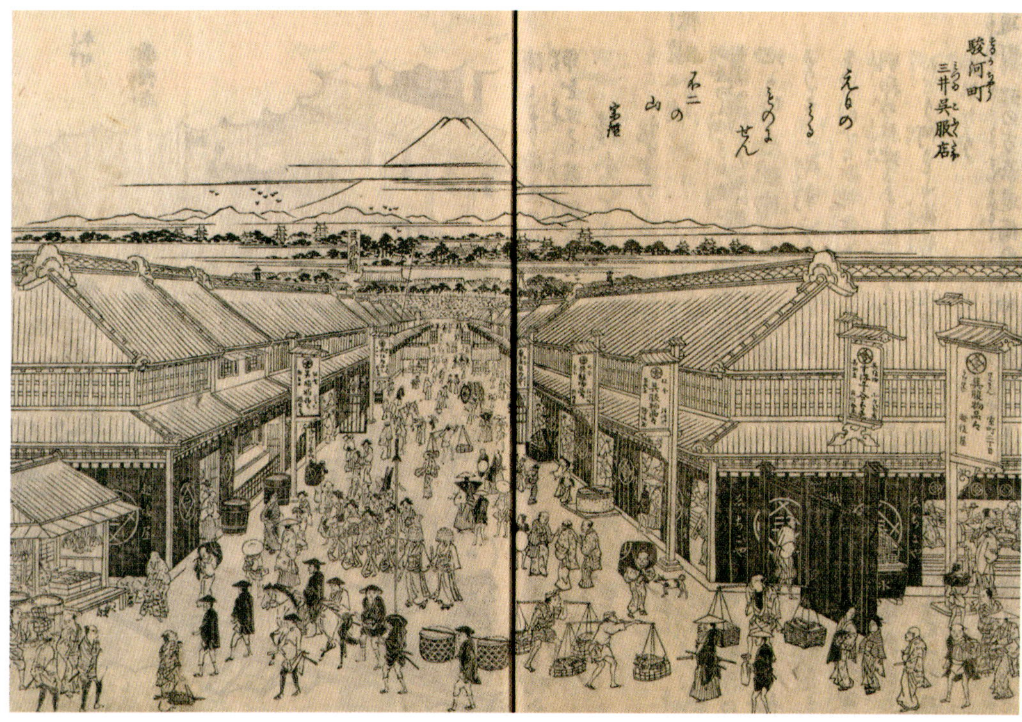

37 Hasegawa Settan, 'Suruga-chō', from Saitō Yukio et al., *Edo meisho zue* (Illustrated Famous Places in Edo, 1834), monochrome printed book. The monumental compendium of Edo's famous sites demonstrates that here was a similar view to that offered at Nihon-bashi, now with a mercantile edge.

result of townspeople's own acumen. The layout was created by Edo's most enterprising retailer, the Mitsui Echigo-ya. Its successor in the Mitsui Company still exists (it hailed from Echigo, while *ya*, again, denotes a house, shop or firm). The Echigo-ya purchased land close to Nihon-bashi at Suruga-chō, named after its fine view of Mount Fuji, which was in Suruga province. They built shops down either side of a street, running equivalently to those on either bank of the Nihon-bashi river. Rather than a trajectory of awesome power, it was a trajectory of wealth, down which anyone could walk, and the Echigo-ya shops, with their huge range of textiles and home goods, were there for any prospective purchaser to enter. The vista terminated in Fuji, but the street was constructed in such a way that the castle was not visible.

As commoner space, Suruga-chō could be depicted by artists without fear of reprisal. A representative illustration comes from

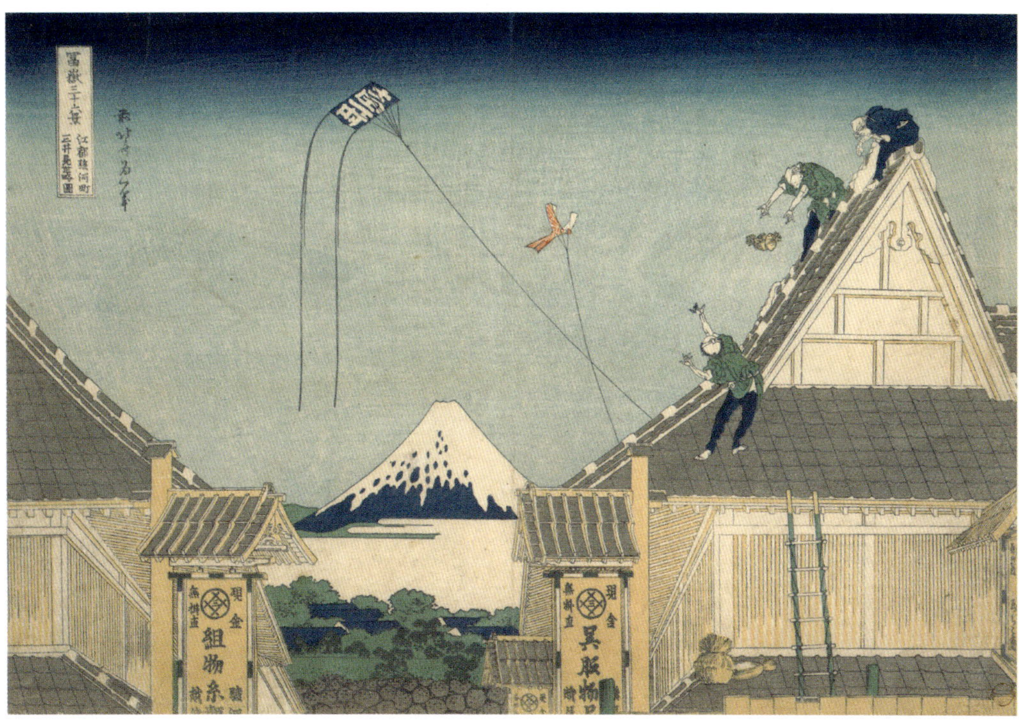

38 Katsushika Hokusai, 'Mitsui Shop at Surugachō in Edo', from the series *Thirty-six Views of Mount Fuji (Fugaku sanjūrokkei)*, c. 1830–32, multicoloured woodblock print. Fuji is snow-capped and New Year kites fly, suggesting another flourishing year ahead.

Famous Places in Edo (*Edo meisho zue*), a voluminous compilation put together over three generations by the Saitō family and published in 1836, illustrated by Hasegawa Settan (illus. 37). It is a treasure trove of Edo lore and imagery. Settan shows that, as with the views from Nihon-bashi, indeed, the straight alignment of Suruga-chō looked good in perspective, but now without the dilemma of how to retain priority for the castle. As an anonymous comic senryū put it, using the Japanese term for Western perspective, 'floating picture' (*uki-e*),

> Going to the Echigo-ya –
> You enter
> One of those 'floating pictures'.[42]

Another image from Hokusai's celebrated *Thirty-six Views of Mount Fuji* (*Fugaku sanjūrokkei*) shows the Echigo-ya at New Year (illus. 38).

Felicitous kites are being flown, adorned with the character for 'long life' (*kotobuki*). Thanks to the peace that the shogunate had ensured, all Edo could celebrate continuous seasonal rounds. Or, at least, it was politic to make pictures suggesting this.

Three
Edo as Sacred Space

ihon-bashi was Edo's monumental centre, but another part of the city, constructed analogously, also gathered structures that articulated a collective meaning. This site was less political than religious and had been constructed to sacralize the shogunate, rather than to illustrate its power. This iconic nexus was not in the centre but in the northeast, the geomantically sensitive *kimon*, the 'gate of demons'. As explained in Chapter One, this was the sensitive direction by which *ki*, or spiritual forces, entered the city. Edo was protected by its castle and its numerous moats and was rendered a site of benevolent rule by its central bridge, but in the northeast quarter it was also protected by Buddhist temples.

Japanese geomancy, or the 'way of yin and yang' (*onmyō-dō*), stipulated that the northeast should be guarded. The shoguns ensured this by positioning the residences of their most loyal hereditary warriors, the *fudai* daimyo, there. This protection had begun earlier in a religious sacralization of the vector, which is the subject of this chapter.

Placing temples in the northeast was standard practice. Japan's first complete capital, Heijō-kyō (Nara), had a colossal compound in that direction. It was fulsomely named the Temple of the Protection of the State by the Gold-Wondrous Kings and the Four Heavenly

Kings (Kongō myōō shitennō gokoku-ji). Being a mouthful, the place was popularly known (and still is) as the Great Eastern Temple (Tōdai-ji). Properly it should be the Great Northeastern Temple, since its purpose was to project the *kimon*. A whole 'outer capital' grew up around the temple as an excrescence on the city grid. Heian-kyō (Kyoto), the capital for much of Japanese history, was constructed in the knowledge that Heijō-kyō had been overwhelmed by the power of its clergy. Its northeast was also protected by a temple, but one located far out of town. Not merely some 20 kilometres outside the city, it was also on top of a mountain, Mount Hiei, 850 metres high. The temple also had a fulsome name, but of a different kind. It subordinated Buddhist to civil power. Most temples have names invoking religious concepts, but this one was named after the era of its foundation, as the Enryaku-ji, or Temple of the Enryaku ('extending calendar') era, which spanned the years 782–806. Its precincts on Mount Hiei were very lavish and entirely crucial to the running of the state, but Enryaku-ji's name defined it as subordinate under the secular sphere.

Warrior cities of the medieval and civil war periods tended to have temples in the northeast, and it was to be expected that Edo would have one. When Tokugawa Ieyasu established his base in Edo in 1590, it so happened that there already was a temple more or less to the northeast of the castle, and long pre-dating it. The history of the institution is lost, but it was certainly old. Places of local worship had existed all across the archipelago for centuries, and this one, in the village of Asakusa, a short distance up the Great River from Edo, was enlisted by the Tokugawa.[1] It was known as the Asakusa-dera (*-dera* is appended to Japanese-language temple names, as *-ji* is to the more numerous Chinese-derived ones). When Ieyasu moved to the region the monks of the Asakusa-dera saw a chance to aggrandize their cloisters. It was by lucky chance – or was it providence? – that it sat in the *kimon* of Ieyasu's castle. Ieyasu naturally visited it, and the monks offered services for his cause. They pointed out to him that the temple's principal icon was wonder-working, and since Ieyasu always won his battles, its power was suitably confirmed. The Asakusa icon laid the ground for the creation of his shogunate.

The icon did not represent a Buddha but a lesser figure, a bodhisattva or 'Enlightenment being' – that is, one who at the point of Enlightenment deferred it, in order to remain immanent in this world and help others on the way to wisdom. Bodhisattvas are many, but that enshrined at Asakusa represented Kannon (C: Guanyin). It is he who will convey the deceased to rebirth in the Pure Land (*jōdo*). This icon, the monks asserted, was an *acheiropoieton* (as such things were known in Europe), a miraculous image not made by human hand. Legend had it that two fishers had found the sculpture in their nets and, terrified, had thrown it back, moving their boat elsewhere. When they fished again, the same object was dragged up. This happened repeatedly, until they realized the image wanted to be taken to land, and so they placed it on the bank and erected a little shrine. Knowing nothing of Buddhist precepts, the villagers called this the Asakusa-dera, from the location. They could however recognize it as Kannon, whose iconographical marker is a crown with a buddha image on it. The shrine came to be known as the Asakusa Kannon. Thereafter, the two fishers always had wonderful catches, and the fame of the icon spread. Word came to the attention of a wandering monk, who conducted the first formal service in front of the Kannon. Then he went blind. The image appeared to him in a dream, telling him it did not wish to be seen, so the next morning it was sealed in a shrine, and the monk's eyesight returned. The Asakusa Kannon became a 'secret Buddha' (*hibutsu*), of which there are several in Japan, only rarely revealed at moments of special sanctity. It may have been this monk who upgraded the temple name to something more formal. As well as Asakusa-dera, it might be called the Senso-ji. However, this is just the characters for Asakusa pronounced in the Chinese way, Sensō, with *-dera* accordingly changed to *-ji*.

As a northeast protector temple, the Asakusa-dera, or Sensō-ji, had some deficiencies. It had not been built to project the castle as it existed long before, so it was not well aligned, more east than northeast. Moreover, it was on the riverbank, whereas protective temples should be on an eminence. The mountaintop Enryaku-ji was extreme, but even Heijō-kyō's Great Eastern Temple was on a hill. Also, while Kannon had a cultic following as the conveyor of the dead to blissful rebirth, he is not a buddha as is required at a protector temple. These discrepancies were tolerated at first, but as Edo grew, they became problematic.

With a requirement for something that fitted the bill more precisely, a new temple was founded in 1625. Ieyasu was dead, and this was the work of his grandson Iemitsu, installed in 1623 as the third shogun when his father, Hidetada, went into retirement. The Tokugawa regarded it as worthwhile to take the considerable step of protecting their city and sacralizing their regime with an entire new temple complex. The timing also meant that the temple would be ready for the millennial anniversary of the finding of the miraculous Kannon by the fishers, which the monks dated in accordance with 645 – the myth is just as likely to have been given a date retrospectively to match. The new temple would be properly in the northeast, on a hill, and would enshrine a buddha.

Work was put under the care of a senior monk, Tenkai, who had studied at the Enryaku-ji on Mount Hiei. He had been close to Ieyasu, who had awarded him a temple at Kawagoe, a strategic town close to Edo; the precinct was named the Kita-in ('cloister of much happiness'; *-in* denotes a small temple). Though not initially large, the Kita-in was given an impressive additional name. All temples have a 'mountain name' as well as their normal designation, and the Kita-in was proclaimed Tōei-zan ('Mount Hiei of the East'). This brought the capital's protector temple and its long, pious traditions into Ieyasu's orbit, albeit outside Edo proper.

Tenkai was fully aware that Edo had a hilly area exactly northeast of its castle. It had been allocated to *fudai* loyalists of the Ueno daimyo family, but they agreed

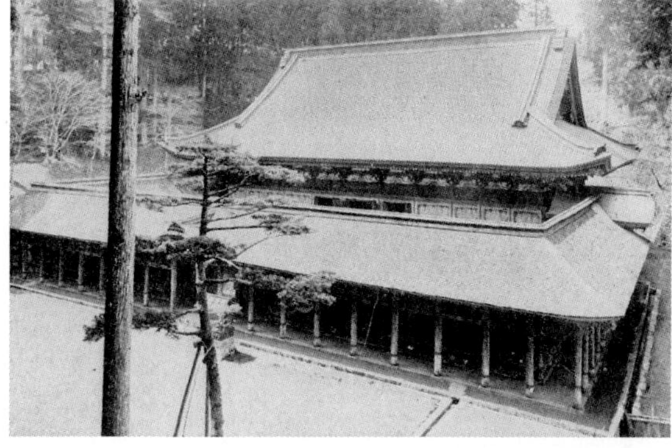

39 Konpon chūdō, Enryaku-ji, Mount Hiei, as rebuilt 1660. The principal hall of the capital's great northeastern protector temple, destroyed by Hideyoshi but rebuilt under the Tokugawa.

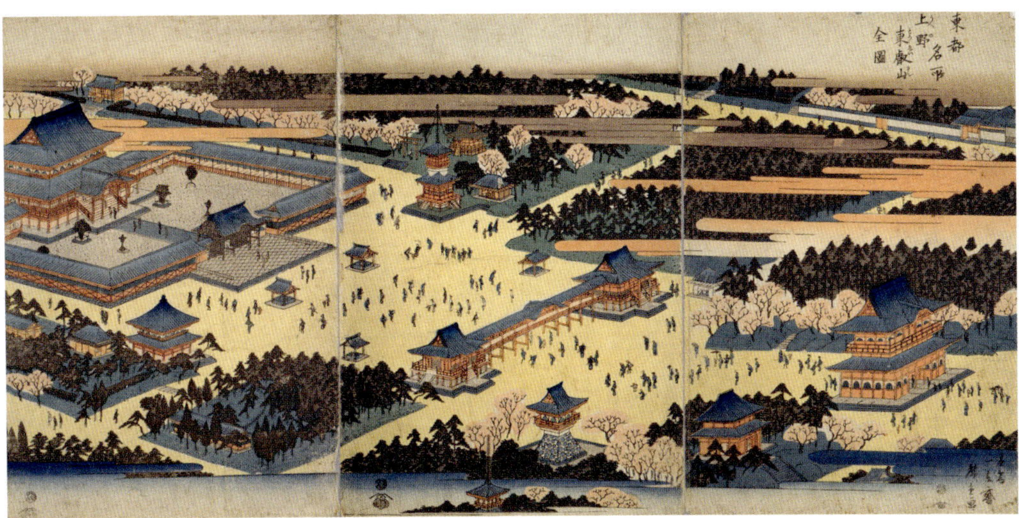

40 Utagawa Hiroshige, 'Complete View of Tōei-zan Temple in Ueno', from the series *Famous Places in the Eastern Capital*, c. 1832–4, multicoloured woodblock print. The Edo temple copied the name and general appearance of the protector hall outside the capital.

to relinquish it. The place had become known as Ueno, which fitted, since it literally means 'upper plain'. The name selected for the new, projected temple is telling. It was to be Kan'ei-ji, where Kan'ei ('long lenience') was the era then under way (1624–43), promulgated upon Iemitsu's accession as shogun. This matched the Enryaku-ji, also named after the era of its foundation, eight hundred years before. Hardly any Japanese temples have era names, so the Kan'ei-ji was very clearly copied after the model of the protector of the capital.

Parallels were further reinforced. Tenkai's colleagues at the Enryaku-ji sent a magnificent buddha, very ancient, to be the principal icon. It was said to have been made by the Enryaku-ji's founding abbot, Saichō. This eminent cleric had studied in Tang-dynasty China and won great renown. He is not known to have been a sculptor, so the attribution is not accepted today, though association with his hand would have justified special veneration at the time. The specific figure was the Medicine Buddha (J: Yakushi nyōrai), which was also the Enryaku-ji's own principal icon, so the Kan'ei-ji matched here too, with Edo protected by the same buddha (there are many) as the capital. A huge central hall was erected to install the piece, called the Ruri-den ('hall of lapis lazuli'), from the Medicine Buddha's associated colour, blue. This hall had a second name, Konpon-chūdō ('hall of the central fundament'), which was also the name of the Enryaku-ji icon's sanctuary. Or, rather, it had been. The Enryaku-ji Konpon-chūdō was no longer there. It had been lost in the civil wars, its icon now temporarily housed elsewhere. As part of the sacralization of Edo, the shogunate borrowed, but also subsumed, the capital's aura. Only once work on the Kan'ei-ji had begun did Iemitsu pay for the rebuilding of the Enryaku-ji's originating structure. Both halls were so vast that they took many years to build. The Enryaku-ji's Konpon-chūdō required eight years, while the Kan'ei-ji's was not completed until 1697 (illus. 39 and 40).[2] For its 'mountain name' the Kan'ei-ji was accorded Tōei-zan ('Mount Hiei of the East'), with the title therefore removed from the Kita-in (it was suitably compensated). Tenkai was nominated to be first abbot. The shogunate now had a protector precinct perfectly in accordance with requirements, both mirroring and supplanting the protector temple in the capital.

The Kan'ei-ji was reserved for government use. The shogunate endowed it with an income of 5,600 *koku*. This largesse compared with the older Asakusa Kannon, on an endowment of just 500 *koku*. The latter was now turned over to city use. As it needed commercial activities to survive financially, the Asakusa precinct became almost like a fairground, with shops even inside the temple grounds. Most commoner families had, or would acquire, graves here, ensuring crowds of visitors, and when the Kannon image was revealed, huge throngs came. This atmosphere contrasted with the Kan'ei-ji, where the halls were quiet and sober. Between them, the temples provided for all Edo's social classes, and together they offered a swathe of sanctity across the whole northeastern area, in a projective arc covering almost a quarter-circle. Before long, the suburbs of Asakusa and Ueno merged into one urban mass, conjoined with Edo.

The difference in the mood of the two temples was captured by a best-selling guide to Edo, already mentioned in Chapter Two as the three-generation work of the Saitō family. The illustrator, Settan, shows the Asakusa Kannon teeming with visitors. Pilgrims, tourists

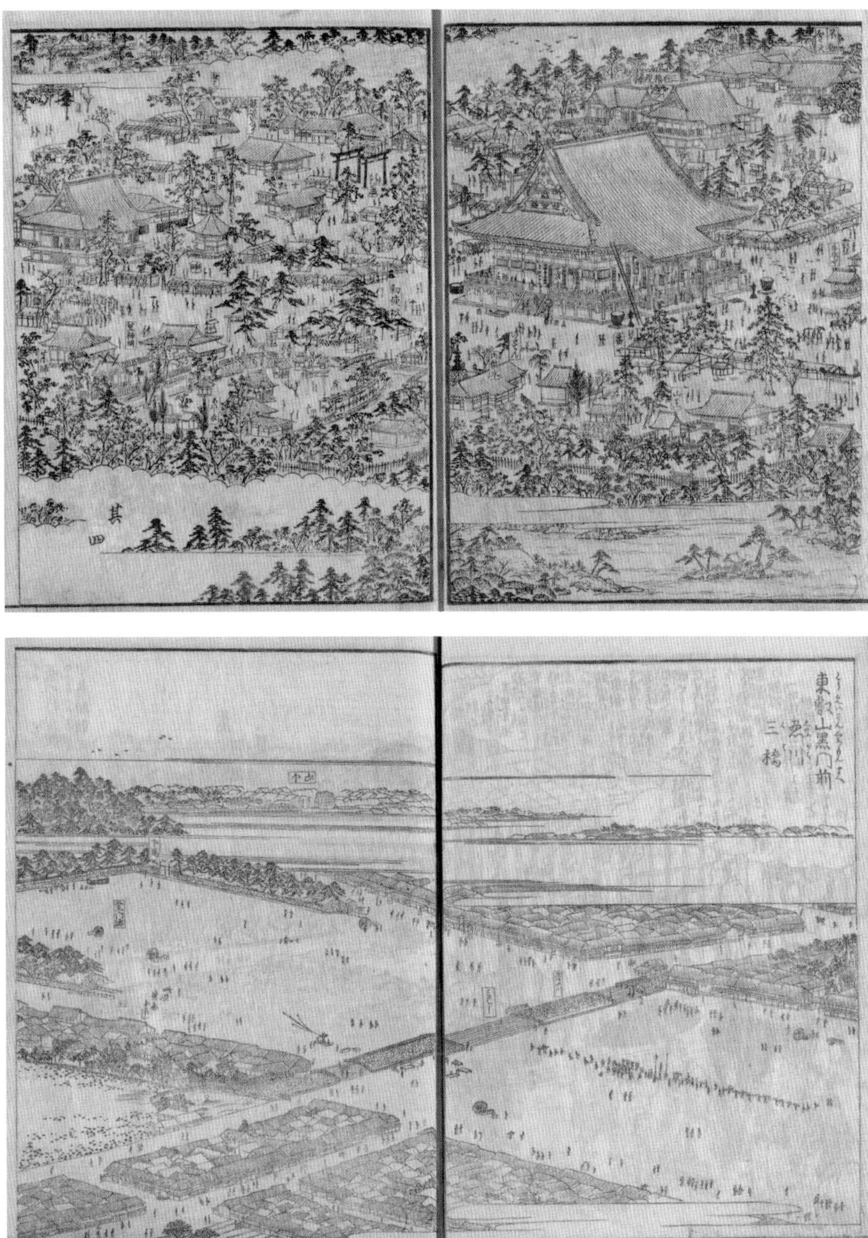

41 Hasegawa Settan, 'Sensō-ji [Asakusa Kannon]', from Saitō Yukio et al., *Edo meisho zue* (Illustrated Famous Places in Edo, 1834), monochrome printed book. The popular temple is shown crowded with worshippers and visitors.

42 Hasegawa Settan, 'Kan'ei-ji', from Saitō Yukio et al., *Edo meisho zue* (Illustrated Famous Places in Edo, 1834), monochrome printed book. The temple, used for high-level government rituals, is shown in respectful quiet and cloud-hidden, a sober official retinue crossing its forecourt.

and people just coming to enjoy the outdoors and walk about. The Kan'ei-ji, by contrast, is devoid of people, apart from an official retinue making its way across open space, the temple buildings wreathed in cloud (illus. 41 and 42).

Having the temples side by side was a recipe for rivalry, not least as the Asakusa monks were unhappy at their reduced status, despite their early – and successful – assistance of the Tokugawa. The shogunate did not forget the debt, but its own institution had to take priority. The Kan'ei-ji was given hierarchical as well as financial precedence, and in 1647, when Tenkai died aged 109, and a successor was needed, the shogunate requested a prince-abbot (*monzeki*). Certain prominent temples in the capital had the long-standing privilege of a dharmic prince (*hōshinnō*), or ordained member of the dairi's (emperor's) family, as their abbot. Iemitsu's now-reigning son, Ietsuna, demanded that the court accept the Kan'ei-ji into this hallowed fraternity. The dairi, Go-Kōmyō-in, must have been shocked, but negotiations resulted in the arrival of his brother, Dharmic Prince Suchō. For the rest of the Edo period, the Kan'ei-ji would have a prince-abbot.

It was not possible for Asakusa's abbots to equal this. Although they conceded status, rivalry festered. In 1685, the Sensō-ji abbot rebelled against the situation and was expelled from office. Much later, in 1740, the abbacy was abolished, and the Asakusa Kannon headship was reduced to a deputy, chosen from among monks of the Kan'ei-ji. By contrast, the Prince-Abbot of Ueno, as he was called, had a plum clerical preferment, as well as, surely, a more thrilling life than was available in the capital. He would also serve as a back-channel for court–shogunal politicking and the easing of frequent tensions.

‟

Having borrowed the name style of the Enryaku-ji and of the mountain on which it stood, the shogunate valorized the Kan'ei-ji further. Not far from the capital is Lake Biwa, Japan's largest body of fresh water and a place of considerable historical importance. In the middle is the holy island of Chikubu-shima (*shima* meaning island), with an

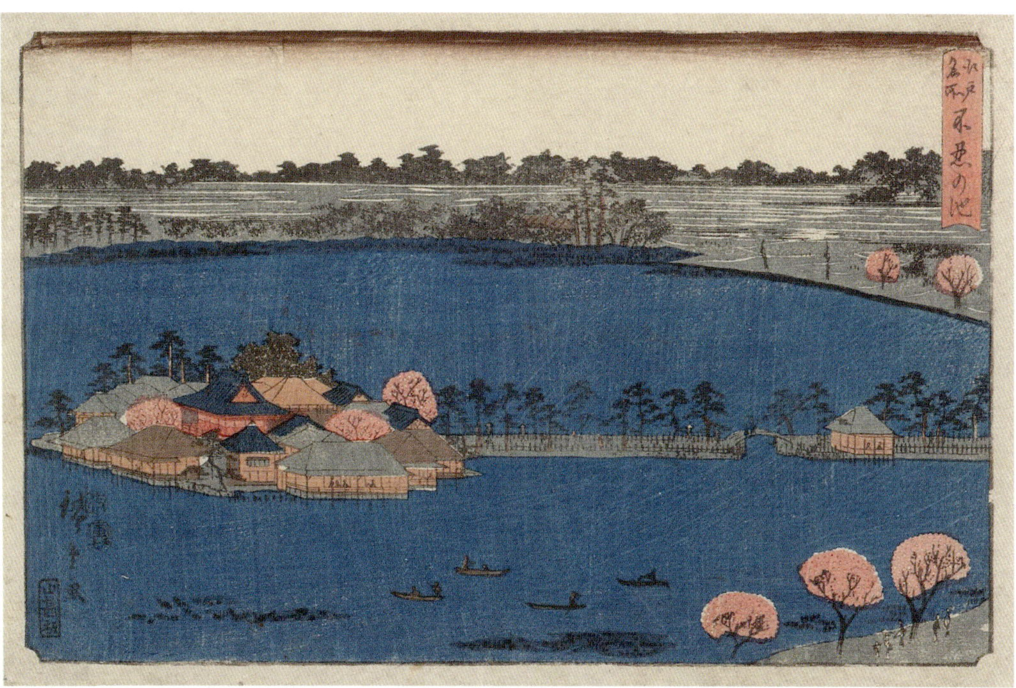

43 Utagawa Hiroshige, 'Shinobazu Pond', from the series *Famous Places in Edo*, 1854, multicoloured woodblock print. A small pond was expanded to replicate Lake Biwa and the island of Chikubu-shima, near the capital.

ancient precinct. Ueno hill had a natural pool at its base, and this was turned into an 'Eastern Lake Biwa', and although that name was not specifically used, an island was built to be an 'Eastern Chikubu'. A shrine put on the island, reached by a short causeway, was dedicated to the same divinity as at Chikubu, Benzaiten, originally the Hindu goddess Saraswati, goddess of the arts (illus. 43).

The reason for invoking the Enryaku-ji and Mount Hiei is obvious, but the relevance of Lake Biwa and Chikubu-shima is less evident. The likely prompt was a *nō* (Noh) play. An anonymous work named *Chikubu-shima* tells of an ancient courtier who made a pilgrimage to the island sanctuary known as the Tsukubusuma Shrine. He encountered a woman, who startlingly declared: 'I am the goddess Benzaiten.' The divinity herself had come to live in Japan. She explained, 'I make my dwelling upon this island to protect all sentient beings.'[3] Thereupon magical music was heard, and the goddess danced until nightfall. A dragon emerged from the lake, presenting the courtier with a jewel

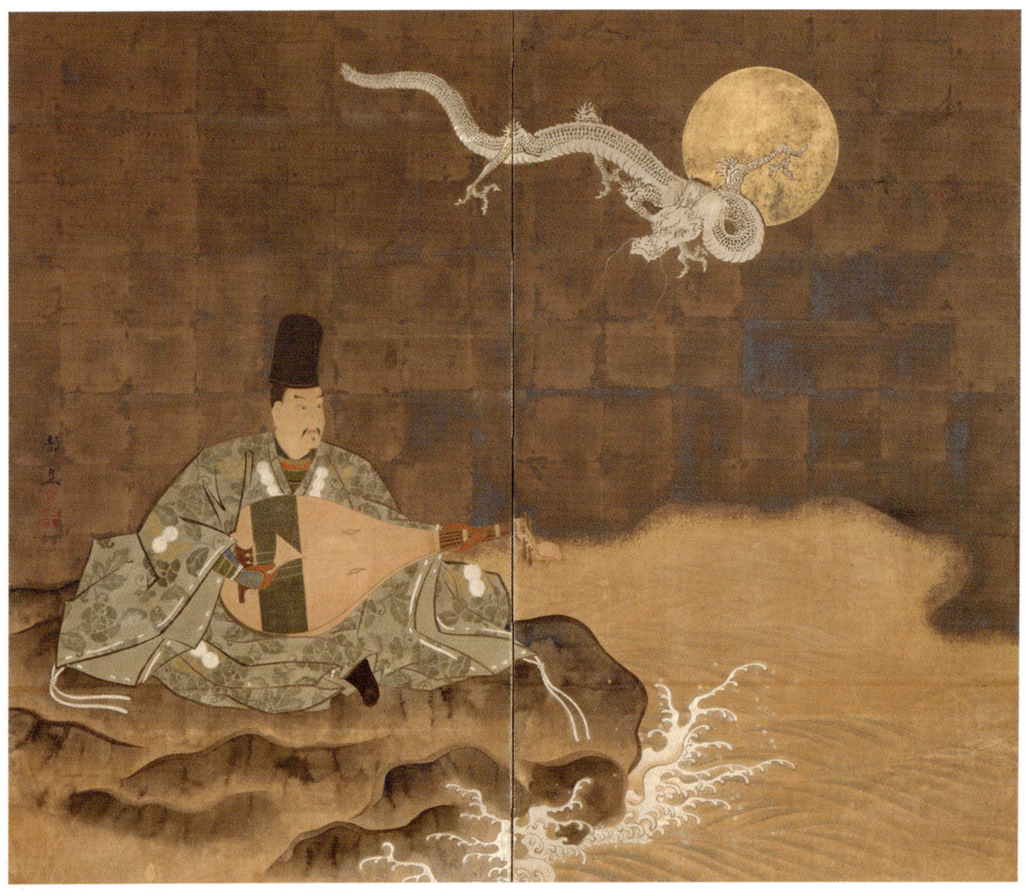

before disappearing back into the waters. To the Tokugawa, the tale was crucial for their particular standing. Other versions of the story associated the pilgrim-courtier with Taira no Tsunemasa, nephew of the warrior leader Taira no Kiyomori and a famous *biwa*-player. He had come here in 1184 to pray for the defeat of the Minamoto. But they had not been defeated; on the contrary, Tsunemasa had been killed, and the Minamoto had gone on to found the first shogunate at Kamakura.[4] This was historical fact. Kamakura was not far from Edo, and the Tokugawa claimed descent from the Minamoto, using that shogunate as the precedent for their own. To Edo period audiences, the appearance of the goddess and the dragon implied that a

44 Suzuki Shuitsu, *Taira no Tsunemasa Playing the Biwa at Tsukubusuma Shrine*, second half of the 19th century, two-panel folding screen, ink, colour, and gold on silk, 145 × 164.8 cm. Myth had it that this refined warrior visited the island in Lake Biwa before a great battle, which he lost.

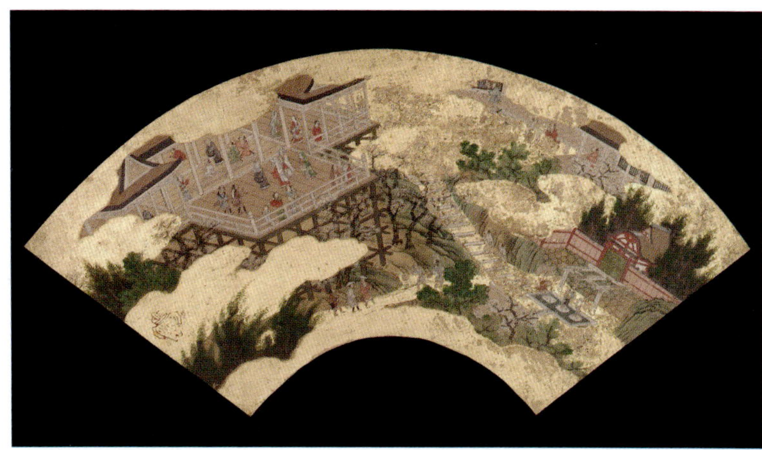

45 Kano Shōei, 'Kiyomizu-dera', from *Famous Places in the Capital and Legendary Figures*, mid-16th century, fan painting, ink, colour and gold on paper. Fans were essential in summer, and finely decorated ones were made. This shows one of the capital's best-loved temples, originally perhaps part of a set. Note the temple gantry to the left, and the three canals of the Otowa falls to the right.

mystic promise had been made for the success of the Minamoto, as Tokugawa forebears. The noble refinement of Tsunemasa makes his end quite tragic, but nonetheless inevitable. The Taira would go down in history as warriors who did not adequately maintain the line between warriorhood and courtliness.

Nō plays were seldom made into pictures, and public depiction of Tokugawa ancestors fell foul of the 'iconography of absence': they would be talked about in the glorious tones of nō chant, but could not easily be depicted. All known images of the play *Chikubu-shima* show the courtier unambiguously as Tsunemasa, but all date from the nineteenth century, after the fall of the shogunate (illus. 44).

Replicating Chikubu-shima and its shrine in Edo was another way for the shogunate to sanctify themselves and their city. But it was also a means of arrogating power from their last, deposed rivals. Until 1615 the Toyotomi had controlled Osaka, and Hideyoshi had extensively patronized Chikubu-shima. The shrine halls were all Hideyoshi's gifts. His successor, Hideyori, commemorated his father's death (or his advisers did, since Hideyori was a child) by performances of *Chikubu-shima*. Tellingly, as first Edo shogun, Tokugawa Ieyasu donated a great formal gateway to the Chikubu-shima shrine.[5] The complex could only be approached through a Tokugawa access point.

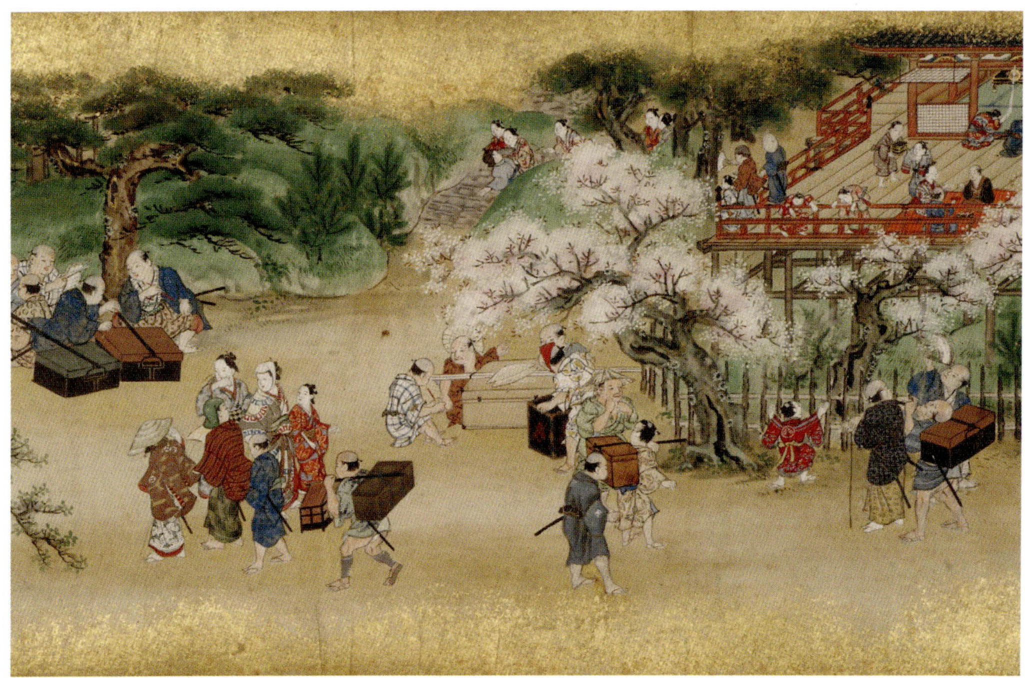

46 Follower of Sumiyoshi Gukei, 'The Kiyomizu Hall', from *Scenes of cherry-blossom viewing in spring in Ueno, from Hirokoji (south) to Sanno shrine (north)*, 1716–36, pair of handscrolls, gold and colour on paper. Among the many structures in the Kan'ei-ji compound was a reduced-size replica of the capital's Kiyomizu-dera, with its famous gantry.

The Edo Lake Biwa was named Shinobazu Pond, and it and the island shrine were completed in 1642. Other referents were also going up. Although the public were kept away from the main halls of the Kan'ei-ji, they were welcome within its wider grounds. Visitors wandered the hilly parkland. Here the shogunate gathered references to other ancient and hallowed sites.

Any traveller to the capital would infallibly marvel at the Kiyomizu-dera ('temple of fresh waters' – unusual in having a non-theological name), founded in 778. Its wonder-working image represented the bodhisattva Kannon and was a 'hidden Buddha' – truly hidden, as it had not been seen for centuries. The temple name came from the curative Otowa Falls, their water channelled into spouts under which visitors bathed. Most sensational was a gantry projecting before the main hall, jutting out on stilts from the steep hillside. Raised high over the treetops, it was designed to give worshippers a sense of floating off ethereally towards Kannon's paradise, Potalaka (Fudaraku).

The Kiyomizu Temple burned down no fewer than nine times over the course of history, though the icon was always saved. After a fire of 1469, the then shogun, Ashikaga Yoshimasa, helped fund a rebuilding. In 1629, while the Kan'ei-ji was under construction in Edo, the Kiyomizu Temple burned down again. Its abbot was so desperate that he revealed the 'hidden' Kannon to encourage donations. Iemitsu, aware of the shogunal precedent, also stepped in to rebuild the temple, but in Edo. The Kiyomizu-dera was recreated at reduced scale in the grounds of the Kan'ei-ji, without a waterfall but complete with hanging gantry. Since it was not a temple in its own right, it was known as the Kiyomizu Hall (*dō*). It was set at the highest point in the temple, with wide views over Edo, thus turning the shogun's city into Potalaka (illus. 46).[6] Once the Edo hall was complete, and only then, did Iemitsu provide funds to rebuild the original in the capital. Edo, again, both mimicked and replaced. The abbot's gratitude may not have been unalloyed, but he still sent up one of his finest images to be installed in the Edo hall, also as a 'hidden Buddha'. In 1698 the Kiyomizu Hall was moved to its present location, less dramatic, but now overlooking Shinobazu Pond and the shrine to Benzaiten, as modern tourists can see.

The Kiyomizu Temple was copied in Edo a second time. Although unrelated to the northeastern *kimon*, it is worth mentioning. This was

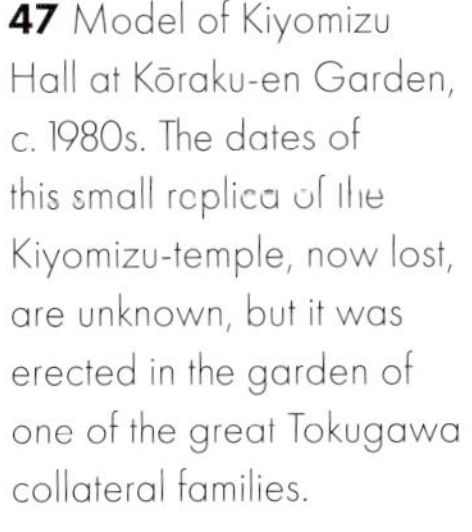

47 Model of Kiyomizu Hall at Kōraku-en Garden, c. 1980s. The dates of this small replica of the Kiyomizu-temple, now lost, are unknown, but it was erected in the garden of one of the great Tokugawa collateral families.

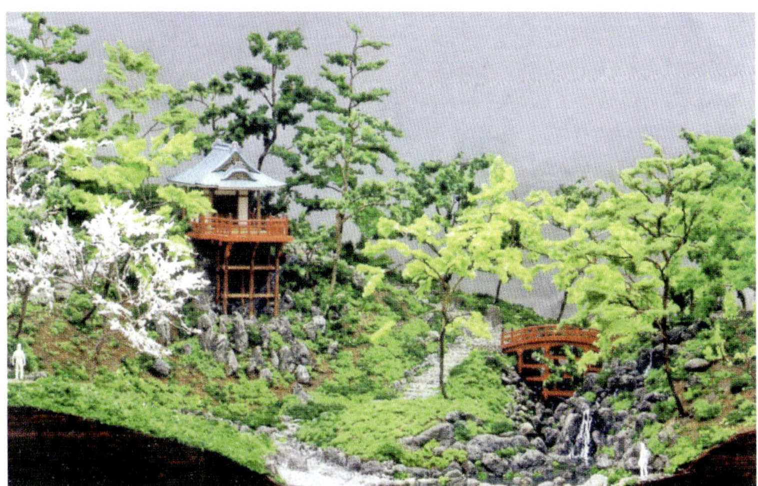

even more diminutive still, with just enough room for one person to sit on the gantry. It was constructed at the villa of the daimyo of Mito, whose much-applauded garden, the Kōraku-en ('garden of pleasure taken afterwards'), still remains. The hall is gone, but it exists in a modern speculative model (illus. 47). The daimyos of Mito were Tokugawa collaterals, functioning as deputy shoguns. They had begun their garden in 1629 – that is, the year that the Kiyomizu-dera in the capital was lost. It is not certain when the miniature hall was put up, but it was at the highest point in their garden, on a considerable cliff with views over the garden, giving the daimyos of Mito their own private Potalaka.

The original Kiyomizu-dera in the capital had an associated shrine where young women would go to pray for a husband. It was said that when a woman's chosen partner resisted, she could force the hand of fate by leaping off the gantry; if she survived, Kannon would ensure the man's heart turned to her. Stories tell of women who resorted to such measures. This lover's leap did not transfer to Edo, and the gantry was not high enough to be much of a test. Edo visitors nevertheless recalled their desperate sisters in the capital. As one poet put it in around 1760, in another anonymous comic senryū verse, apparently written in the rain,

> Looking as if they
> Intend to leap off.
> Kiyomizu's
> Raindrops.[7]

The celebrated Edo artist Suzuki Harunobu made pictures of women on the gantry, seeming to ponder their next move, or even leaping off. Since Harunobu only made views of his home city, he was at least imagining the lover's leap being transposed to Edo (illus. 48).

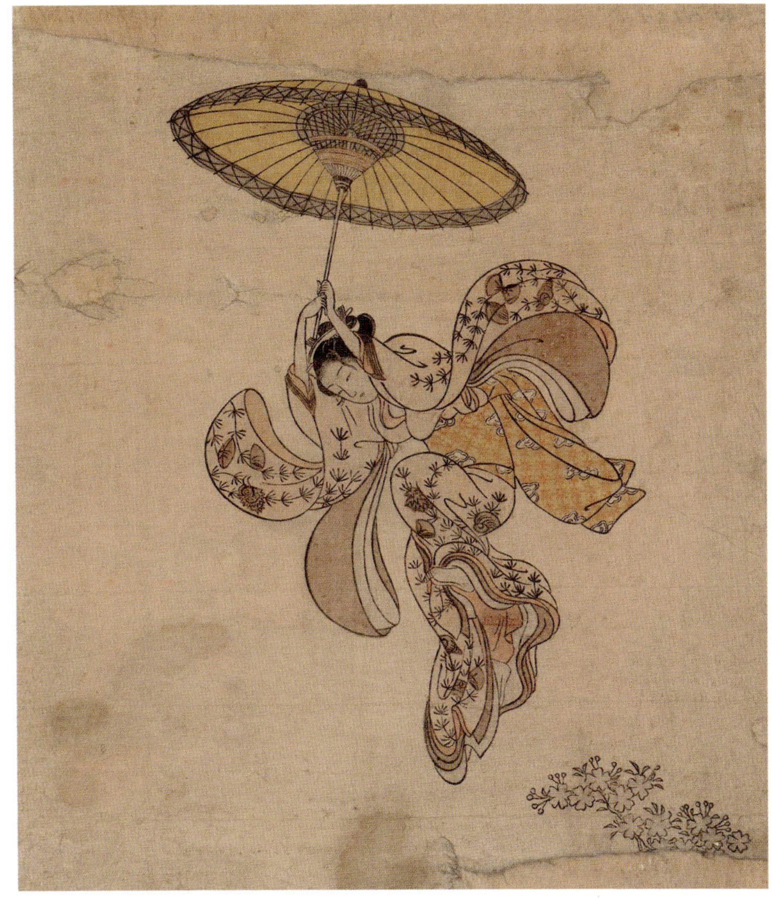

48 *Suzuki Harunobu, Young Woman Jumping from the Kiyomizu Temple Gantry with an Umbrella as a Parachute*, 1765, multicoloured woodblock print. It was recorded that young women would leap off the temple gantry in the belief that if they survived they would be successful in love.

The northeasterly protective temple for Japan's first complete capital, Heijō-kyō (Nara), set one clear precedent. The Great Eastern Temple contained a colossal buddha statue, some 16 metres high. Cast in 752, and damaged by the passage of time, it still remained a stunning sight. The equivalent temple of the capital, the Enryaku-ji, did not have a great buddha, but Hideyoshi had presented one in 1588 as part of his new Hōkō-ji ('temple of widening expansion') complex, across the River Kamo. The size of this image is not certain, but Hideyoshi's Great Buddha Hall was 20 metres high, the biggest free-standing wooden building ever erected on earth, so the buddha cannot have

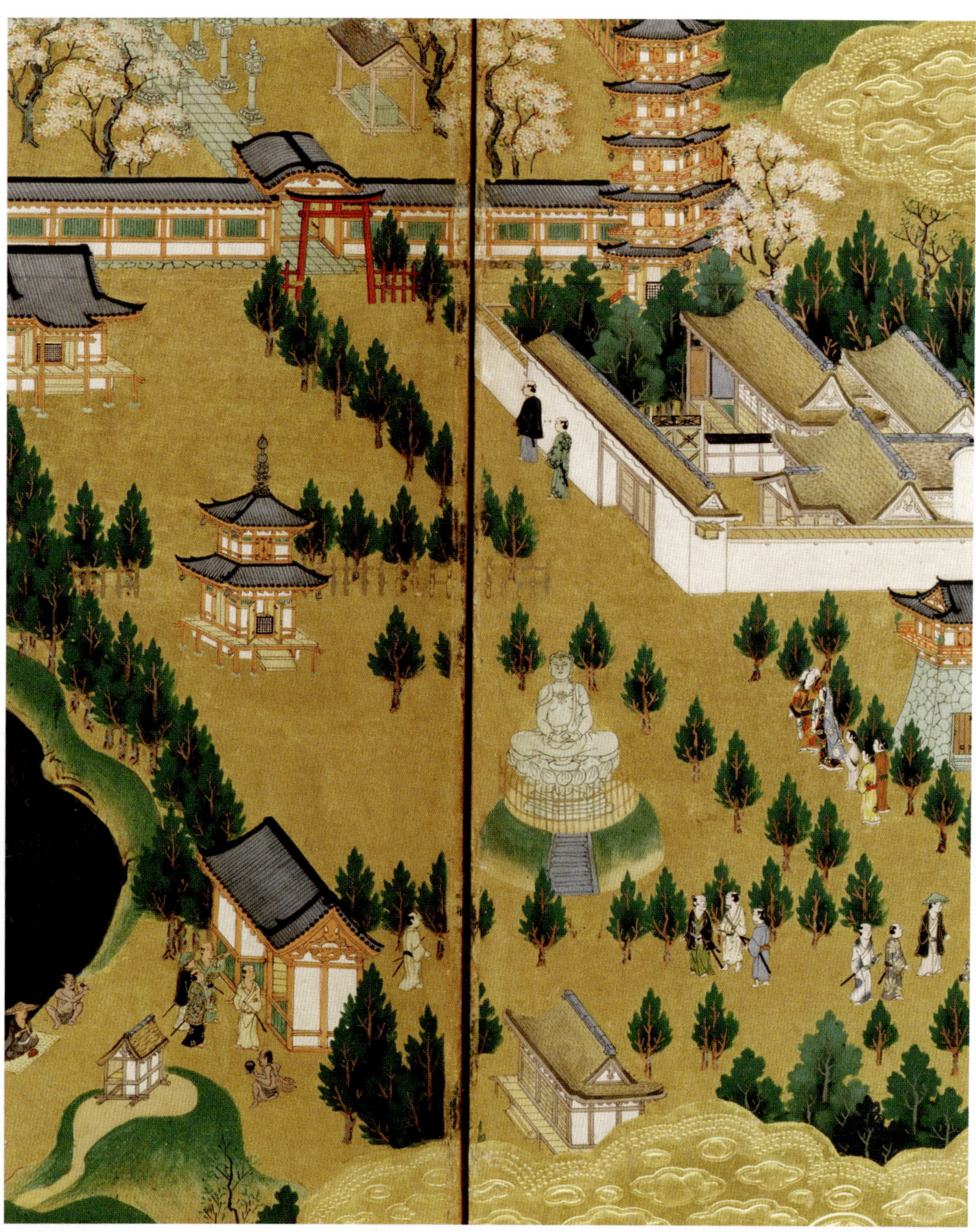

49 Detail of illustration 5, right panel, 'Great Buddha'. The Great Buddha of Edo was not very large but was set on a hillock. It was later rebuilt and provided with an enclosing hall.

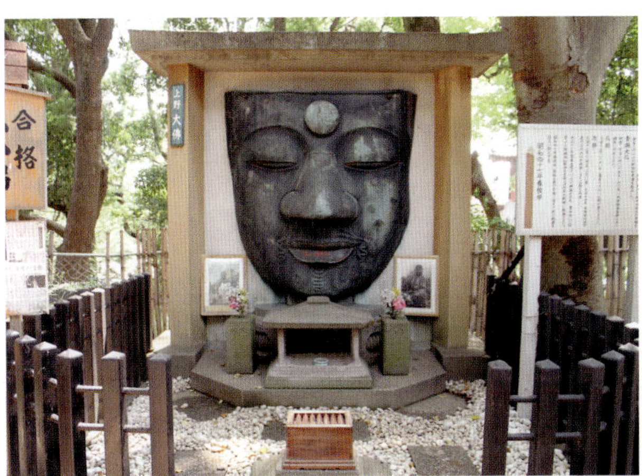

50 Unknown artist, *Face of the Great Buddha of Edo, c. 1647*, bronze, Ueno Park, Tokyo. Today only the Buddha's face survives, encased in concrete, though still with ritual instruments before it.

been less than about 15 metres. Between the Heijō-kyō buddha and Hideyoshi's, another had been built, by the Minamoto family in 1252, at their shogunal seat of Kamakura. Naturally, as the Tokugawa consolidated their regime, they would build a Great Buddha too. They would put it in the Kan'ei-ji. Work began in 1631, with funds coming not from the shogunate itself but from one of Ieyasu's most loyal allies, Hori Naoyori. He desired it to secure repose of the Tokugawa and Toyotomi dead. The result was rather small, but it was set on a mound, which increased the height. It can be seen in the Rekihaku Edo screens (illus. 49). Records claim that the icon was made of clay, but if so, it is hard to see how it could have survived. Whatever the material, it was destroyed in an earthquake in 1647 and replaced several years later, smaller, at just 5 metres, though in durable bronze. In 1698 the Prince-Abbot of Ueno donated a hall to be built around it. This too was lost, in 1841. All that survives today is the Great Buddha's face, forlornly set in concrete (illus. 50).

&cxy;

If the Kiyomizu-dera was the capital's most astounding piece of lofty architecture, and the Great Buddha its biggest icon, then the Rengeō-in ('cloister of the Lotus King') was the most astounding temple in terms of length. The hall was 120 metres long, built to accommodate 1,001 standing images of Kannon. Constructed in 1164, it had been lost to fire in 1249, but several of the statues had been rescued and were augmented with replacements for the lost ones, carved in identical style in the workshop of the revered icon-maker Tankei. A new hall was put up to house them in 1266. It was also one of the capital's oldest structures. The hall and images, still there today, were and are

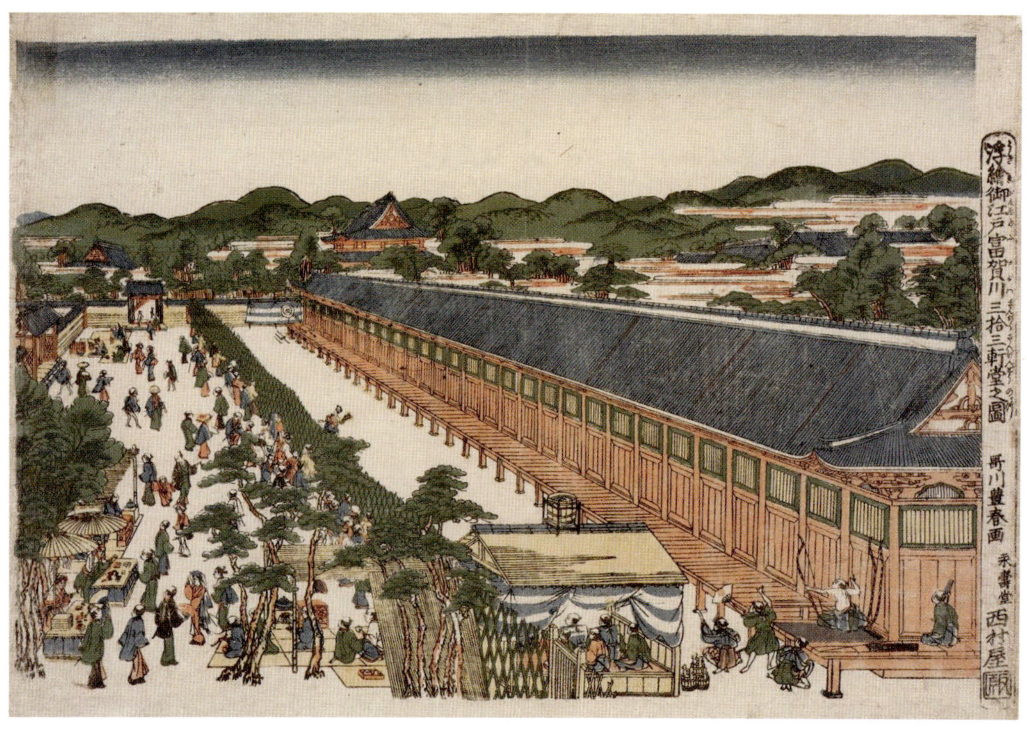

popularly known as the Sanjūsangen-dō ('hall of thirty-three bays'); a 'bay' (*ken* or *gen*) being the interval between pillars, about 2 metres.

So it was that a Sanjūsangen-dō was built in Edo, too, in 1642 (illus. 51). It was not sponsored by the shogunate, nor even by a loyal ally, and neither was it at the Kan'ei-ji. It was still in the northeast, but at the Asakusa Kannon, with funding coming from the common people. The hall was the same length as the original but only half as wide and containing just a single statue. It was not really the building or the image that accounted for the replication, but an event that took place there. Since about 1610, an archery contest had been held at the hall in the capital, with contestants sitting on the veranda and shooting arrows the full length of the building, trying to hit a target at the end. This was hard to do without striking the eaves, and a person had to be exceptionally strong to succeed. The event became famous in 1686 when one Wasa Daihachirō loosed 13,053 arrows in rapid succession,

51 Utagawa Toyoharu, 'Perspective Picture of the Hall of Thirty-three Bays at Fukagawa in Edo', 1770s, multicoloured woodblock print. Use of perspective allows Toyoharu to show the hall to dramatic effect. The work is reverse-printed, so would be viewed in a mirror for heightened realism. Archers try to shoot the length of the hall without striking its beams.

of which 8,033 hit the target.[8] The Edo building was built before this feat, but to hold a similar competition, and a master of archery, unnamed, is said to have petitioned for permission to erect it and to solicit funds. In the capital, the archery was confined to the back, as it was peripheral to the religious purpose, but in Edo, the archery contest was the whole point.

Within eighteen months of completion, in 1644, the hall was moved. Apparently the archery master had been unable to pay the lumber merchant, not having collected as much money as anticipated. Seeing the potential of archery, however, the lumber merchant moved the structure across the river and re-erected it in the residential district of Fukagawa. There it stayed until 1698, when it fell victim to fire. Another lumber merchant obtained a site close by and built another version. In 1839, a truly amazing feat unfolded there when a ten-year-old boy shot 122,015 arrows in the space of ten hours (one arrow loosed every three seconds), all but 255 hitting the target.[9] A dozen years later, Hiroshige included this third hall in a pictorial guidebook of 1850, *Edo omiyage* (Gifts from Edo). He then reused the image in his colour album *Edo meisho hyakkei* (One Hundred Famous Views of Edo) of 1856–9, though by then the hall was gone, lost to an earthquake in 1855 (illus. 52). Hiroshige did not show the contest but depicted the hall at a rising angle, giving the sense of an arrow in flight.

Plentiful comments exist on the many and various Edo arrogations of the capital's revered sacred spots. But few are of an evaluative kind. It would not be proper to pass judgement. We do not know if commoners correctly absorbed the referents intended, nor whether clerics in the capital felt validated or slighted. But thanks to the rise of a genre of comic verses, senryū (mentioned above), we can get an idea. These anonymous snippet poems on urban fads were published annually in Edo from 1765 to 1840.[10] One makes a pun on the two northeastern temples of Kan'ei-ji and Asakusa Kannon. It derives its humour from a copper coin in widespread use, the *kan'ei tsūhō* ('Kan'ei piece'), first minted in the Kan'ei era and sharing a name with the temple. The

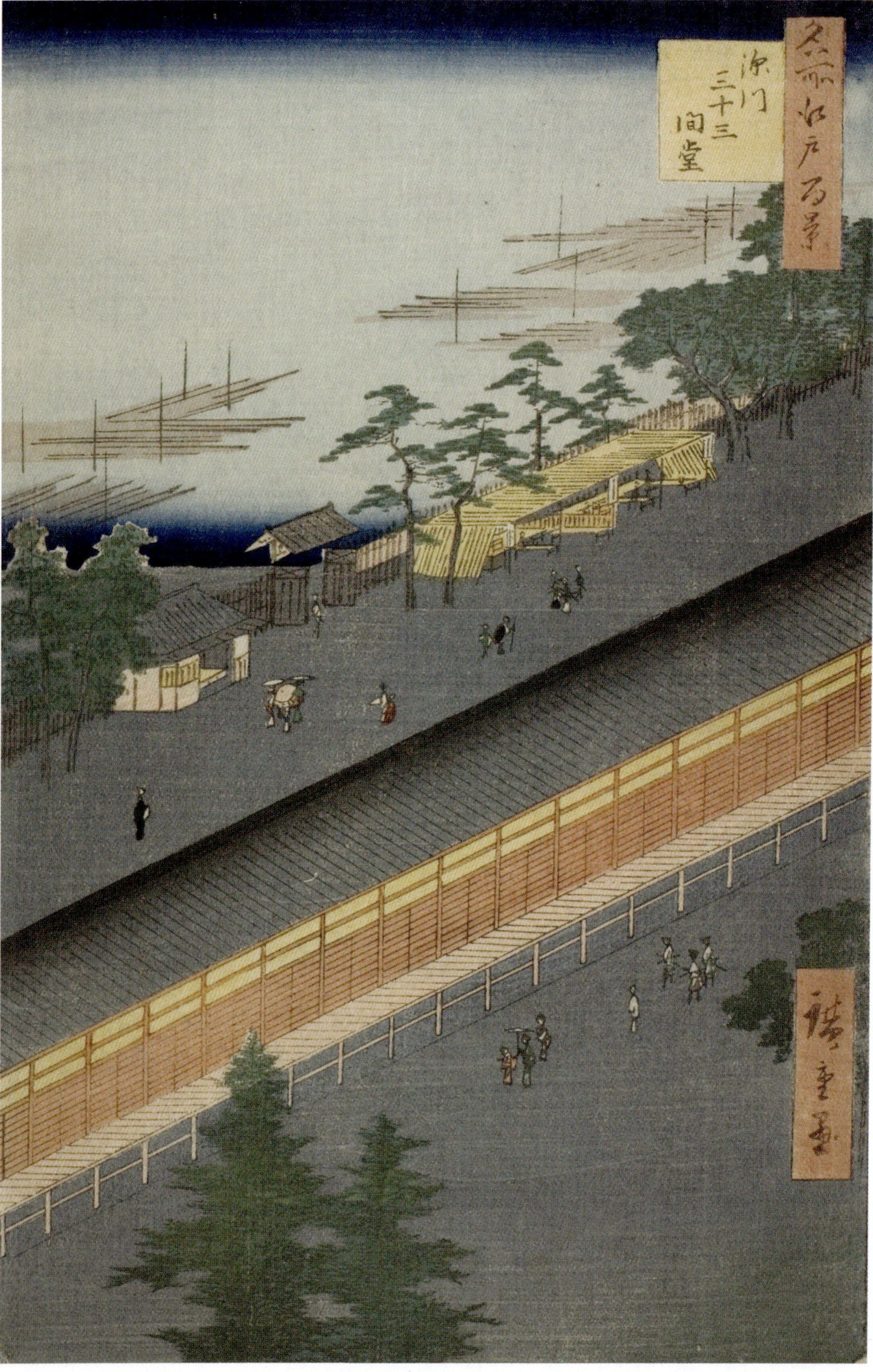

名所江戸百景
深川
三十三
間堂
廣重画

versifier then links this to the Asakusa Kannon's 'mountain name' of Kinryū-zan ('mount gold dragon'). Thus,

> The things to see in Edo
> Are no more than this:
> 'pieces' and 'gold'.[11]

The poet pretends to sniff at Edo as having no sites of cultural interest, and at Edoites as obsessed with money. But most senryū are really self-validating statements mocking lightly in a kind of praise. Another makes a similar point, comparing the Kan'ei-ji and Asakusa Kannon, again, but matching them against two temples in the capital, not replicated but well known. These were the Golden and Silver pavilions:

> Gold and silver
> For the jewelled seat.
> Coin
> For the lap.[12]

The 'jewelled seat' is where the dairi sat, while Edo was the 'shogun's lap'. The capital's beautiful precincts are set against Edo's grubby cash. But Edoites liked to see themselves this way. The two pavilion temples are referred to in another senryū:

> Temples of the capital,
> After currency conversion,
> Built in Edo.[13]

The tone of the verses all pretend scorn, but the point of senryū is to be scornful of everything, tongue-in-cheek.

☙

The northeast, above all, needed to be protected. Behind its purifying barrier of temples, the shogunate positioned things that no city could

52 Utagawa Hiroshige, 'The Hall of Thirty-three Bays at Fukagawa', from the series *One Hundred Famous Views of Edo*, 1857, multicoloured woodblock print. The hall was replicated in Edo, though more for fun than worship. Hiroshige shows it rising like an arrow in reference to the archery competitions held there.

do without but which were polluting – as they put it, the 'vile places' (*akusho*). These sites contaminated *ki*, but the location ensured all negativity would be erased by what was passed over next.

The 'vile places' were associated with violence, death and ritualized dirt. The most prominent was Edo's execution ground, Kotsugahara ('field of bones'). It has now disappeared under the railway lines at Ueno Station, but the street that led to it is still there, called Kotsu-dōri ('road of bones'). The temple, used for giving criminals their last rites, is still there too, mordantly named Enmei-ji ('temple of prolonged life'). Other 'vile places' were slaughterhouses, tanneries and ateliers for leatherwork. A caste of hereditary 'untouchables' performed these jobs, cruelly called *hinin* ('unpeople'), forced to inhabit the hamlet of Senjū, beyond Asakusa. Though such discrimination is no longer legal in Japan, Senjū is still one of the cheapest parts of Tokyo and full of sellers of shoes, belts and handbags.

After the great fire of 1657, Edo's official pleasure district, the Yoshiwara, was relegated here too. Prostitution was not 'vile' for sexual reasons, and the shogunate had no position on licentiousness itself. It was vile because of extravagance and, worse, sex work's inherent lack of 'sincerity' (*makoto*). Courtesans relied on deceit and swindle, making protestations of love but only in exchange for money, as the clients who squandered gifts on them fully knew. Funds and energies could be put to better use.

Late in the Edo period, in 1841, the theatres were also relocated here, beyond the temple band. The kabuki stage was also a place of insincerity, as actors spoke lines, laughed and wept, all according to a script. The nō theatre, by contrast, was a semi-religious enterprise, fully 'sincere': it was therefore not considered 'vile'.

ↂ

The northeast was where *ki* entered, and after passing through the city it duly exited in the southwest. If the northeast was the 'gate of demons', the southwest was their 'back gate' (*ura-kimon*). Neither Heijō-kyō (Nara) nor the capital had mechanisms for the guarding of this place of outgoing, but Edo did. This was perhaps because danger

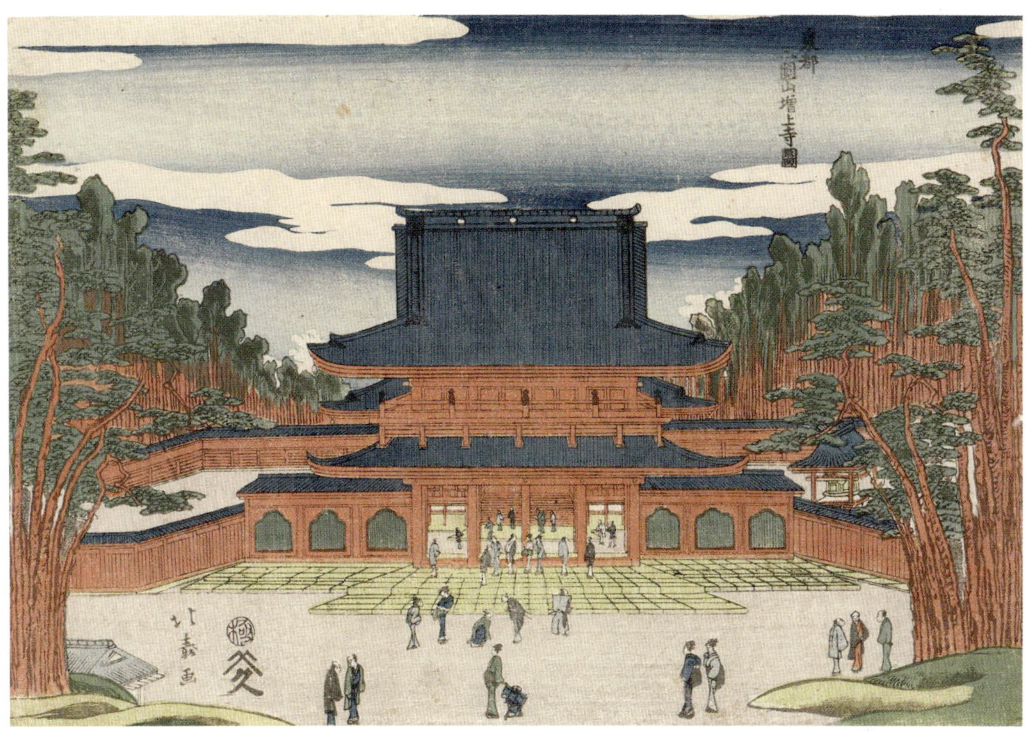

53 Shōtei Hokuju, 'San'enzan Zōjō-ji Temple', from the series *The Eastern Capital*, c. 1818–30, multicoloured woodblock print. The Tokugawa family's own tutellary temple in Edo is shown, or rather hidden behind its great gate. In the centre, Hokuju deferentially shows a commoner bowing to a military person, suggesting that here, above all, decorous behaviour is observed.

might genuinely emanate from that direction: it was, after all, where the Tōkaidō highway entered, and where real alarm was likely to occur. Here, Edo was given a set of institutions to match those in the opposite quarter, to repurify *ki*, ensuring that the countryside abutting the city was also clean. Again, the foci were two temples, one built to accommodate the populace, one for government use.

Not long after the Tokugawa gained possession of Edo in 1590, they took steps to cater for their family's spiritual needs. Buddhism is broadly divided into schools (Zen being perhaps the best known). The Tokugawa were devotees of Pure Land Buddhism. This meant that they venerated Kannon, and it accounts for their initial enthusiasm for the Asakusa-dera and its icon. But the Asakusa Kannon was anomalous: although enshrining an image of Kannon, it actually belonged to another school, Tendai. The Kan'ei-ji, next to it, was also Tendai, in emulation of the capital's northeasterly protector, the Enryaku-ji, which was institutionally Tendai. The Tokugawa were therefore without a suitable temple to meet their familial requirements.

In 1598, Ieyasu ordered the relocation of a Pure Land precinct to this area, to be his tutelary temple (*bodai-ji*). The place would hold prayers for the Tokugawa family and contain the graves of a hoped-for line of warlords, wives and children, and, from 1603, shoguns. It was positioned so that travellers coming in from the capital would see it almost immediately on arrival, reinforcing the Tokugawa imprint on the city.

Ieyasu could have endowed a whole new institution, but perhaps historicity lent more weight. He relocated a temple established in time immemorial, and refounded in 1385, at which point it had changed its name from Kōmyō-ji ('temple of radiant light') to Zōjō-ji ('temple of high elevation'). Its abbacy was awarded to the great cleric Zon'o, later given the supreme title of National Teacher (*kokushi*).[14] The Zōjō-ji's 'mountain name' was San'en-zan ('mountain of karmic links to the three'), where 'three' meant the Buddha, the dharma (Buddhist truth) and the sangha (clergy). But this 'mountain name' appealed to Ieyasu because it could also be interpreted differently. The Tokugawa hailed from Mikawa (near modern Nagoya), a place name literally meaning 'three rivers' (*mi* and *san* both mean 'three'; *kawa* is a river). San'en-zan could thus be glossed as 'mountain of karmic links to Mi[kawa]'. The name seemed to be a prediction that the Tokugawa would one day leave Mikawa and rule from here.

Upon relocation, the Zōjō-ji was vastly expanded and given accommodation for 3,000 monks, with an endowment of over 10,500 *koku*. In 1622, the year before his abdication, the second shogun, Hidetada, donated a massive gate, still standing as one of Tokyo's oldest structures (illus. 53). He also gave a precious printed *Tripitaka* ('three baskets'), or

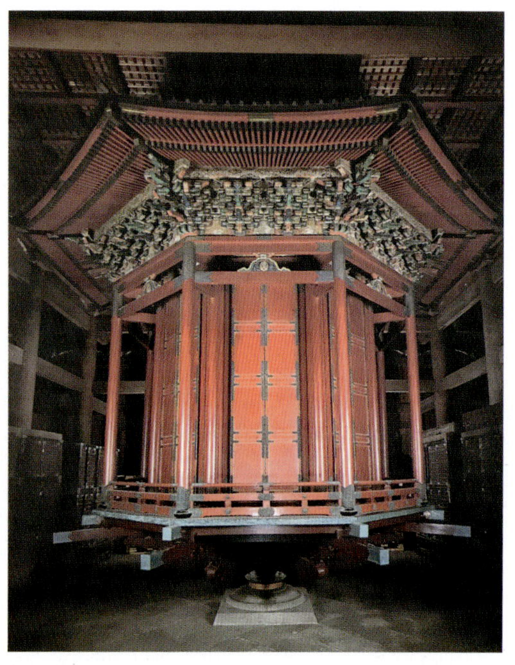

54 Pivoted library housing the printed Tripitaka, c. 1625, Zōjō-ji, Tokyo. Few temples possessed the entire canon of Buddhist sacred texts, which were seldom printed. Rather than reading the books, devotees would rotate the library on its spindle.

complete set of Buddhist scriptures – another 'three' – so voluminous that few temples had one, plus a revolving library to hold the books, also extant (illus. 54).

The Zōjō-ji had a principal icon, but on Ieyasu's death it was given another. This was the statue he had personally venerated and which he had habitually taken on campaigns. It represented the buddha Amida (Skt: Amitabha), lord of the Pure Land, whom Kannon attends. It was said to have been carved by the great tenth-century evangelist of the Pure Land, Genshin, whose treatise the *Essentials for Rebirth* (*Ōjōyō-shū*) of 985 was a classic text (today, Genshin is not thought to have been a maker of images). Crucially, the image was said have been used by the first Kamakura shogun, Minamoto no Yoritomo. Centuries of devotion using incense and candles had covered it in soot, so this Amida was called the 'black icon' (*kuro-honzon*). At one of Ieyasu's most crucial battles, his forces facing defeat, a black warrior appeared, killing adversaries while taking no wounds. This turned the tide, and Ieyasu carried the day. He asked his generals who the hero was, but no one knew. On returning to camp, Ieyasu opened his shrine to give thanks, but the icon was gone: *it* was the black warrior. The icon itself had secured a Tokugawa victory. The image later returned to the shrine, where it was treated with the utmost honour and declared a 'hidden Buddha'.[15] Nowadays it is revealed three times a year, drawing great crowds to the Zōjō-ji.

With the provision of this official southwestern temple, a parallel popular one was envisaged. Travellers heading towards the capital would want to buy charms and amulets, and those arriving into Edo would need to offer thanks. In 1633 the shogunate decreed a temple for this purpose, and they gave it another unusual name: Tōkai-ji ('temple of the Tōkai[dō]'), after the highway (illus. 55). Among Edo's main temples, Zen was not yet catered for, so the Tōkai-ji was affiliated with that school. On establishing it, Tokugawa Iemitsu invited as first abbot a famous cleric from the capital, Takuan Sōhō, originally a Pure Land monk who had changed to Zen and become abbot of a premier Zen temple, the Daitoku-ji ('temple of great virtue'). Takuan had been

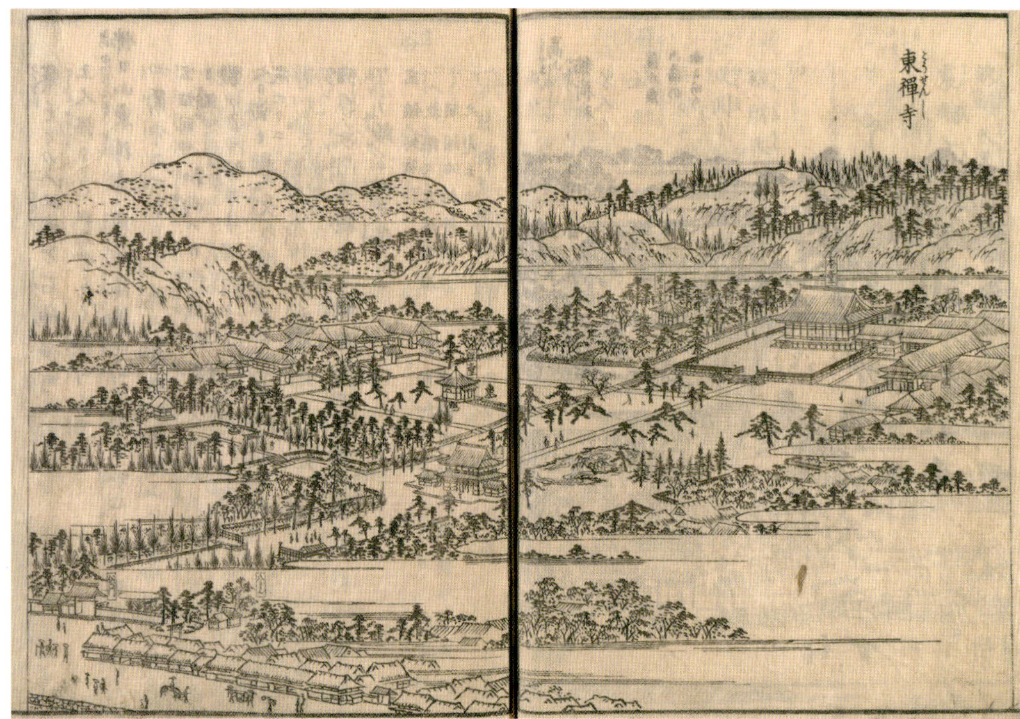

disliked by Hidetada, who exiled him, but Iemitsu was well known for countermanding his father's wishes, and on Hidetada's death he amnestied Takuan. Takuan came to Edo in triumph to take up the abbacy. The Tokugawa were Pure Land Buddhists, but most warrior families were Zen, and Takuan gained a huge following. He conceptualized many notions that have since become core Zen ideas. His magnum opus, *Record of Unmoving Wisdom and Divine Mysteries* (*Fudōchi shinmyō roku*), is still read, available in English as *The Unfettered Mind*. Takuan is thought to have secured the most famous garden architect of the period, Kobori Enshū, to lay out the Zen temple grounds, and if that is true, it was Enshū's only work in Edo.

Takuan was from peasant stock, and he never lost a sense of the importance of religious outreach. The popularizing intentions of the Tōkai-ji suited him well. His training in two different Buddhist schools (most unusual) freed him from sectarian bias. Takuan's most

55 Hasegawa Settan, 'Tōkai-ji', from Saitō Yukio et al., *Edo meisho zue* (Illustrated Famous Places in Edo, 1834), monochrome printed book. This temple protected the 'demon's back gate' (*ura-kimon*), and was much visited by those using the Tōkai-dō highway that ran 500 km to the capital.

56 Model of the central sanctuary of the Taitoku-in, Mausoleum of Tokugawa Hidetada (1632), 1909–10, wood, lacquer, copper alloy, painted and partially gilded. The second shogun's sumptuous mausoleum was destroyed by enemy action in 1945, but a model of it has recently been discovered in London and is on permanent loan back to the Zōjō-ji.

famous achievement was the invention of a cheap, nutritious radish pickle, still widely eaten and eponymously called *takuan*. It could be carried by travellers and must have saved the life of many a person fainting by the roadside. When he died in 1645, his gravestone, which is extant, was carved to look like a stone press for *takuan* production.

Ieyasu had been buried outside Edo at Nikkō, as Iemitsu would be; but the second shogun, Hidetada, was buried at the Zōjō-ji, in 1632. The stunning mausoleum was destroyed in the Second World War, though photographs of it survive. Recently, a large architectural model has come to light, somewhat implausibly in the British Royal Collection. In 2016 it was returned to the Zōjō-ji on permanent loan (illus. 56).[16] The Zōjō-ji monks knew Iemitsu had expressed the desire to be buried next to Ieyasu at Nikkō, but strongly opposed his wishes. After conducting his death rituals, they considered refusing to give up the body, only relenting on condition that future shoguns would be buried at their temple – a promise which, if made, was reneged on.[17] The fourth shogun, Ietsuna, was buried at the Kan'ei-ji, as was the fifth, Tsunayoshi. From then on, burials alternated between the Kan'ei-ji and Zōjō-ji. The dual system ensured shogunal graves further purified *ki* at both main and back 'gates' of the city.

❧

Other holy sites were replicated in Edo too, not concentrated in geomantically significant vectors but in locations that suited the intended parallel. Mount Atago, for example, is a steep hill in the capital with an important temple on top, dedicated to the Atago avatar. An avatar (*gongen*) is the Shinto divinity emanating from a Buddhist one, in this case from the bodhisattva Jizō. One of central Edo's several hills was set up to be an equivalent to Mount Atago. Just 30 metres high, Edo's Mount Atago was not very tall, but it did have excellent views.

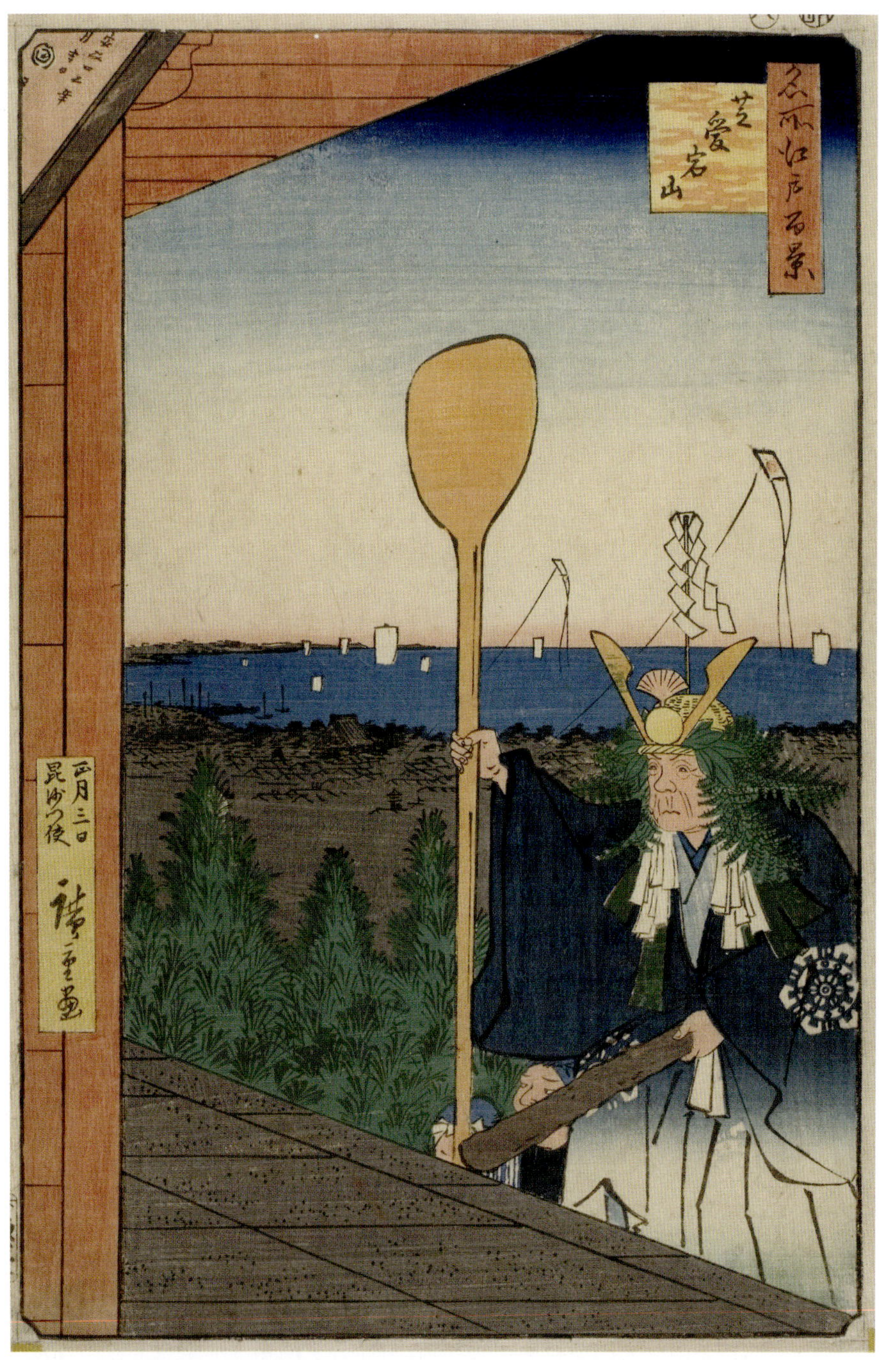

57 Utagawa Hiroshige, 'Mount Atago, Shiba', from the series *One Hundred Famous Views of Edo*, 1857, multicoloured woodblock print. One of Edo's hills was named to match Mount Atago in the capital. The panoramic views ensured it was much visited.

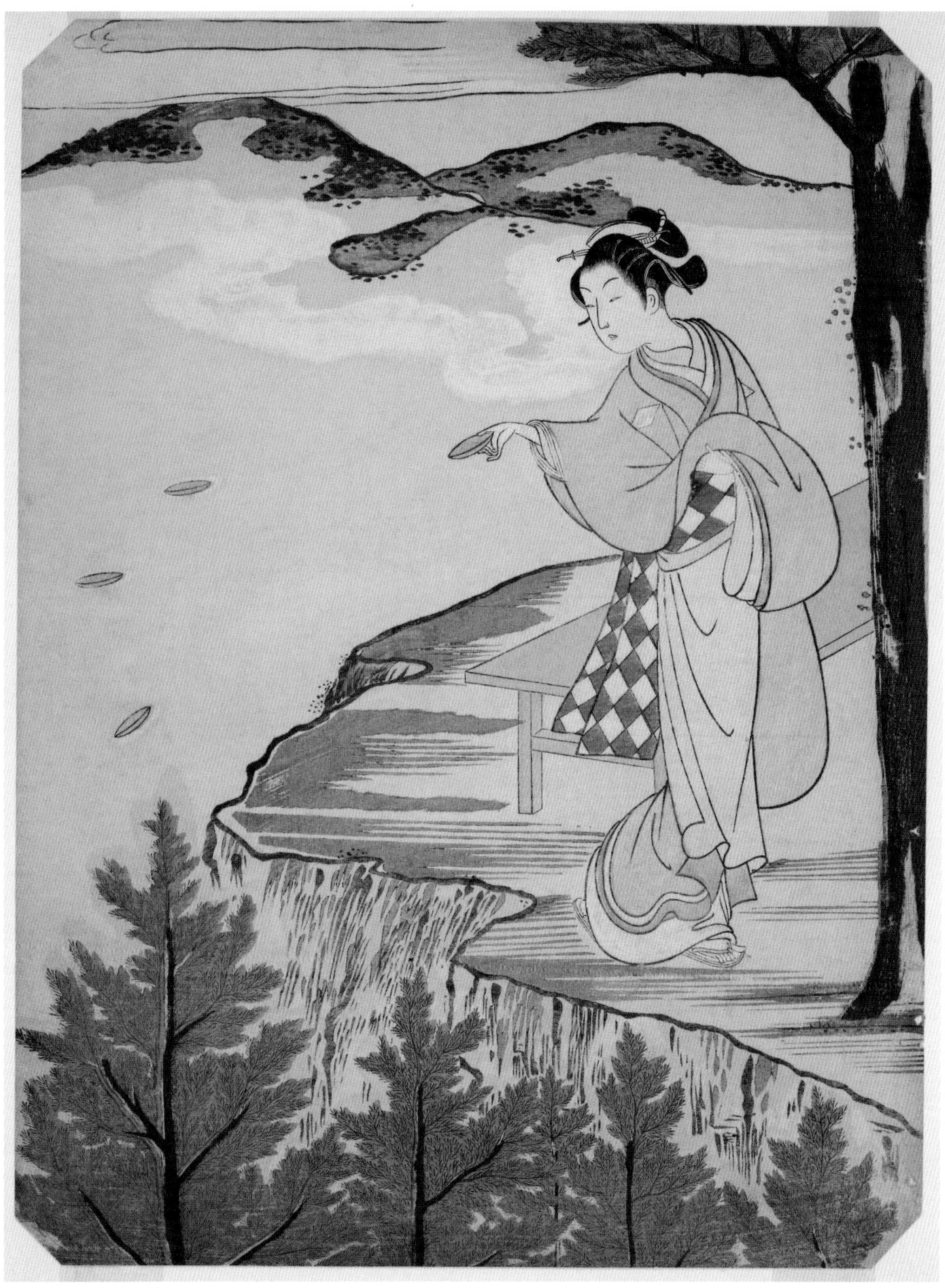

58 Suzuki Harunobu, *Tossing Dishes Over a Cliff*, c. 1766–7, multicoloured woodblock print. The practice of hurling one's troubles away in the form of ceramic tiles thrown over a cliff was imported from the capital to Edo.

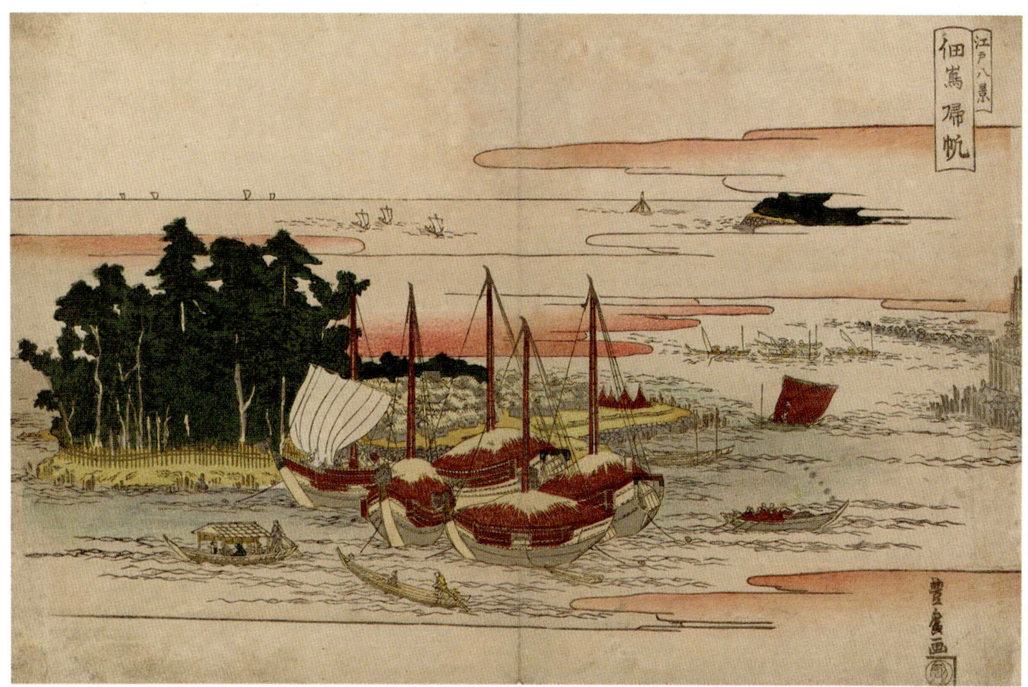

59 Utagawa Toyohiro, 'Returning Sails to Tsukuda-jima', from the series *Eight Views of Edo (Edo hakkei)*, 1790s, multicoloured woodblock print. Boats come home to the fishing families' island under an evening glow. The place was named after the fishers' island in Osaka.

Hiroshige depicted it in his guidebook *Edo omiyage*, mentioned above. He showed a ritual under way, specific to Edo and not copied from the capital, where an elder presented a huge rice spoon in prayer for plentiful food, as the caption explains. Hiroshige recycled this image for his colour collection *Edo meisho hyakkei*, as he did with the Hall of Thirty-three Bays (illus. 57).

Another ritual took place at Edo's Mount Atago, this time appropriated not from the original but from another hill, outside the capital, called Mount Takao. There, pilgrims spun ceramic dishes into the valley below. Edo people similarly flung away their troubles by 'dish-throwing' (literally 'tile-throwing', *kawara-nage*), as depicted by Harunobu (illus. 58).

Finally, there is one instance of a religious site borrowed from another city – not the capital, but Osaka. This was done because its parishioners had been relocated and they did not want to be deprived of their habitual deity. Edo had abundant fisheries but not enough fishers, so as the city grew, Ieyasu offered Osaka's fishing community good terms to re-establish themselves in Edo. He set aside two small islands in Edo Bay, rather like where the Osakans had come from, and as their old home was the island of Tsukuda-jima, Edo's islands were named Tsukuda-jima too (illus. 59). As another senryū put it,

A map of Edo
With dots added:
Tsukuda-jima.[18]

The two islands were like pinpoints in Edo Bay. In 1644 reclamation work joined the islands together, expanding the space to some 200 metres along each side to accommodate the thirty or so households now resident.[19]

The fishing families brought with them the Radiant God of Sumiyoshi. A 'radiant god' (*myōjin*) is a Shinto divinity and also a Buddhist one, akin to an avatar except that both parties are equal. His shrine on Osaka's Tsukuda-jima had no special architecture or rituals, but soon the displaced families created a ceremony, held every three years, on the day when Ieyasu had invited them to Edo (the 29th day of the sixth month).

This Radiant God served fisherfolk but also doubled as the deity of literature. The curious combination came from a nō drama thought to have been written by the greatest proponent of the genre, Zeami, early in the fifteenth century. The play tells of the arrival in Japan of a revered Tang dynasty poet, Bai Juyi, in English sometimes written Po Chü-i. In Japanese he is called Haku Rakuten, which is also the play's title. It is not a factual event, but the play has Bai Juyi pull his boat in near Osaka, in front of the main shrine to the Radiant God of Sumiyoshi. Bai Juyi has been sent by his emperor to test the Japanese skill at verse, which the Tang court assumes will be weak. Still in his boat, without deigning to step ashore, Bai Juyi challenges the first Japanese he sees to a poetic competition – totally unfairly, as the man is a fisherman. Yet actually, he is the Radiant God of Sumiyoshi, who has taken the guise of a fisherman to defend the Japanese honour. He produces a peerless poem, to Bai Juyi's great surprise. Importantly, the issue was not one of skill. Bai Juyi's verse for the bout was peerless too, but it was, naturally, in Chinese. The god refuses this mode, and though elite Japanese routinely wrote in Chinese, he offers a verse in Japanese. The play is about Japan's demands for recognition as an autonomous culture while still respecting the norms of the continent. In the play, Bai Juyi concedes this. Thereupon a *kamikaze* (divine wind) arises, expelling him back home. The encounter was occasionally made the subject of paintings (illus. 60). Shrines to the Radiant God of Sumiyoshi were often located on the seashore, so he came to be associated with both fishing and letters. He now had an Edo precinct too.

A salient addition to this panoply of borrowings came in 1793. A group of enterprising commoners decided their city needed a second Great Buddha, in the southwest, to parallel that in the northeast. The shogunate did not sanction the project, but it did not oppose it either, at least not initially. An image was put up at the Kaian-ji ('temple of peaceful seas'), a Zen institution close to the Tōkaidō, so convenient for visits. There were no resources for a statue in bronze, nor even in wood, so one was created in basketry. This allowed for rapid production, though not much resilience. Amazingly, the object was over 40 metres tall – higher than any Great Buddha ever attempted. Pilgrims flocked in until, records state, the whole area turned black. No picture of it seems to have been made, other than a tongue-in-cheek story pretending to expound the miraculous origins of the image; 'origin legends' (*engi*) were told about many icons. Enthusiasts took boats across the bay to view the statue from the other side, sometimes with the aid of a telescope (illus. 61). This was all too much for the authorities, who demanded that the structure be pulled down. The Great Basket Buddha (*kappa ōbotoke*) lasted just sixty days.[20]

৩

The erection of temples and shrines was (usually) a permanent way of sacralizing space. But icons were mobile, and over the course of history

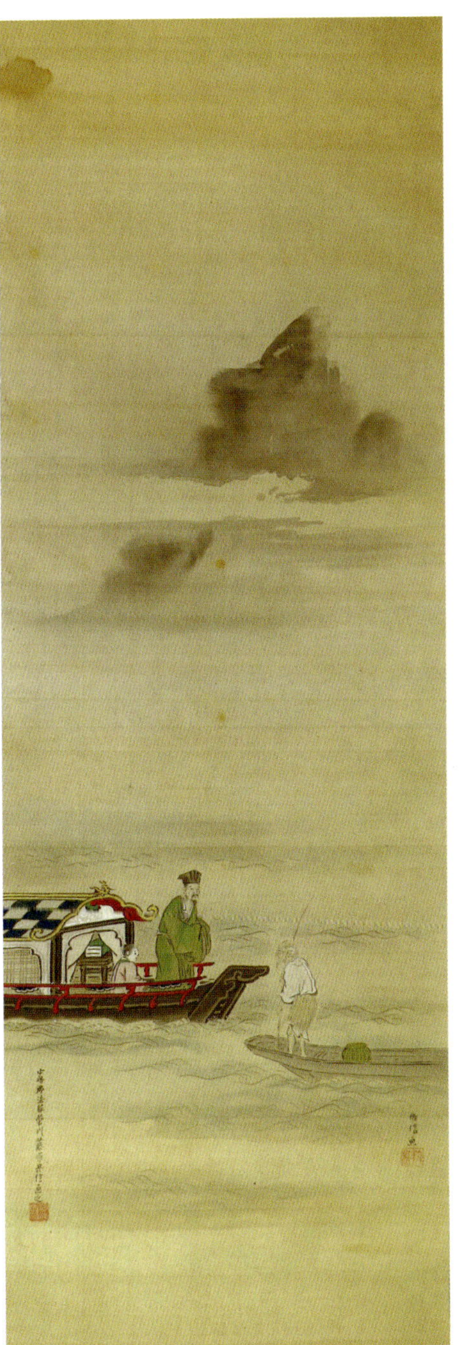

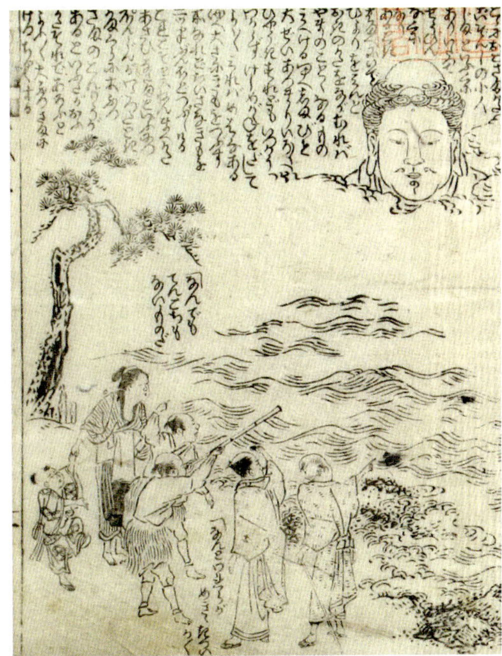

60 Kano Eisen and Korenobu, *The Poet Bai Juyi* (*Haku Rakuten*), 18th century, handscroll, ink and colour on paper. A nō (Noh) play fictionally told of the great poet coming to Japan to hold a verse competition. Unfairly, he challenged a local fisherman – who turned out to actually be the god of Sumiyoshi, and so produced a peerless verse. The Chinese is shown as pompous, while the Japanese is simple and uncontrived.

61 Katsushika Hokusai, 'Great Buddha of the Kaian-ji', from *Nanasato fūki* (1794), monochrome printed book. The short-lived 'great basket Buddha' could be viewed from across Edo Bay.

many had shifted between precincts. A system for temporary borrowing became popular in Edo too. Taking the lead from occasional displays of 'hidden Buddhas', known as *kaichō* ('opening the curtains'), loan exhibitions were called *de-gaichō* ('out *kaichō*'). It was a way for venerated images, most of which were in the capital, to lend authority to Edo. Donations made were useful to both host and lending institutions. *De-gaichō* were religious but came close to art exhibitions, with aesthetic or historical interest as evident as piety; and fashionable people wanting to be seen attending. The Asakusa Kannon was perennially short of funds, so hosted many. One Edo temple became specialist for *de-gaichō*, the Ekō-in ('cloister of rotations'), founded in 1658 for repose of those killed at the terrible fire of the year before (the name refers to transmigration). The precinct was conveniently on the Great River, across a bridge that had been built after the fire both to serve as a future escape route and to open up new districts for expanding Edo's development. Among many icons that came to the Ekō-in was the 'hidden Buddha' of the Kiyomizu-dera.[21]

Not all *de-gaichō* icons came from the capital. The hallowed buddha of the Zenkō-ji ('temple of good radiance') in remote Nagano came several times. Or rather, as it was too holy to travel, it was brought in replica, people along the route touching the strong-box containing it. A member of the Dutch East India Company recorded an icon leaving Nagasaki in 1796:

A Japanese deity was escorted on board a barge amid many ceremonies. It will be transported to Edo to exercise its miracles there. On this occasion [Nagasaki] Bay was filled with pleasure boats and other vessels. The priests on board gave out blessings to many people, which made them all happy.[22]

In the rapidly expanding area across the bridge, further on from the Ekō-in, was perhaps Edo's most extraordinary temple, the Gohyaku Rakan-ji ('temple of the five hundred arhats').[23] Arhats (J: *rakan*), said to number either five hundred or sixteen, were persons who had heard the Buddha preach a mystic sermon on Vulture Peak, the highest place on earth, and been Enlightened. They were particular objects of devotion in the Obaku school of Buddhism, a form of Zen introduced by Chinese emigrées in Nagasaki. With the collapse of the Ming dynasty in 1644, some eminent Chinese monks came to Japan. The most senior, Yinyuan (J: Ingen), had been permitted by the shogunate to open an Obaku temple near the capital at Uji, named the Manpuku-ji ('temple of ten thousand blessings') following the name of the temple he had left in China (C: Wufan-su). Ingen's home temple was in the district of Huangpo, pronounced 'Obaku' in Japanese (meaning a cork tree), and hence this name was given to the Chinese school. The Manpuku-ji was completed in 1661 with the surrounding area given the name Obaku. So here was another borrowing, though it was unrelated to Edo.

Before long there were Obaku temples across the country. A Japanese Obaku monk named Shōun arrived in Edo in 1687. He began

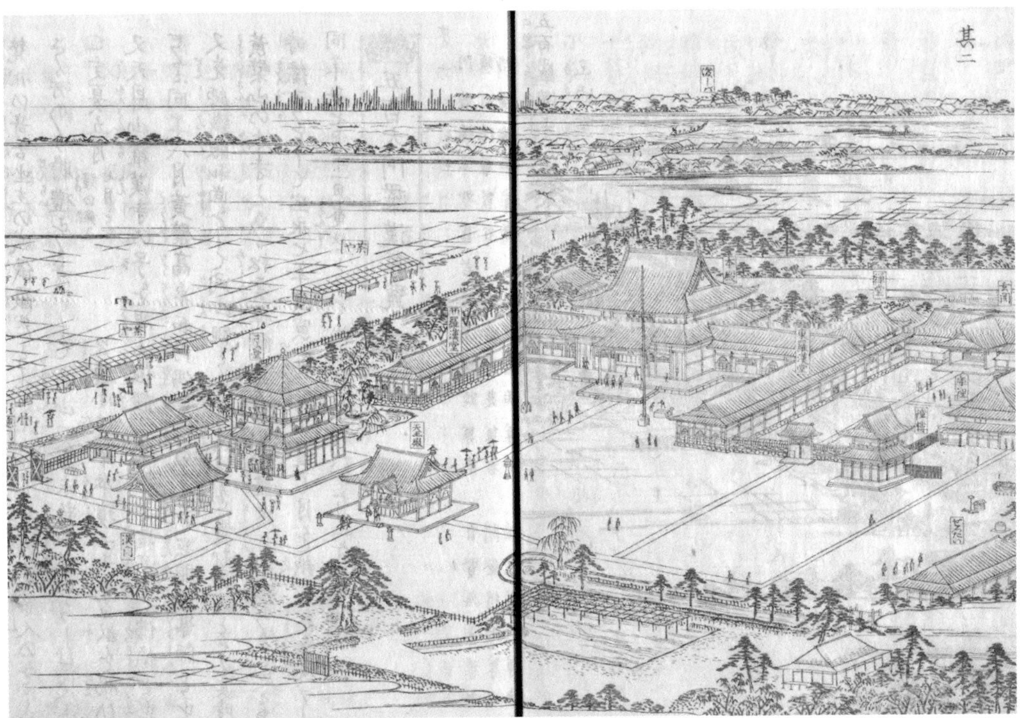

carving five hundred arhat images, each life-sized – an epic endeavour. Shōun set up at Asakusa, so throngs passed, offering donations.[24] The shogun's mother, Keishō-in, came to hear of him and sponsored several images. Shōun completed the 450th arhat in 1695 and was offered a plot in the development district across the Great River. After all five hundred images were made, he sculpted a massive buddha to be placed in the centre, with two attendants, seated on realistic rocks. It made a stunning diorama of the mystic sermon at Vulture Peak (illus. 63). The dating is unclear, but Shōun died in 1710, the Temple of the Five-hundred Arhats all complete. The shogunate continued to support the temple, even erecting a special gate (*onari-mon*) to be used by shogunal retinues (illus. 62). However, they required its monks to be Japanese, not foreign. Still, Edo had acquired an international Buddhist site, and, given that the Ming had crumbled, it could be proposed as continuing the faith of the continent in the shogunal city.

The arhat temple was hugely exciting to Edo people, who could not travel abroad. It had foreign-looking images and unknown rituals, and its temple food was interesting and tasty. But it had no parishioners, so was reliant on offerings, which were many, since the allure of the Rakan-ji (as it was abbreviated) made it one of the most visited sites of Edo. A senryū compared it to the Sengaku-ji ('temple of the spring peak'), which was among Edo's top sites owing to the graves there of the Forty-seven Rōnin (masterless samurai), self-sacrificial warriors who died in 1703 – still famous from samurai movies. The versifier imagined tourists planning their sightseeing while resting in Edo's cheap hotel district, Bakuro-chō:

63 Shōun Genkei, from set of five hundred Arhats (present layout), c. 1695, gilded wood. This Chinese-style temple boasted five hundred life-sized statues of the arhats, arranged with other images to recreate the Buddha Mystic Sermon.

Bakuro-chō.
The morning after the 500,
It's the 47.[25]

The first thing a visitor did on arrival in Edo was visit the Rōnin graves, but that afternoon they went to visit the Five Hundred Arhats. Even the Rōnin came second to that.

The Rakan-ji thus offered sacralization in most unusual terms. Obaku monks were allowed the privilege (or were forced) to wear the Tokugawa crest on their vestments (as they still do), so the alterity of the Ming was clearly built into the shogunal structure.

The project came to fruition in the time of the eighth shogun, Yoshimune, who was known as an art-lover. In a separate move, Yoshimune had decided to create a shogunal painting gallery, acquiring foreign work to match his peerless Japanese collection. He commissioned pieces from the new Chinese dynasty of the Qing, and also some from Europe – the only shogun who ever did so. Yoshimune's commission was taken to Amsterdam by the Dutch East India Company or VOC and resulted in five canvases arriving in Japan in 1726. Three were on military themes (a battle, a siege and a hunt), which Yoshimune kept for himself. The other two were mild (flowers and birds), and these Yoshimune wanted to make publicly available. He came up with the Rakan-ji as the best site of display, since, after all, it was a place of foreignness. The two paintings would have been seen by tens of thousands of people, though we have almost no written descriptions of them, nor were copies produced, because of 'awe' over shogunal gifts. Just one sketch of each painting is known to have been made, shortly after the works were exhibited, by an otherwise unrecorded person called Zaiga. These were published, but discreetly, deep within the pages

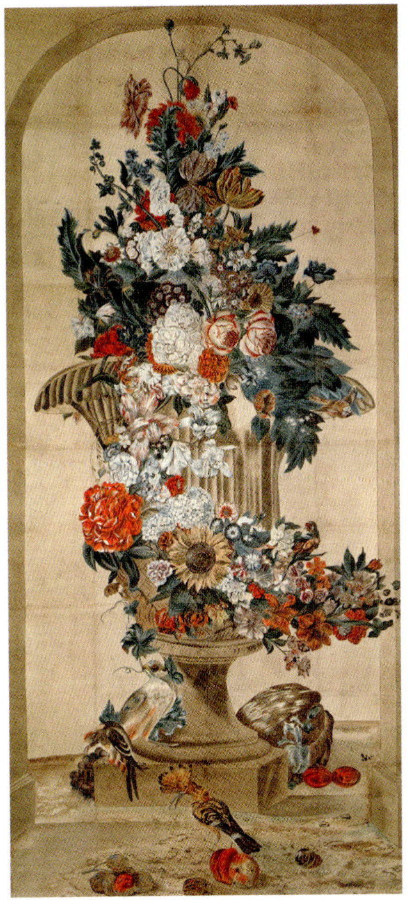

64 Tani Bunchō, copy after Willem van Royen, *Flowers and Birds*, c. 1730, hanging scroll, colour on silk. The shogun Tokugawa Yoshimine commissioned paintings in Amsterdam and then donated two to the Gohaku Rakan-ji. Over time their surfaces darkened, so precise copies were commissioned.

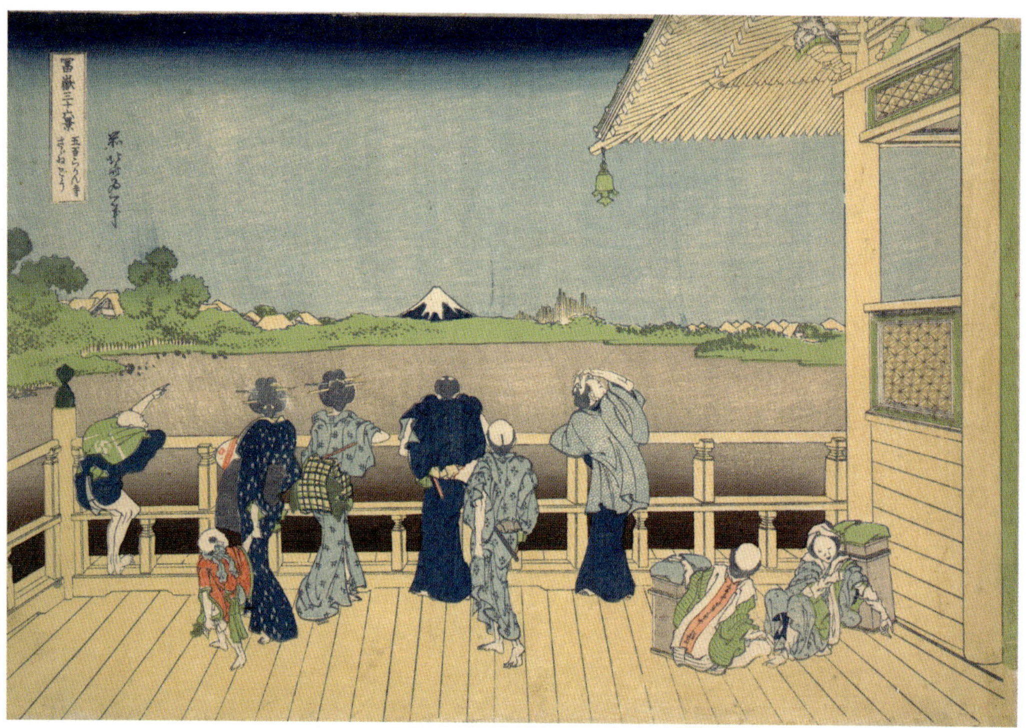

of a long book by Yamashita Sekichū (also otherwise unknown) on 'bird and flower painting' (*kachō-ga*), a Japanese genre with which the Dutch works seemed to fit.[26]

Around one century later, the authorities noticed that the pictures had darkened. They sent an official painter to copy them, or at least one of them – probably both, but only one copy is extant. Tani Bunchō's rendition was so meticulous that it even included the artist's signature, thanks to which the maker can be identified as Willem van Royen (illus. 64). Not a household name today, van Royen was popular in early eighteenth-century Amsterdam for nature painting, though he is unlikely to have painted the military themes. Edo thus acquired a kind of European sacralization, too, turned Buddhist, to cleverly avoid outlawed Christianity.

Later, another building was added to the Rakan-ji, in about 1780, furthering its strangeness and inserting yet another dimension. The

65 Katsushika Hokusai, 'Turbo Hall at the Temple of the Five Hundred Arhats', from the series *Thirty-six Views of Mount Fuji (Fugaku sanjūrokkei)*, c. 1830–32, multicoloured woodblock print. At the top of the Gohyaku Rakan-ji's Turbo Hall, viewers look out towards Mount Fuji.

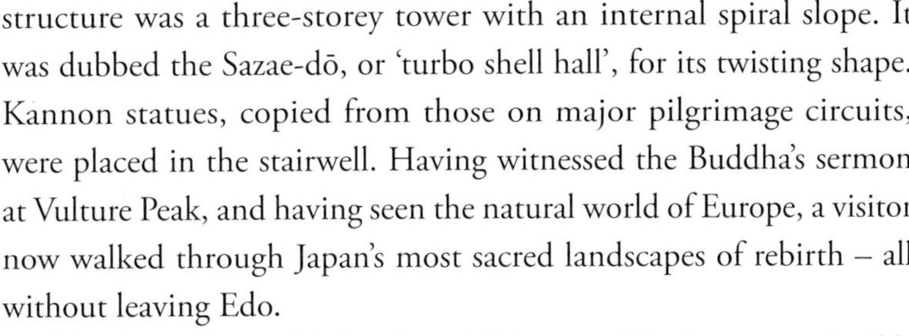

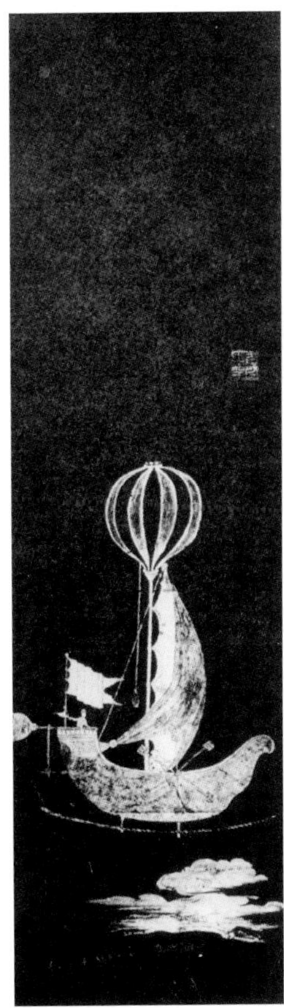
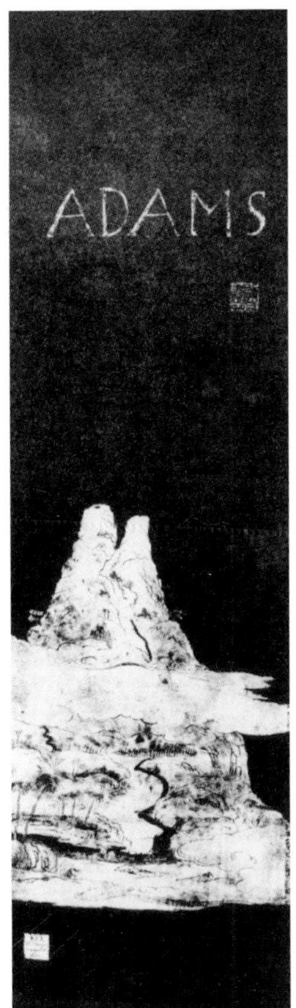

66 Shiba Kōkan, c. 1790, pair of hanging scrolls, gold on blue paper. Sadly now lost, this diptych shows the site of the Buddha's Mystic Sermon on Vulture Peak (called by the Dutch 'Adams Berg'), together with a *charlière*, or hot-air balloon. Both scrolls have shogunal crests on the mounting (not visible here).

structure was a three-storey tower with an internal spiral slope. It was dubbed the Sazae-dō, or 'turbo shell hall', for its twisting shape. Kannon statues, copied from those on major pilgrimage circuits, were placed in the stairwell. Having witnessed the Buddha's sermon at Vulture Peak, and having seen the natural world of Europe, a visitor now walked through Japan's most sacred landscapes of rebirth – all without leaving Edo.

The Sazae-dō was Edo's only publicly accessible three-storey building. No visitor had ever gone up so high, yet they hardly seemed to ascend because the slope was so smooth. At the top was a terrace affording wonderfully liberating views, as captured by Hokusai in his *Thirty-six views of Mount Fuji* (illus. 65). Visitors looked down at the Rakan Hall and the shogun's processional gateway, recalling how all this was thanks to Tokugawa dispensation. 'Awe' was owed. Looking over their glorious city, they saw in the distance the sacred peak of Fuji.

Then Vulture Peak was found. This was about the time the Turbo Hall was erected, and the hall may have been built in response to the discovery. Though assumed to be legendary, the voc reported in Japan that it was true. The Company traded with many places, and one was Ceylon (Sri Lanka), which had a holy mountain with sacred footprints at the top. The Buddhists asserted they were the Buddha's own footprints, while Muslims and Christians said they belonged to Adam, and Hindus said they were Shiva's. Being so high, Buddhists further claimed that this place must be Vulture Peak. A Dutch print was brought to Japan, labelling the peak 'Adams Berg'. This was copied for publication in a book on Western affairs, *Kōmō zatsuwa* (European Miscellany, published in 1787).[27] The author, Morishima Chūryō, was from an elite intellectual family, and had the image transcribed by the Western-style townsman artist Shiba Kōkan.

Chūryō's book is full of interesting facts, one regarding the invention of the hot-air balloon. A print showing this curious device came to Japan too, not depicting the first ascent by the Montgolfiers but that by Jacques Charles one month later, in November 1783. Chūryō also had Kōkan copy this for inclusion in his book.[28]

Of great interest is that Kōkan also worked the two imported images as paintings. He made them into a diptych, lavishly rendered in gold on a purple ground, a combination generally reserved for Buddhist scriptures. He placed Adams Berg to the right – that is, in first place. To the left he put the charlière, or hot-air balloon. The world's highest point and a machine for ascending to such levels were thus paired. Hanging scroll diptychs are rare in Japanese art, but triptychs are common, most frequently with a buddha or other admired figure in the centre, the flanks particularizing the composition as desired by the user. That was probably the case here, though we cannot be sure. Likely, however, there was a buddha in the centre. Sadly, Kōkan's works are lost, and today all we have is a pre-war monochrome photograph (illus. 66). However, its caption states that the paintings were mounted on cloth adorned with the Tokugawa crest.[29]

Four
Reading Edo Castle

eyasu had been awarded the well-situated but ruined Edo Castle in 1590. One of his first actions upon deciding that Edo would become the seat of his power was to thoroughly remodel its defensive and residential areas. During the early years of the seventeenth century the site was provided with massive walls, like most castles of the period, though because of the deficiency of stone and the risk of earthquakes, these were generally stone claddings built around an earthen core. The Portuguese and Spaniards had introduced ballistics, so a castle's outer defences had to be further from the centre than a cannonball could fly, and Ieyasu gave Edo a perimeter of some 16 kilometres. A soaring keep or donjon would be expected of a first-rate castle, allowing surveillance of territory and warning of enemy attack.

Castles had service towns, so outworks and towers were beautified. People living in their lea were given something to venerate. A castle might be fearsome to look at, but a sense of safety emanated from it too. Keeps were recent innovations, and it was European practice that had inspired them. The Japanese language originally had no term for such structures, so one was generated, *tenshu-kaku* ('turret of the lord of heaven'). *Ten* (heaven) could be thought of as an abbreviation of *tenka* ('all under heaven'), the pan-East Asian word for a realm. Using it indicated that warlords aspired to cosmic authority, though at this time in Japan many were pretty paltry in fact. Toyotomi Hideyoshi, who was not paltry, had announced his aim as 'unification of the tenka' (*tenka tōitsu*), and he referred to himself as Tenka. Ieyasu, perhaps more mild-mannered, proclaimed: 'The tenka belongs to the tenka' (*tenka wa tenka no tenka nari*); that is, the realm is for all those 'below heaven', meaning the people.[1]

While *ten* is 'heaven', *shu* is 'master', or the territory's ruler. But *tenshu* could also mean something else. Lord of Heaven might be a generic self-asserting name for civil-war strongmen, but it was also what Christian missionaries called their god. Other terms were used too, and in the end the missions gave up and called God *deus* in Latin, or *deiusu* in Japanese. A keep, then, had a foreign tinge, not only because it emerged from cannon warfare but because it associated the lord inside with a monotheistic Almighty. Over time, and certainly after the expulsion of the missionaries in 1614, the *shu* came to be rewritten with a homophone, not 'master', but 'protection'. Keeps were cleansed, as it were, of foreign overtones and became more indigenous, as the 'protectors of heaven'.

The keep was the only part of a castle commoners would see, and then mostly viewing it from afar. They could never penetrate the interior. A keep was thus both for use and a symbol. There may have been some towers before, but Ieyasu built Edo's first fine keep in 1604.[2] This was probably under construction when he retired the following year, in favour of his son Hidetada. It was a multi-storey single tower, but little more is known of it. Hidetada rebuilt it in 1622, perhaps to increase its size, since he was remodelling the castle to take account of the advancing bureaucratization of Tokugawa rule. The new keep was multi-level, with several subordinate towers. In 1637 the third shogun, Iemitsu, demolished his father's structure and replaced it. Iemitsu's finished keep appears on the Idemitsu and Rekihaku screens (see illus. 20 and 21). Depictions cannot be relied upon to convey

67 Kano Naonobu, 'Dawn over the Golden Castle', from *Twelve Views of Musashi Province*, 1648, handscroll, ink and light colour on paper. This set depicts various places in the area around Edo, including the shogun's castle, reproduced here, on what is probably intended as New Year's morn, ushering in another year of bounty. It is among the first dated views of Edo Castle keep.

exact appearances, but by 1640 Edo Castle keep seems to have been a massive, but trimly attractive, single-tower, five-storey affair, white, but with heavy eaves and tiling. It rose to 60 metres, which is nearly a third taller than Japan's tallest extant keep, at Himeji Castle (though that also stands on a hill). It may have been the largest ever erected in the archipelago. Aesthetic value as well as military functionality was clearly the objective. A loosely rendered ink-wash work of 1648 is the first securely dated representation, included in a set of twelve Edo views (illus. 67).

The great fire of 1657 wiped out much of Edo, burning the castle and razing Iemitsu's glorious keep. The sketch for a proposed rebuilding exists, and if the intention was to replicate what was lost, not to innovate, this may be our most accurate likeness of what had stood for about two decades.[3]

However, the keep was not rebuilt. Its stone base was retained and is still an impressive indicator today (illus. 68). But Japan's most important castle, its grandest and the place from which rule emanated, lacked a keep for the next 250 years of shogunal residence. Why? On what grounds was Edo's most visible shogunal building consigned to memory? There are several opinions. Some scholars have argued that by 1657 a keep was no longer necessary. It is true that the last major Tokugawa battle had taken place long before. But that is to think in retrospect; it is not what the shogunate knew at the time. Indeed, in 1648, for example, 4,000 soldiers had marched on Edo to assassinate Iemitsu and overthrow the regime; they failed, but this Keian

Disturbance shows that the need for vigilance had not retreated. Another interpretation is that the shogunate was experiencing financial problems and could not afford the colossal expense of rebuilding. This may be true. Yet all governments have money for what they deem essential, even at the sacrifice of other things. Most likely is a third option. The keep was left unbuilt for reasons neither military nor financial, but to do with iconography. Such a bombastic structure no longer fitted into the shogunal symbolism of rule. The Tokugawa had fought their way to power, superseding all competition. But as peace prevailed, they shifted to a different kind of rubric. A shogunate was always a military government, with swords and ranks. Yet more widely, the symbolic language of rule switched from force and compulsion to invocation of rule by 'virtue'. Indeed, 'virtue', *toku*, was in their name (along with *gawa*, meaning river). The Tokugawa were a 'river of virtue' flowing from a distant past into an unknown future. The shogunate deployed what has been termed 'genesis amnesia', smothering recollection of their actual rise to power.[4] They clouded it with a language of moral lessons. Now, it was not by killing their rivals but by being good that they had succeeded. The Tokugawa called their stronghold, we recall, not Edo Castle (by which name it is generally known) but Chiyoda Castle, 'castle in the rice fields for one thousand generations'. It was barely a castle at all, they proposed, more like a strong agricultural storehouse. It was about succour and security, not oppression. After the fire of 1657, and without its keep, Edo Castle indeed did not look much like a fort. The Tokugawa no longer needed – or wanted – their paramount and obvious instrument of attack and defence; they preferred to imagine that they rejoiced in the love of the people, who recognized upright rule and were grateful for abundant supply. So the skies above Edo closed over and healed.

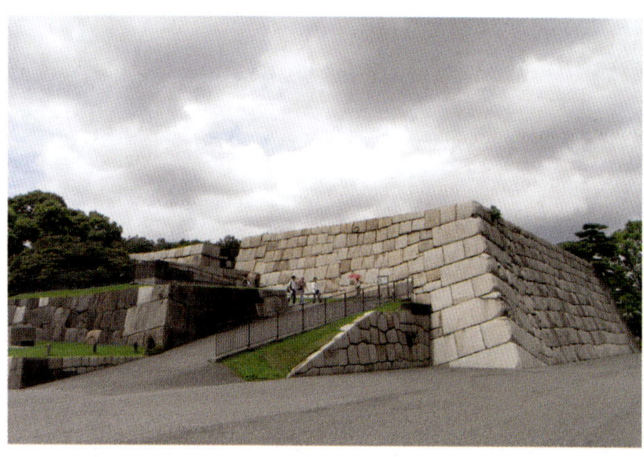

68 Stone base of Edo Castle keep, c. 1625. All that is left, this nevertheless indicates the colossal dimensions.

The shogun had other castles. He did not wantonly dismantle them, but when time or disaster took their toll, they were not rebuilt. The lofty keep of Nijō Castle, in the capital, stood until 1788, but then fell victim to fire. It was not rebuilt. The capital's skies healed over too. The regional daimyo followed suit. After fire or earthquake, keeps and subsidiary towers were not rebuilt. Active disempowering strategies were to plant trees in the honour courts where warriors had once paraded and to encourage lotuses to clog moats, once dug to repel intruders. This compromised utility, but that was the purpose: to suggest that emergency was not envisaged. In fact, the shogunate did not dismantle his readiness. It only dismantled the appearance of readiness. The prints by Hokusai discussed in Chapter Two show Edo Castle with only secondary towers and looking rather more like a forest than a redoubt, though Hokusai and his publisher knew that if they showed it otherwise there would be repercussions (illus. 29 and 31). The compound was still clearly the site of government, but as a military entity it seemed no longer really there.

As rule changed from the language of violence to ethics, rulers withdrew. A preference for non-seeing and non-showing is apparent across all East Asian systems of kingship. As mentioned above, this has been termed the 'iconography of absence'. It was not something that the shoguns invented. In China, the palace was called the 'forbidden city' (properly 'purple forbidden city', Zijincheng), not just inaccessible but invisible too, though everyone knew it was there. It is often forgotten that the dairi's palace in the capital had the same name, in Japanese pronounced Kinjō. The Japanese fondness for massive architectural gates was related to protection, of course, but it was also a means of concealing power. The point of a gate is to be taller than the buildings behind, and so to hide them. The shoguns imposed a meticulous protocol on gate construction in Edo, with size pegged to status.[5] Gates kept intruders' bodies out but also prevented ocular and aural ingress via strictly encoded patterns. Nomenclature too followed a tendency towards hiding. Today we casually say 'the shogun', but this strongly military title was softened and made elusive. He was more often referred to as 'the governmental personage' (*kubō*) or as 'the great tree' (*taiju*), naturalizing his presence. Proper names were also adapted. Hideyoshi was Tenka, while Tokugawa Ieyasu, one of the greatest fighters in world history, was known as Ankoku-sama, 'Lord of the Peaceful Country'.

One articulation of this, to the level of obsequiousness, appears in a print by Hokusai from the series *One Hundred Views of Mount Fuji* (*Fugaku hyakkei*), published in 1834 but often reissued. It is labelled 'Fuji of Edo' (*Edo no fuji*) and shows the peak rising up behind a finial of Edo Castle, made in the shape of a mythical fish, for fire prevention (see illus. 8 and 69). The location is at once recognizable. Hokusai does not show the castle, in fact: what he shows is *not* showing it, out of 'awe'. Instead we see a bird. This might seem rude, for where birds perch, they leave droppings. But that is not the meaning. Birds are timorous and fly away at the slightest movement. Here, a bird is at rest, even sleeping – the ultimate sign of harmony and the absence of all alarm.

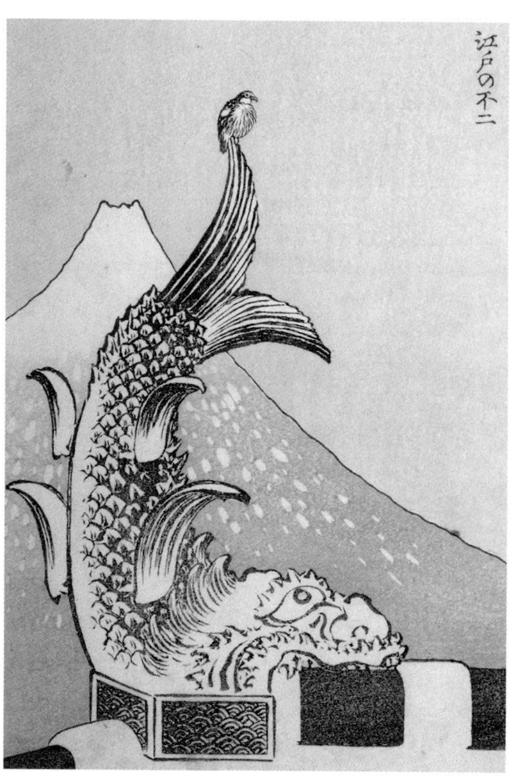

69 Katsushika Hokusai, 'Fuji from Edo', from *One Hundred Views of Mount Fuji* (1834), monochrome printed book, c. 1849 edition. This best-selling book suggests the most iconic view of Fuji from Edo is as seen behind the upturned fish finials of the castle.

Few gained access to the interior of Edo Castle, but to those who did, every part of the buildings and their decoration was pregnant with meaning. Both structures and fittings have long since disappeared, but there are sources that allow us to envisage them. Elite temples were patronized by military figures, with abbacies decorated quite like warrior mansions. This is not surprising, since abbots were the sons and brothers of warlords and tended to use the same artists. The overriding intent of castle interiors (and thus also of abbacies) was to prove that the long civil war, which had lasted from the 1460s to the 1590s, was over. The greatest painting master of this period was Kano Eitoku. He had been extensively patronized by Hideyoshi, and though he died too soon for the Tokugawa to use, he left a formidable school behind him. During the wars the Kano (also written Kanō) built a reputation for excellence across the range of work required to meet the warriors' needs. Eitoku homogenized a manner out of pre-existing styles that had immediate impact. It could be rapidly executed and it deployed a recognizable vocabulary via identifiable modes and symbols.

Eitoku's work took two main forms, both of them political. One was so-called 'continental pictures' (*kanga*). This was used to depict matters of universal importance, proper to the rulers of all places and in all times, pan-geographical and transhistorical. This included scenes illustrating the wisdom of ancient sages and the timeless cultivated activities of intelligent people. 'Continental', literally 'Han', meant the classical past, akin to what Europeans mean when they speak of 'the Classics', or 'Greece and Rome'. It had little to do with the actual modern states of the Ming, then the Qing, dynasties, nor the Joseon court on the Korean peninsula. Rather, *kan* (Han) referred to a lost antiquity during which ethical existence had first been adumbrated and lived, now accessible only in books. 'Continental pictures' implied such subject-matter, but also style. The work attempted to replicate that of the historical times under discussion, using a wan palette, close to monochrome, since it was through such painting that 'continental' modes had been handed down. In parallel, Eitoku had a second type, 'Japanese pictures' (*waga*). These were used to depict matters pertinent to the local polity and to governing the Japanese states. Universal norms had to be paralleled with Japanese specifics, defined for the here-and-now, not necessarily relevant in other lands or at other times. 'Japanese pictures' replicated the look of works from ancient Japanese times, which had come down in paintings with bright colours and gold grounds.

This Kano division was not so simplistic in practice, and the two modes overlapped and blurred. But not all warriors were aesthetically confident, and they required clear legibility in their castle spaces.

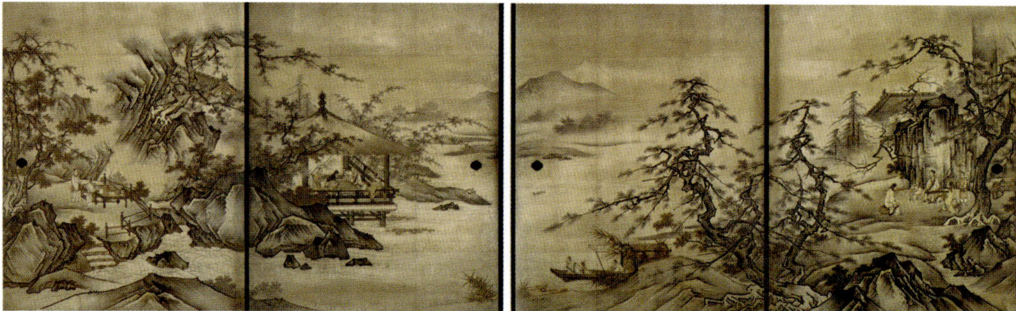

70 Kano Shōei and Eitoku, detail from *The Four Accomplishments*, 1566(?), wall paints, ink on paper. Details of an extant room painted with this hallowed theme in monochrome. The 'accomplishments' together constitute civilization, and are music (the *kin*), games of skill (*ki*), calligraphy and painting.

The Kano school produced copybooks laying out the assortment of modes and themes, passed on within the school. This allowed warrior clients to be assured of what they were ordering. A person entering a Kano-painted space was immediately aware of what pictures denoted, informing them of where they were, who they were and what was likely to unfold. The statements were as lucid and clear as military orders. In battle a mistake can lead to death, and in castles too. A barked command was turned by the Kano into something lovely, and uncontested.

For an example of 'continental pictures', let us consider an early work by Eitoku, probably undertaken with his father, Kano Shōei, in about 1570 (illus. 70). It survives *in situ* in a temple just outside the capital (within modern Kyoto), the Jukō-in ('sub-temple of gathered rays'). The work shows the Four Accomplishments (C: *siyi*; J: *shigei*), or the activities that constitute cultural behaviour – always had and always will, everywhere. Being four, the theme worked well in interiors, painted across a room with one accomplishment per wall. The artists have included additional elements to augment the visual interest and allow for the fact that the sliding screens can be opened, hiding one part of the painting behind another. The 'accomplishments' are music, games of skill, calligraphy and painting. What better way to define culture? Music was specifically the *kin* (C: *qin*), an almost-silent instrument that players used to attune their minds with the cosmos; it is not for concerts, much less for rowdiness. Games of skill specifically referred to *ki* (C: *qi*), a board game akin to chess; victory goes to the deepest thinker, not to the richest or strongest person, nor the one with most soldiers waiting outside. Calligraphy refers to the keeping of records, transcription of emotions and explanation of ideas, in elegant form. Finally, painting, last because it is the most workmanlike, allows the keeping of knowledge that cannot be transmitted in words, like colours or the forms of ritual objects, or faces. Works in the 'continental' manner will be set in times and places that are deliberately indeterminate. No buildings or paraphernalia particularize depiction in a given moment or country.

The 'Japanese' mode was quite different. It spoke of the here and now; it did not depict an abstracted everywhere but dealt with the controlling and regulating of land. Being in the local style, it spoke specifically of *this* land. One example by Eitoku is a folding screen probably executed shortly before his death in 1590 (illus. 71). It must have been one of a pair, but only half the composition survives. Inevitably, movable screens survive in greater numbers than wall paintings, though not always completely. Protruding from the left is a dead branch, suggesting that the lost part showed the world in a frigid, wintry state. Into this dolefulness, from the right, come two mythical Tang lions, symbolic animals said to appear when the world is good and to flee when the world is bad. Tang refers to the ancient Chinese dynasty,

71 Kano Eitoku, *Tang Lions*, late 16th century, single screen, gold and colour on paper. The stunning pair survives only in its right-hand element. Two mythical lions (either male and female, or a lion with its cub) descend on golden clouds, bringing ongoing happiness into a wintry world.

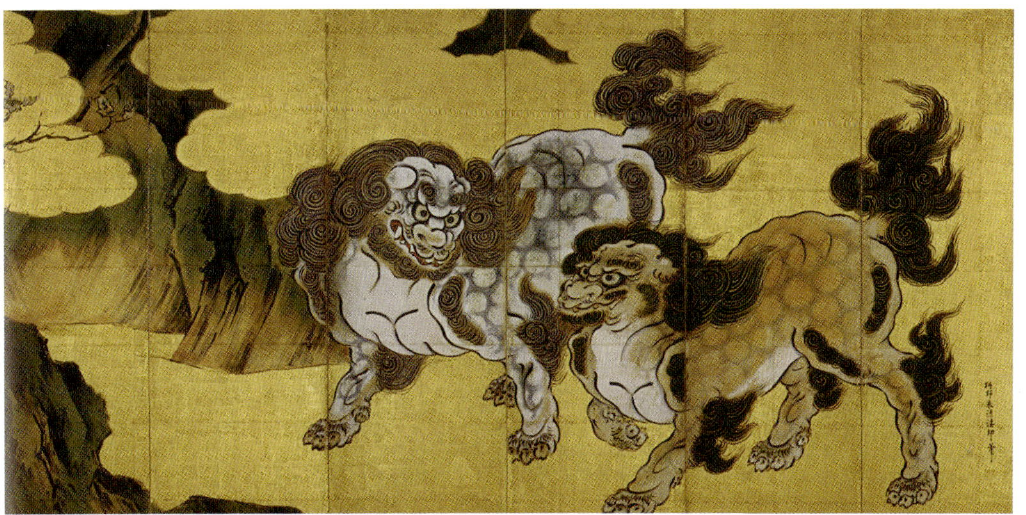

but only insofar as their legendary forms hailed from there. These animals speak of governing Japan. They are painted as arriving into a chill environment. The work is an admission that war is ongoing, but law and peace are coming back. One lion is large with a generous mane, the other small, so they are either male and female, or a lion with its cub. In either case, the pairing promises procreation and succession. A post-war world is coming, the viewer sees, and will continue into the future, here, in Japan. Such a screen might be given by one warrior to another, to indicate approval or to endorse territorial gain. While works of 'continental painting' require prolonged viewing, and are supposed to invite the viewer's immersion, 'Japanese' ones do not. Their impact is instantaneous. When put out in a room, the person of higher status would have the screens to their back, while the person of lesser status would have their eyes on the floor. The paintings were not, in the end, much looked at. Eitoku conveys a terse message that can be deciphered in seconds. This does not preclude it also being a great painting, and today it is regarded as one of the masterpieces of the age.

At the dawn of the Edo period, Kano paintings adorned many castles. It was Eitoku's grandson Kano Tan'yū who was called to Edo in 1617, the year after Ieyasu's death, to become official painter to Hidetada, who appointed the fifteen-year-old prodigy to a newly created post, Painter-in-Attendance (*goyō-eshi*). Tan'yū entered the regime itself, not as an external operator but as part of the shogunal chain of command. He was given an office within the confines of Edo Castle and a government emolument. His family took hereditary military status. Tan'yū and his assistants worked along lines established by Eitoku, but since Edo Castle was lost in the fire of 1657, we cannot know what its interior looked like. We know something of the rebuilt version, post-1657, as discussed at the end of this chapter, though that was lost too. To grasp the visual effect of Edo Castle we are assisted by folding screens, but they are mostly without documentation and it is seldom clear who commissioned them or where they were placed. We need to turn to a surviving building. The second shogunal castle, Nijō in the capital, still has its set of audience suites. These are partial and would not have been used identically, but they can usefully be read to indicate how Edo Castle might have looked, and also how it might have been perceived.

℘

A castle at Nijō had existed for much of the civil war period, but it had been relocated and entirely reconfigured in 1603 when the new shogunate was declared. This early appearance is unknown, but surviving well is the redecoration of 1624–6, overseen by Tan'yū, now in his mid-twenties. Nijō was reworked again in the nineteenth century, though not overriding much of the work left by Tan'yū and his pupils. In 2017–19 the wall paintings were removed and facsimiles installed, attempting to be true to how the originals would have looked when first created some four hundred years before. Today, the castle interior is again radiant with gold, though perhaps without some of the brush details it once had. Tan'yū and his staff's rather battered originals are now in the castle museum. In the absence of Edo Castle, we can use these removed wall paintings, and to gain their full effect, walk through the reproductions in the surviving suites at Nijō.[6]

A visitor leaves the city street by crossing a moat – only one, though Edo had several. They pass through a heavily fortified gate and enter into an area with flagstones and high walls. The sense of enclosure is fearsome. An abrupt 90-degree turn is required to progress further. A confused intruder could be pinned here and shot. Even a legitimate visitor registers extreme levels of preparedness by the castle occupants. The visitor is confronted by a T-junction. The route appears to continue to the right, and a person forcing their way in would naturally turn that way. However, the path peters out in exposed, open ground. Entry is actually to the left. After a short distance, a full 180-degree turn is required. The person wheels about and sees before them a gloriously ornamented gate, in lacquer, paint and gold. It is without apparent military function. It is there to convey 'awe'. The gate is unprotected, yet it could not be stormed because the approach is at an angle. The gate is thus impressive and does not seem fierce, but is

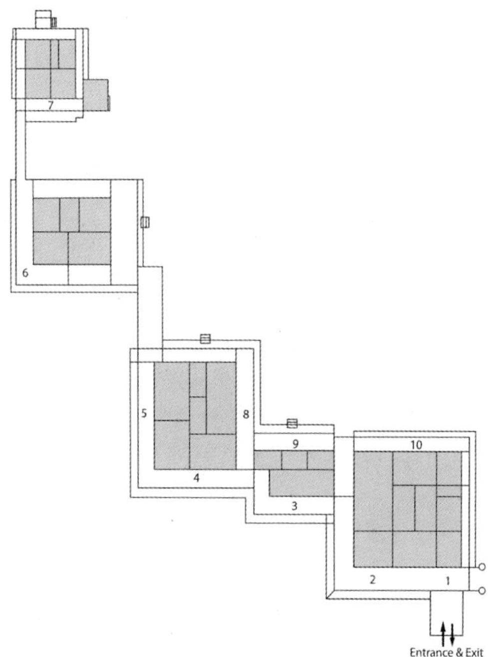

72 Plan of Ninomaru Palace of Nijō Castle.

1 Yanagi-no-ma (Room of Willows), Wakamatsu-no-ma (Young Pine Room;
2 Tozamurai-no-ma (Outer Waiting Area);
3 Shikidai-no-ma (Ceremonial Platform);
4 Ōhiroma: San-no-ma (Third Great Room);
5 Ōhiroma: Ichi-no-ma (First Great Room), Ni-no-ma (Second Great Room), Musha-kakushi-no-ma (guardroom);
6 Kuroshoin (Black Study);
7 Shiroshoin (White Study);
8 Ōhiroma: Yon-no-ma (Fourth Great Room);
9 Rōju-no-ma (Ministers' Offices);
10 Chokushi-no-ma (Court Messengers' Room).

The suite moves leftwards and upwards, or northwest, called the 'geese-flight pattern', probably for geomantic reasons and to secure good light. How far a visitor penetrated depended on their status, and room decoration was carefully calibrated to the level of the user.

actually impossible to assault. Visitors are made to realize they have progressed beyond terror and are now welcome guests. The scintillating gate has only one immediately apparent ornament, and that is a cusped gable. Known as a 'Tang gable' in Japanese (*kara-hafu*), it refers to antique continental practices and the classical rule of the past, as the lions did, but in the bright colours associated with indigenous work. Cusped gables were used often on Edo period buildings to confer honour at the highest level. No normal visitor would pass under such an ornament. Transfixed, they would not know what to do. If beckoned in, they would feel a humbling honour. The gate is also multiply ornamented with the Tokugawa triple-hollyhock crest – or rather it was: these were despoiled and replaced with Japanese Imperial crests in the late nineteenth century.

The gate is oriented southwards, meaning a visitor approaches heading north. This is the correct vector to deferentially meet superiors. Having summoned the courage to pass through, a person comes to a wide honour court giving a view of the impressive line of chambers, the audience suite, all that remains today. The chambers extend leftwards in a retreating line without visible end. A gilded entrance is ahead, and visitors remove their shoes and step up. The degree to which they will be allowed to penetrate through the suite depends on their status. Rooms are grouped in five blocks, connected by integral corridors. Their retreating line to the left means they run northwestwards, that is, in a geomantically neutral direction. The deeper one enters, the higher a person's standing, but the inner rooms do not give magical protection to the outer ones, as would be the case had the sequence run northeastwards, towards the 'gate of *ki*' (or 'demons', *kimon*) (illus. 72). The reason for this is probably that the most important rooms are two-thirds of the way in, and the full sequence terminates in a women's space, which could not be allowed to protect the male spaces that precede it. However, each block has several rooms, mostly four main ones, interlocking in jigsaw-like fashion, and the northeastern one is calibrated to protect the others geomantically, through decoration or function. Given that the line of rooms moves left and backwards, the entrance to each block from the previous one will be in the southeast, and the exit in the northwest. The rooms along the southern aspects will be brightest, as they face the sun. The western ones, being the furthest in and closest to the following block, will be most honorific. However, many additional spaces exist, complicating the interpretation, with irregularities and surprises. A visitor is never certain, which is deliberate as an intruder will be scotched.

A wooden corridor wraps around the whole structure, as is common in Edo architecture. Not every visitor was allowed into the rooms at all, and some would be received sitting in the corridor, their host addressing them from inside. Some were not allowed into the corridor, either, and would kneel on the gravel outside. The rooms are matted, but the corridors have floorboards. Throughout, these are set with nails underneath, so that the pressure of a footfall makes them squeak. Every step is audible; covert access impossible. But in typical Edo style, this military function was both present and denied. These

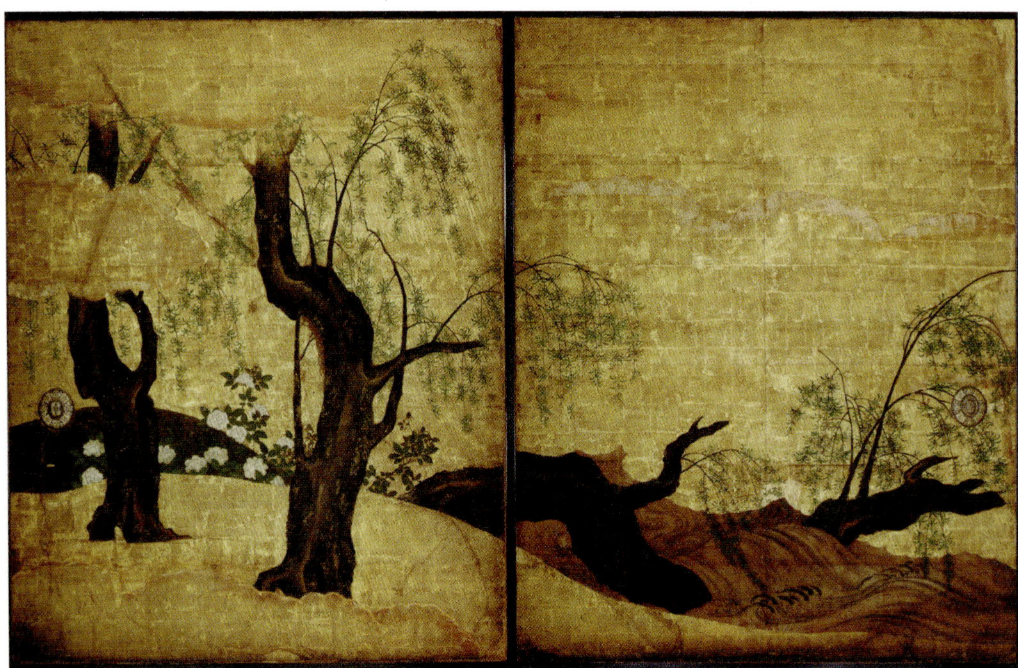

floors, placed so as to record a visitor's presence, are called 'nightingale fixings' (*uguisu-bari*), as if their purpose was no more than to delight with birdsong.

Each of the suite's five blocks has a name to indicate its hierarchical level. Within the blocks, each room is named, as was normal in the period, by the theme of its wall-paintings, which will convey the spatial meaning, or else by a number, indicating seniority within the block, with Room One (*ichi-no-ma*) being the most elevated.

The first block is the Outer Waiting Area (*tōzamurai*). Its layout is the most confusing. A person enters by the Room of Willows, painted with that tree and also with roses. Before the subject-matter is considered, we see that the works are in the 'indigenous' colour-and-gold manner, as is the case in most of the castle, it speaking on rulership here and now. The trees and plants are rendered so as to position the viewer at ground level. Though the building is raised and visitors have stepped up, they feel as if they have not ascended at all. The boles and lower

73 Kano School, *Willow Room, Outer Waiting Area*, c. 1626. Willows have symbolic meaning as the abode of spirits. One has collapsed but still lives, nourished by a stream coming from within the building.

branches of the trees are visible, but their upper parts are lost above. A river flows in from the senior spaces in the northwest, coming towards the visitor as if to succour them. Visitors know they are supplicants hoping to move towards the source of the stream – perhaps up this 'river of virtue'. Willows are dense with meaning, too. Their long, loose branches, in continual motion, make them fine but quivering trees. One is shown collapsed into the stream, unable to meet the strain, yet it still struggles on, in leaf (illus. 73). Because of their swaying form, willows were associated with ghosts, which were said to inhabit them. The tree thus links humanity with another, incommensurable world, like the one that visitors will encounter as they progress onward. Roses, by contrast, lack symbolic sense and are here to contrast with the willows, being tight and rounded, with a whiteness that complements the trees' brown and green. Kano painting had codified pictorial pairings of this sort, and it was uncommon to use single themes. Normally a main topic was assisted by a fixed supporting double.

After the Room of Willows comes the Third Room, relatively low in status within this block but interconnecting immediately with the Second. In effect, this creates one large room, painted with tigers. The beasts appear with their established supporting double, bamboo (illus. 74). Visitors are still at ground level but find themselves surrounded by the greatest forms of this-worldly existence, for the tiger was the king of beasts (as the lion was in European symbolism). Bamboo is lofty too, being evergreen, so constant and unchanging; yet also flexible. It sways in the wind responsively but always returns to its upright posture. Bamboo is also hollow, so without ego. The virtuous military ruler is fierce as a tiger, though as flexible as bamboo, and considerate, though true as bamboo. Since tigers were not seen in Japan, their form was little known. The leopard was misunderstood as being the female, so whether a painted configuration shows tigers only, or tigers with leopards, will make a difference to a room's meaning. These rooms have both, and they therefore speak of coupling, continuity and succession, as did Eitoku's lion screens. The rooms include young bamboo to further suggest that the felicitous conditions of shogunal rule will continue into the future.

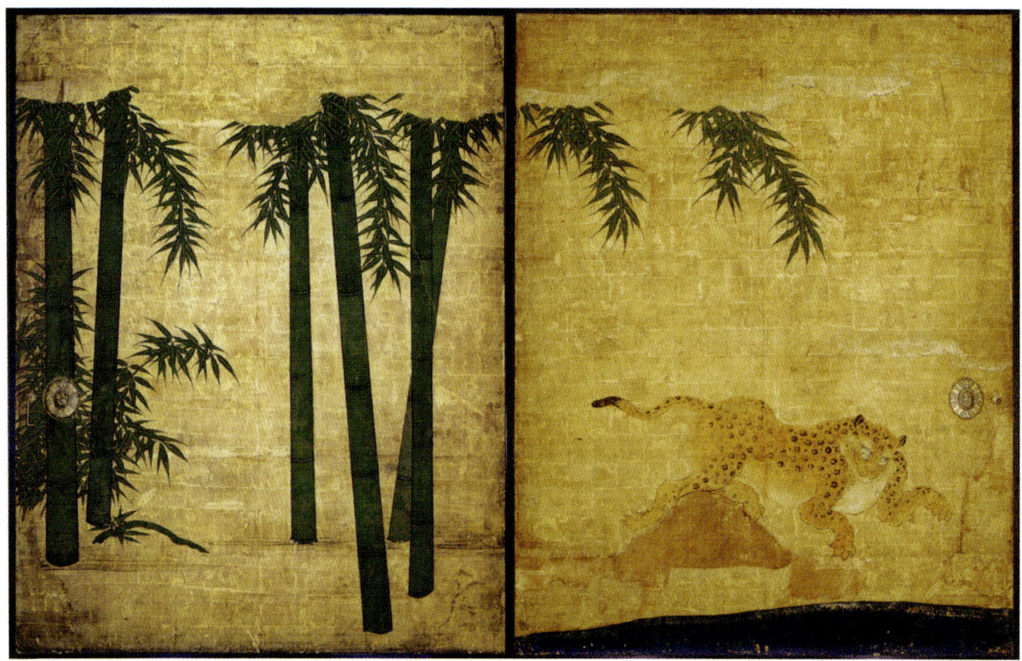

In reality, big cats spend much time sleeping, yet these painted ones are ever-active, undertaking all required endeavours, denying themselves repose. On the walls of these Third and Second rooms, the male and female tigers (*sic*) nourish themselves from the river that appeared in the room before.

Next is the First Room. The stream is now gone because the host would be seated here, not yet the shogun, but some representative, who would entertain the visitor. The visitor had reached the source, but only of the Outer Waiting Area.

Note that there are no depictions of dragons: in fact, there are none at Nijō Castle at all. The Tokugawa made little use of dragon imagery. Dragons are lords of all creation, but external to this world and almost never appearing in it. The painted world of shogunal and daimyo castles was about governing in the here and now, following the world of antique sages. It was not about some abstract empyrean. At most they will show tigers and Tang lions. On the continent, the

74 Kano Jinnojō, *Tigers and Leopards*, from Second Room of Outer Waiting Area, c. 1626. It was believed that the leopard was the female of the tiger, thus this room alludes to family and to the continuity of the great military households. The energetic drink from a stream flowing from the interior of the building.

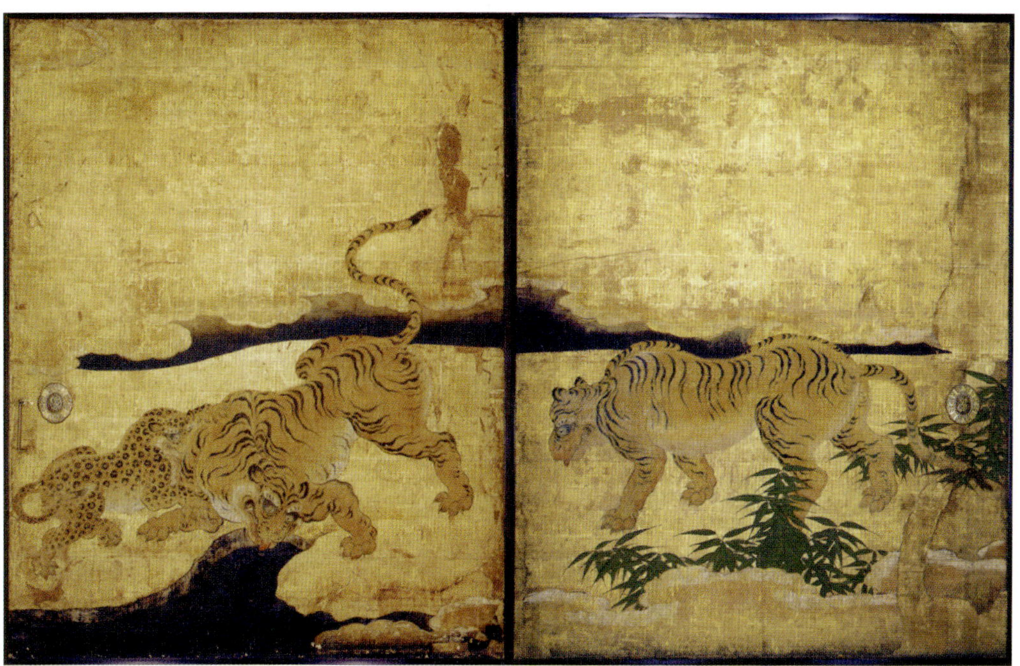

huangdi (Chinese emperor) monopolized the symbolism of the dragon, though in Japan it was more associated with Buddhism.

Overall, the first set of rooms articulates the role and function of great military families – the daimyo ruling Japan's regions. Having entered, trembling, the visiting daimyo is reassured that, yes, he is in control on the ground, and is supported in this role, which will continue. But there is further to go.

This Outer Waiting Area also has rooms in the northeast. Only two are of any size, and these are significant spaces. They are for reception of representatives of the dairi's (emperor's) court, called *chokushi*. The paintings reflect this very different constituency of users. The position of these rooms means that they protect the others geomantically, and this acknowledges the dairi's historic priority. The world depicted is solemn and still. Vast cypresses – deciduous trees, but the longest living – are the theme. The floor of one of the rooms is slightly raised, because that is where the *chokushi* would sit, elevated above the receiving shogunal officer. Despite this deference, another point is made. The layout requires the *chokushi* to sit facing west, the shogunal officer looks east. He does not look north, which is the proper vector of humility. Parity is thus asserted, as neither man looks 'up' or 'down' on the other. Since the shogunal officer looks east, however, he looks towards Edo, which is where his instructions come from, and not from the court. The river enters these rooms, picked out gloriously in silver (since oxidized to black). The Tokugawa also moisten this landscape, with one particularly lavish cedar so well watered that it is able to extend a canopy over the *chokushi*'s head.

Next is the second block, called the Ceremonial Platform (*shikidai*). Until this point, the paintings were by Eitoku's nephew, Kano Jinnojō, who was Tan'yū's cousin in the former generation. Jinnojō was probably enlisted in deference to his seniority within the Kano line; all Eitoku's sons were dead, making him the family patriarch. Jinnojō has first place out of respect, but as he was not a specifically shogunal painter, he did not paint the rooms of high authority. Further in, Tan'yū and his atelier took over.

A single space occupies the whole of the south side of the Ceremonial Platform. It is part-room, part-vestibule. There are three small spaces along the north side, while the southern part is one extended space. This is filled with enormous pines. The viewer is still at ground level, able to look up into the treetops, unattainable but in their field of sight. Pines, too, are symbolic. They are evergreen so share bamboo's meaning of consistency; but, unlike bamboo, pines grow to great size and age. A mature pine may be centuries old, so will have existed when the great events of the distant past took place; future events will be enacted under the same branches that are seen today. Like cedars, pines link people with history, but they are seasonal, altering with the yearly cycle. East Asian symbolism makes much use of puns, and the words for pine allows for several. One term is *matsu*, homophonous with 'wait'. The pine tree bides its time, as must a ruler, without haste. The visitor, too, must await their appointed audience here. Another word for pine is *shō*, the many homophones of which include 'correct'

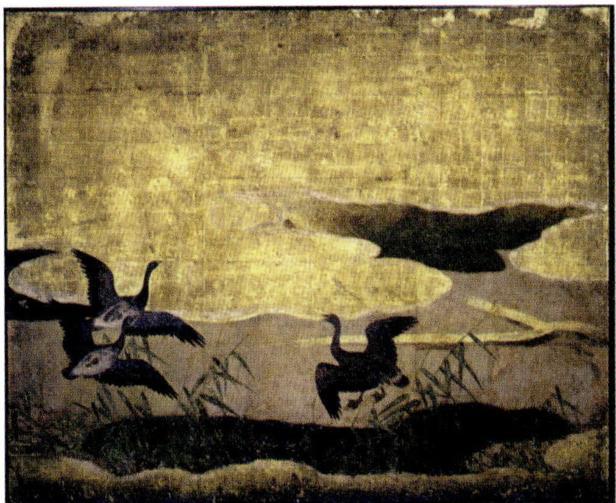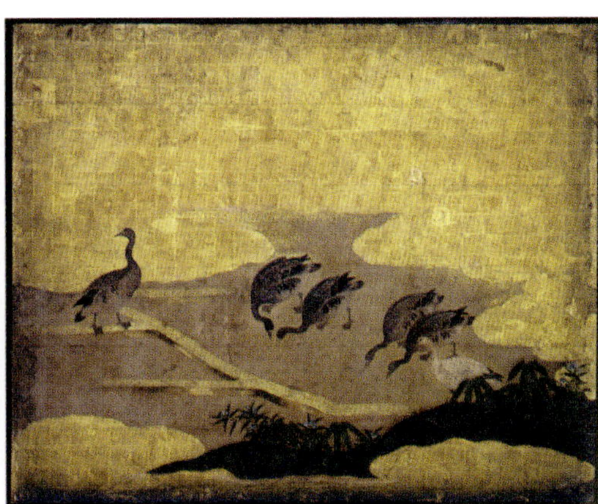

75 Kano School, *Geese After Harvest*, from First Room of Ceremonial Platform Suite, c. 1626. Geese representing ministers of state debate together as they clear up the final remnants of a good harvest.

and 'government'. Pines cover just about all the desiderata of proper rule and loyal service.

The three northern rooms of the Ceremonial Platform were reserved for use of ministers who comprised the Council of Elders (*rōjū*). They are less spaces of audience than of discussion. The room first entered is the Third. It is painted with winter scenery, and so it shows a time of difficulty. Birds are to be seen, cold but resolute, able to meet the climatic challenge. They appear to be engaged in a lively debate. One flies off in the direction of the next room, looking backwards for confirmation, as if entrusted to carry their collective decision. The viewer is still on the ground, but the bird rises above, transitioning from land to sky. The Second and First Rooms particularize this interpretation. They are full of geese, which are traditionally associated with autumn. The season has wound back, though if approached from the other end – as would be appropriate for a senior person, who would emerge from the deeper interior – it is temporally correct. Rice fields have been harvested to feed the people, and the geese peck at the final grains, ensuring no wastage (illus. 75). The next, First Room should perhaps be understood as spring or summer, though the seasonal content is not apparent. The birds continue their disputations, now across a wider landscape of hills and water.

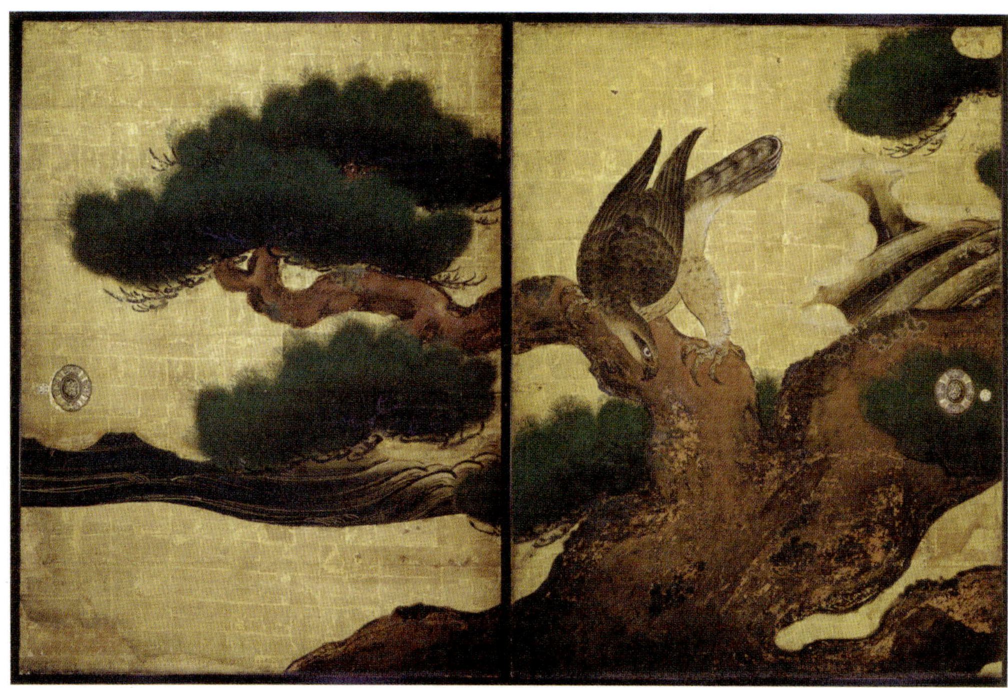

What comes next is the most honorific space, so between the Ceremonial Platform and the next block are fire-retardant doors made of cedarwood. Such doors are common features of important Edo period buildings, but what is uncommon here is their decorative theme. They show cycads. These subtropical plants are rare in central Japan but are common on Kyushu, the southernmost of Japan's main islands, and in the Kingdom of the Ryukyus (an island chain extending all the way to modern Taiwan, now annexed by Japan and called Okinawa). Southern Kyushu was a perennial problem for the shoguns, independent-minded and almost an independent state. The Ryukyuan Kingdom, meanwhile, was an independent state. At Nijō, these borderline, fractious entities are not suggested as threats; on the contrary, they offer safety to the shogunate.

The next, third block is the Great Room (*ōhiroma*), constituting the main shogunal audience area and so the heart of the whole suite. The northeastern room is numbered as the Fourth, which sounds

76 Kano Tan'yū (?), *Hawks on Pine Trees*, from Fourth Room of Great Rooms Suite, 1626. These high-flying birds survey the realm. Pine trees are symbols of continuity and good government.

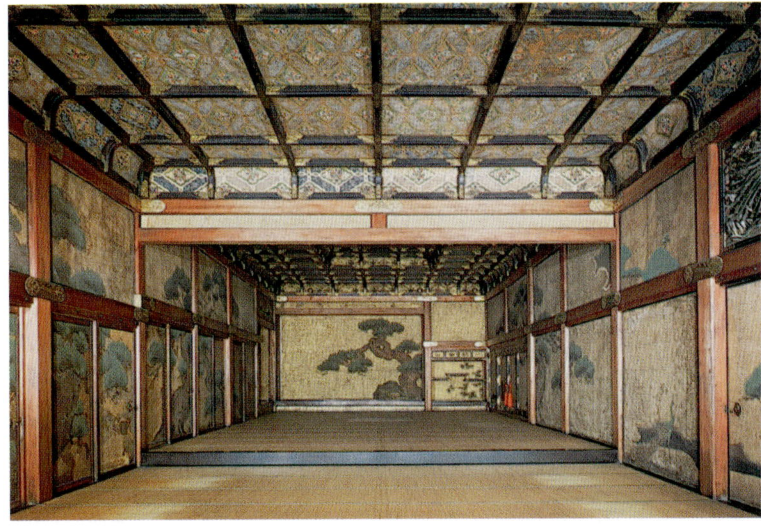

77 Kano Tan'yū, Second and First Rooms of Great Rooms Suite, c. 1626. The most elite of all rooms in the castle is to the rear, slightly raised. The ceiling is higher above the shogun's seat. Paintings are simple and with immediate impact, since visitors' heads would be firmly on the ground.

inferior to the other three spaces because it is not where the audiences occur; rather its location means it offers protection. It is decorated with birds, again, though this time hawks, which are seen amid pine trees. Some in the trees look down, while others on the ground look up, as the river flows past (illus. 76). Pines we already understand, while hawks were painted in military mansions as the self-image of the warrior. They fly above all else and survey all with vigilance. They are trained to hunt, and to kill on command, not wantonly. From the decision-making geese in the former block, we move to a space of preparedness for decisive action, once discussion is passed. The Third, Second and First Rooms form an interconnected L-shape, the point of entry being the Third. These are also ornamented with pines, but these are seen from well above ground level. Few indeed would be admitted this far, and those who were understood their elevated position. The proudest of birds, a peacock, walks with stately gait up an angled trunk, progressing on into the Second Room. Some visitors would move on too, but many would remain in the Third Room. The shogun sat around the corner, so they could not see him. A person might have an audience unaware if the shogun was really there or not. Once in the Second Room, however, the shogun could be seen, ensconced in

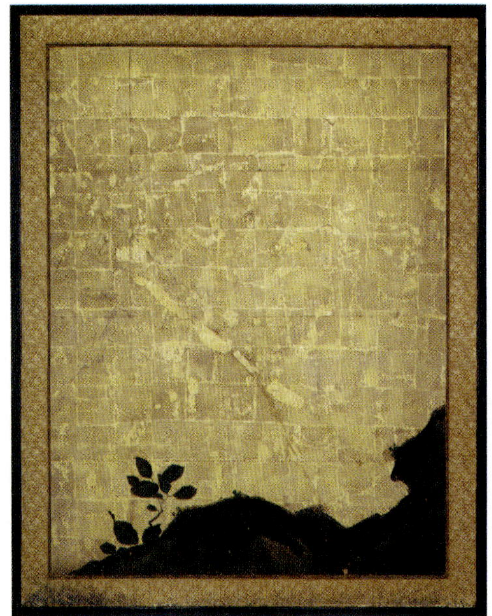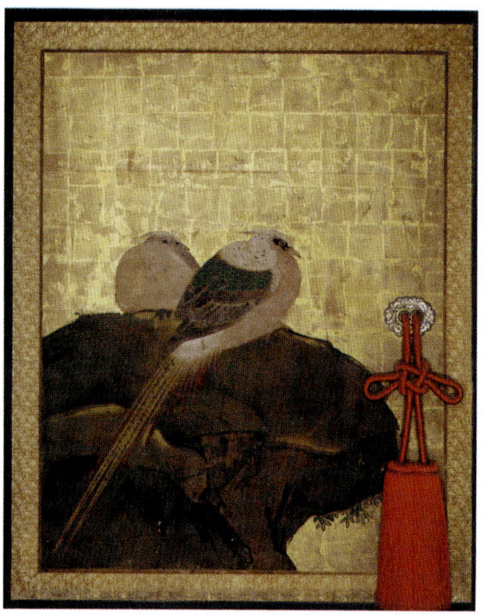

the First Room, which, as with the *chokushi* room, has a raised floor to demarcate status difference (illus. 77). The same peacock, now with offspring, walks in; another has flown across to the opposite wall. However, the Second and First rooms are not much ornamented. A person here would have their eyes firmly on the floor. They would not gaze at the pictures. The shogun was there, but was not really seen at all. There are three massive pines, one per wall, and that is about all. No matter how elite, a person here had only moments to take in the paintings. Intricacy would be redundant. There is a built-in alcove for display of treasures, already seen in some of the former rooms. A tree emerges from this, canopying the head of a person, as in the *chokushi* room, but now the person is the shogun himself. Since this room faces south, the tree is in the geomantically critical northeast, offering protection. A boulder is also present, protecting the shogun's back in the same direction. This room has a raised ceiling in the part above the shogun's seat. He cannot be contained within the limits prescribed for other people, in the architectural equivalent of what Hokusai did

78 Kano Tan'yū, *Sleeping Birds and Red Berries*, doors in First Room of Great Rooms Suite, c. 1626. Birds are timorous and watchful, so sleeping birds indicate profound peace. The berries seem to be nandina, from the Japanese *nanten*, which puns on 'deflecting danger'. To paint these subjects on the door of a guardroom suggests it is unused because the world is so content.

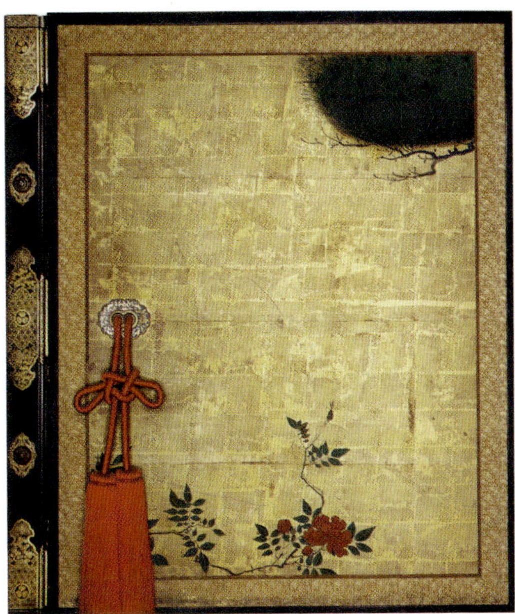 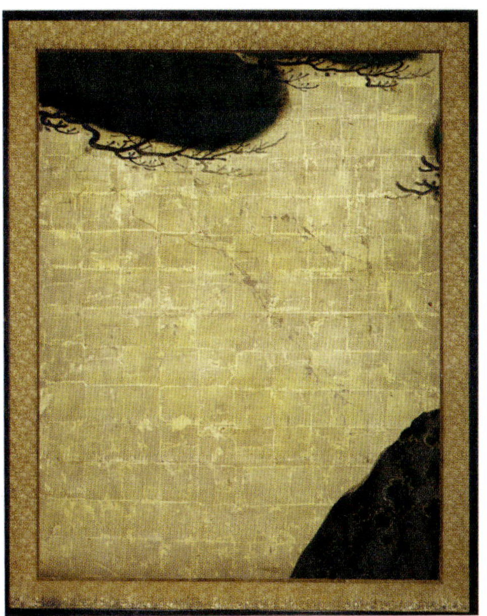

almost two hundred years later when he showed Edo Castle breaking out of the perspectival grid and beyond the picture frame (see illus. 29 and 31). In this northeast corner, young bamboos grow, indicating that this perfect dispensation has a future.

Two large tassels can be discerned on panels in the same northeastern part of the First Room. They indicate the presence of doors, and these give access to a guardroom. Even with their head on the floor, a visitor would make out the door-pulls and know that the shogunate is prepared, with real, as well as symbolic, protection. Yet from where they kneel, the angle is too obtuse for visitors to make out what is painted on the doors (illus. 78). One shows birds at rest. As noted already, resting birds stand for absolute peace, and these also appear to be sleeping (see illus. 69). Resting birds on a guardroom door suggest it is never opened. The soldiers are there, but not needed: the shogun is beloved. Also painted is a second theme, small berry-like flowers. If the door were ever opened these would be crushed, and yet they have grown quite large. Their botanical type is hard to discern, but they seem

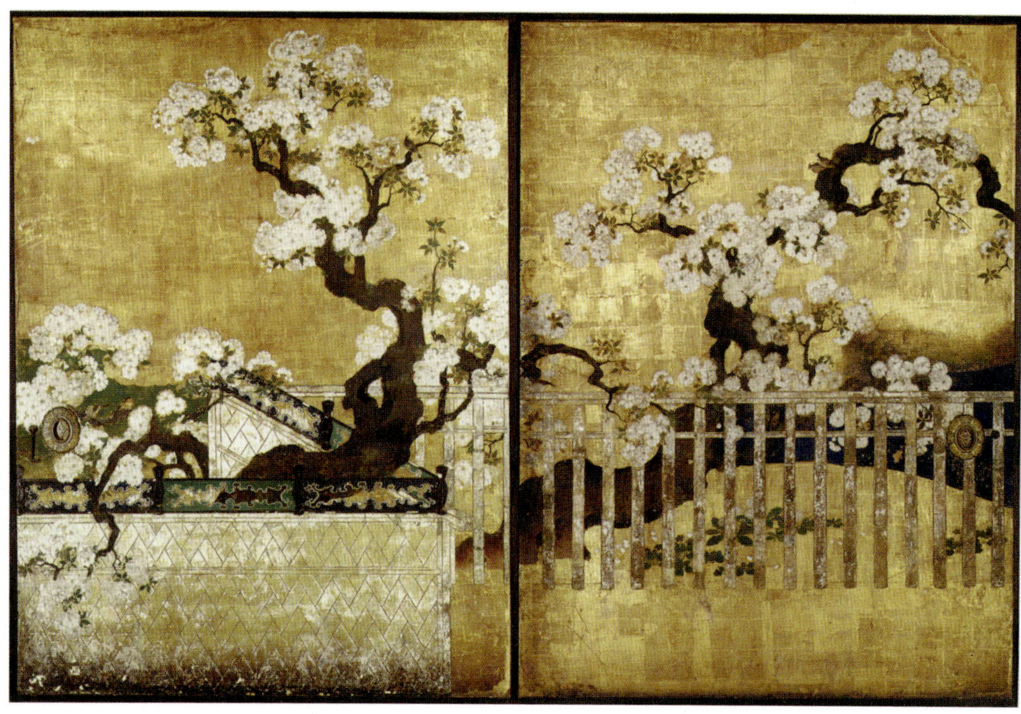

to be nandinas. The English name comes from the Japanese *nanten*, which is a pun: *nan* is 'danger' and *ten* 'deflect'.

This First Room of the Great Rooms was one of the most august places in the realm. But it is a small room. Unlike the throne rooms of Europe, the small space shows how special the honour is to enter here. It is small because those admitted here are so few.

From the Great Rooms, a corridor runs northwards to the next block, called the Black Study (*kuro-shōin*). The name is in parallel with the final block, the White Study (*shiro-shōin*). Beyond the audience rooms, these are both places for the most trusted advisers and family members. The Black Study is brightly painted – 'black' does not imply darkness but, as with black lacquer, luxuriance. It features richly attractive but relaxed scenery with gorgeous cherry blossoms. There are domestic features, too, like garden fences and birds accustomed to humanity (illus. 79). This is the first time a visitor sees nature tended

79 Kano Naonobu, *Cherry Blossom Garden*, from Second Room on Black Study Suite, *c.* 1626. A garden of delights shows the loveliest of all blossoms – the cherry – carefully tended and honoured.

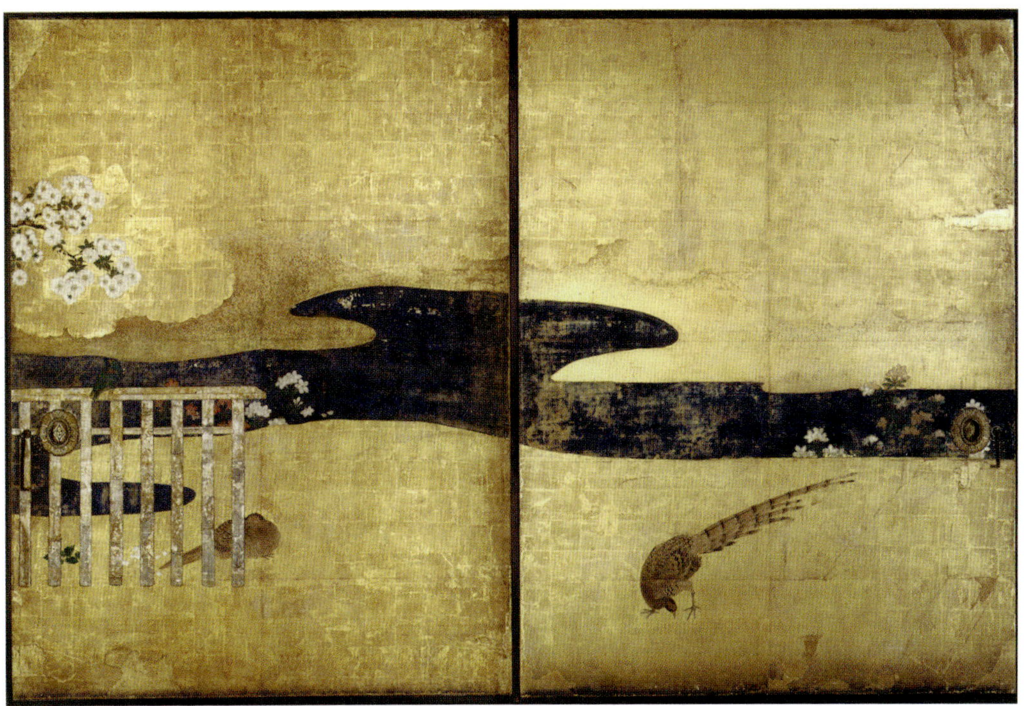

for beauty. Until this point, power has been presented as one aspect of the natural dispensation. Now it is conceded as an artificial imposition, though a lovely one. First is a Room of Peonies, with red and white flowers in bloom. In Japanese thought, red and white are opposites, as are black and white in the West, so here alternatives thrive together, with faction transcended. Some peonies are painted on the outer wall giving on to the corridor. They are in the wild. Those on the interior walls, giving into the room, are trained and improved by human hand. The visitor has now arrived at the ultimate source of the river, in a big pool. The angle of vision is from above, looking down. There is no need to browbeat those who have penetrated so far and risen so high. These spaces need no further protection, real or symbolic, but rather they openly display the fruits of careful management by trusted experts.

The White Study is reached by a narrow, unpainted corridor also running due north. Suddenly the paintings become near-monochrome.

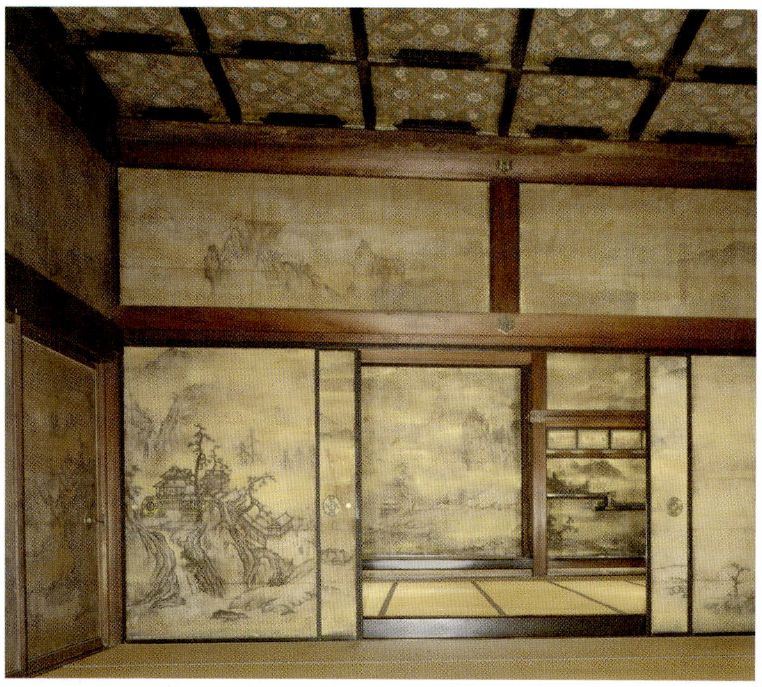

80 Kano Naganobu (?), View from Second into First Room of White Study Suite, c. 1626. In the private interior suite the paintings are monochrome and placid, in the international mode. This sets the Tokugawa on a par with the best-governed continental polities. An entire well-run world is shown across the rooms.

This puts them in the 'continental' rhetorical mode. Until this point, all was polychrome and so 'Japanese'. Here the visitor walks through a liminal corridor into a new world. Rivers and hills are seen, with grand and rustic dwellings in town and country; travellers move; workers labour; elites sit in contemplation. One striking vignette shows a peasant carrying his burden while reading a book (illus. 81). Even the manually employed can hope for betterment. Nearby, a holy monk has befriended a tiger and they sleep together, acolytes joining in, their rakes beside them, tasks forgotten (illus. 82). The previous rooms articulated Japanese government in the here and now, but the ultimate space, the White Study, presents international norms, affirming how the rewards of virtuous rule are the same across all cultures and all times. The shogun's ladies would also be here. Once ethical regulation of the lands is achieved, rulers are entitled to relax.

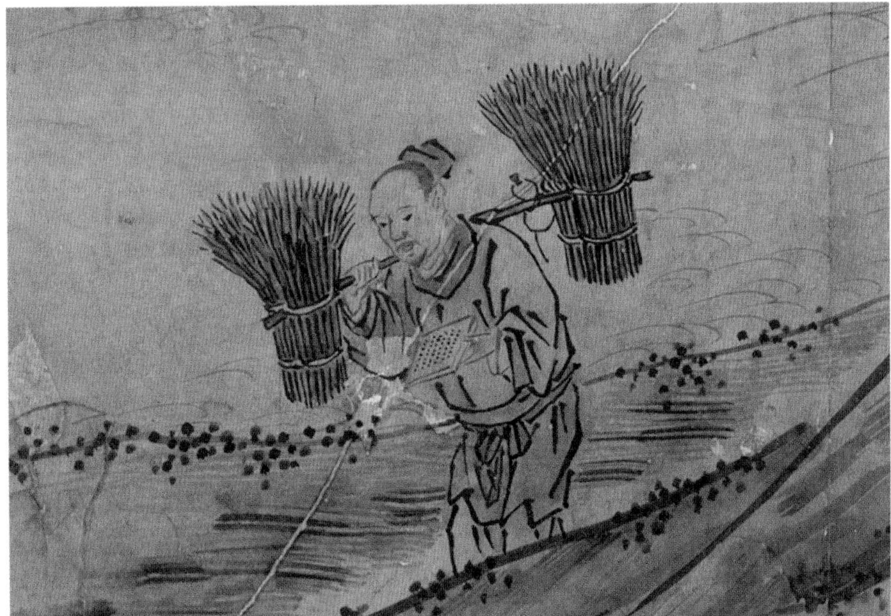

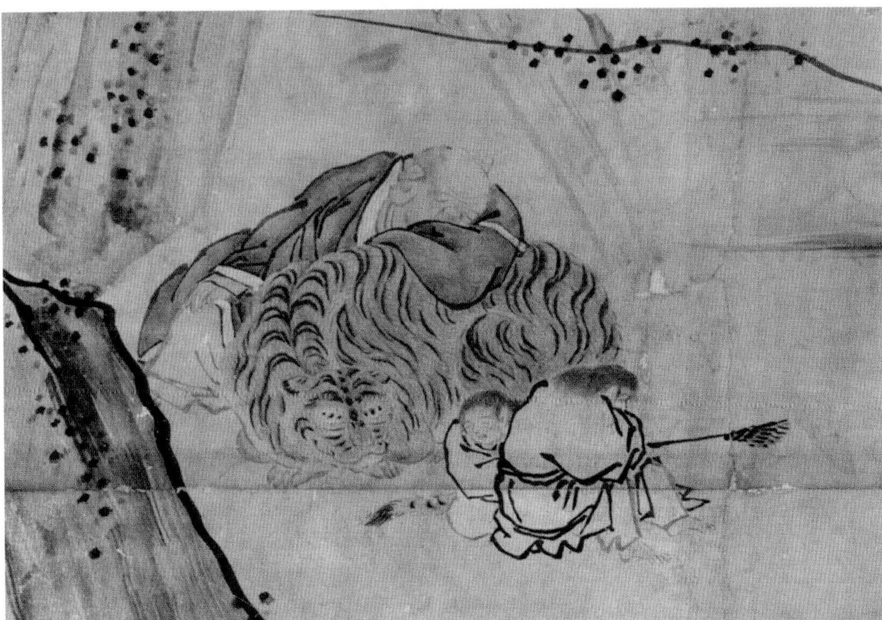

81 Kano Naganobu (?), detail of Third Room of White Study Suite, c. 1626. A peasant carries a load while reading a book.

82 Detail of Kano Naganobu (?), detail of Third Room of White Study Suite, c. 1626. A monk is so virtuous he can render tigers docile, and he sleeps with one he has befriended, while acolytes put down their cleaning tools and nod off too.

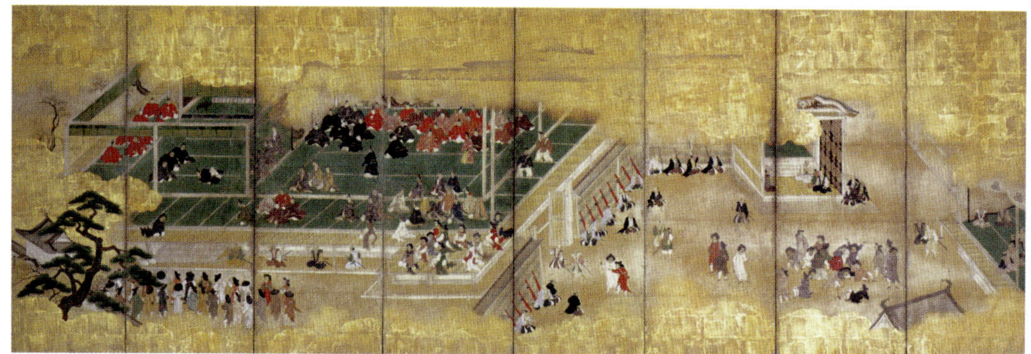

83 Kano Masanobu, *Korean Ambassadors at Edo Castle*, 1655(?), one half of a pair of screens, gold and colour on paper. This half shows arrival and entertainment of emissaries from the Joseon king in the main hall of the castle. Retinues were periodic but this is probably the one of 1655.

The above was an interpretation of the surviving suite of reception rooms at Nijō Castle. Edo Castle was similar, but not identical. The First Room of its main audience block of Grand Rooms was much larger, sometimes referred to as the 'hall of one hundred mats' (a *tatami* mat is about 0.5 by 1.5 metres, or the size of a person lying down). Edo Castle was peopled with more visitors and supplicants than Nijō ever was. Edo Castle is gone, and there are virtually no depictions or descriptions of its interiors, and certainly not of the First Room of the realm. However, a couple of representations exist, one showing something of the interior, as it appeared before the fire of 1657, one showing it after. Both illustrate ceremonial moments, with the reception of foreign emissaries. Precision is avoided. First is a pair of screens of ambassadors from the Joseon (Korean) court. Such embassies were periodic, though this is thought to show the one of 1655 (illus. 83). Tan'yū was living, but this work was commissioned from his son-in-law, Kano Masunobu, categorized as an Outer Painter (*omote-eshi*), that is, on a lower official rung than Tan'yū, who was an Inner Painter (*oku-eshi*).

The image of the First Room of Edo Castle, as rebuilt after 1657, was sketched by a German doctor, Engelbert Kaempfer. He was received here twice as part of Dutch delegations, in 1690 and 1691. His sketch was brushed up for publication in his posthumous *History of Japan* of 1727 (illus. 84). It is apparent from this how large the room was. It has vast pine trees on the walls, just as at Nijō – and these were also painted

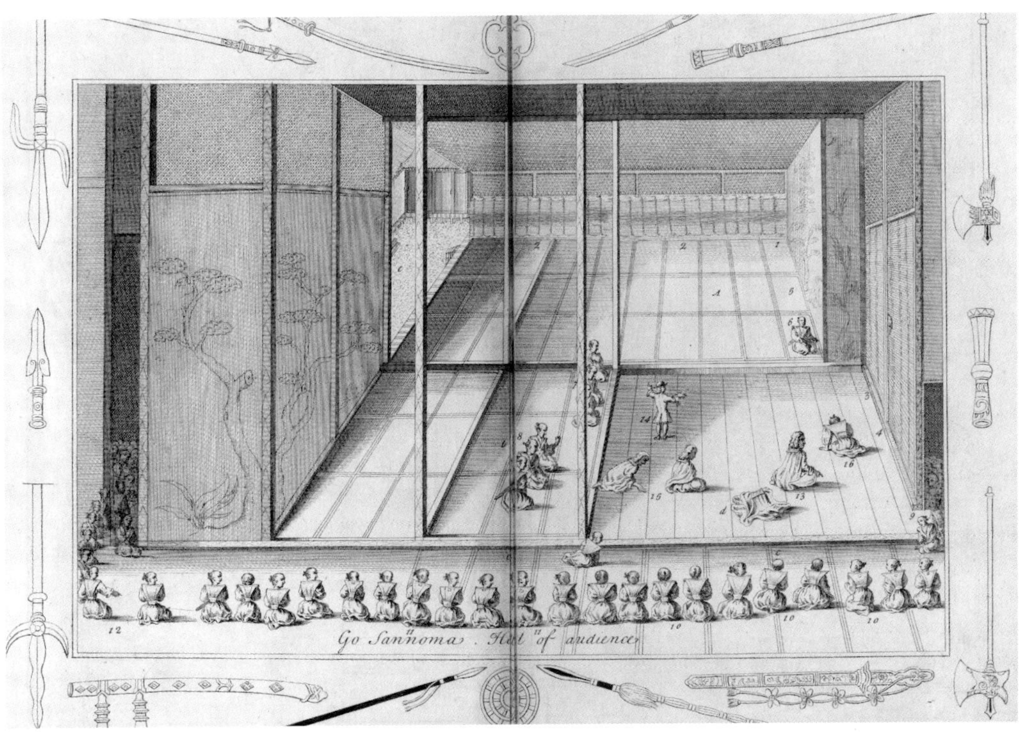

84 First Room of Edo Castle, 'Hall of Audience', from Engelbert Kaempfer, *History of Japan* (1727). Kaempfer went to Edo twice as physician for the Dutch East India Company, and wrote how the shogun (screened off here at the back) asked to witness Dutch polite behaviour and merry-making. Kaempfer's German was translated into English and published posthumously, becoming the main source of information on Japan for over a century.

by Tan'yū and his team – while one end has been screened off, probably a temporary installation to allow the shogun's ladies to peep at the foreigners. The Dutch did not like to take off their shoes, so the mats have been removed in the place where they are. Kaempfer recorded what was going on: the shogun, now Ietsuna's brother, Tsunayoshi, 'had us take off our *kappa*, or ceremonial robes, and sit upright so that he could inspect us'. He also 'had us now stand up and walk, now pay compliments to each other, then again to dance, jump, pretend to be drunk, speak Japanese, read Dutch, draw, sing, put on our coats then take them off again'. Kaempfer was not happy and referred to this as 'innumerable . . . monkey tricks'.[7] But the exercise was not trivial to the shoguns, who would never have mocked their guests. This was an anthropological exercise, to assess the cultural level of the foreigners, of whom they knew little. An evaluation could very sensibly be made by observing Dutch rituals and pastimes.

Although we lack depictions, Edo Castle had two additional spaces not present (or not surviving) at Nijō. Since the shoguns actually ruled from Edo, there was one main hall of government, separate from the Grand Rooms and indicatively positioned to their northeast. This was the Hall of Tigers – tigers only, no leopards, for this room was gendered. It was the prime place of legislation and council, which was perceived as male. The tigers would have been paired with bamboo and depicted in dynamic poses of executive action. Second, given the castle's expansiveness, there was a long, articulated walkway running inwards from the Grand Rooms. This was the Pine Corridor. Along dozens of metres of twists and turns, the all-symbolic trees guided expectant visitors onwards to the deepest sites of 'correct government'.

The paintings executed after the 1657 fire lasted unscathed for almost the entire Edo period.

☙

Tan'yū, the great master of Tokugawa decoration, died in 1674. His last years were blighted by paralysis in one hand, which Japanese doctors had been unable to assist him with. Tan'yū had sought treatment from the physician to the voc, Moijses Marcon, when the retinue made its annual trip to Edo. Sadly, Marcon had to report, 'the man's advanced age presages little chance of a full recovery,' though he felt he could do something.[8] After Tan'yū's death, his brother Kano Yasunobu formulated the theories of the school, compiling them into an in-house text, *Essentials of the Way of Painting* (*Gadō yōketsu*), in 1680. Yasunobu proclaimed the Kano were 'one brush unchanged for ten thousand generations'.[9] Why change painting style, he seemly to imply, unless you wanted to change the government – which of course you did not, the government being virtuous. Castle interiors were painted so as to convince those living in them that there could be no possible reason for desiring change. Accordingly, pictorial style had to be frozen. Actually, Kano painting did alter over time. The forceful, reduced work of Eitoku was adapted by Tan'yū into a milder mode. From images of the *arrival* of felicity, such as descending lions, Tan'yū moved to themes of happy *continuity*. His many depictions of the seasonal round of birds and flowers, and his signature theme of Mount Fuji, viewable from Edo, showed that authority was here for good, and taken for granted. Stylistic morphology continued after Tan'yū' too.

Half of Tan'yū's paintings at Edo Castle were lost in 1838 when a fire destroyed the Western Enceinte, or shogunal living quarters. Once structures had been rebuilt, Tan'yū's successor as Inner Painter, Kano Osanobu, was commanded to redecorate them, and the instructions given to him are telling. Osanobu was told that the pictures must be identical to the ones that were lost (*on-arikata no tōri*).[10] Even after 180 years, change to Kano formulas was not welcome; indeed it was to be scrupulously avoided. Once the decorative scheme was complete, the shogun, Ieyoshi, moved back in, apparently satisfied. Then in 1844 he was forced out again, this time when the Main Enceinte went up in smoke, with the Great Rooms, the 'one-hundred-mat' First Room, the Hall of Tigers and the Pine Corridor all lost. As before, replacements were made, to be just the same as those that had been destroyed. Had Osanobu painted them differently, it would have indicated the world had changed – which it had, but that must not be shown. It was the job of government to retard change, and the job of the Kano school to suggest they succeeded. The Edo Castle interiors could not be altered for an additional, less theoretical reason. The status of a person, whether a daimyo or a high official, was indicated by the degree to which they were entitled to penetrate into the castle and the room in which they were received. Some, for example, might be admitted as far as the Room of Peonies, others to the Room of Peacocks. If the rebuilt structure lost its rooms, with their accompanying protocols of access, the codes of state would fall apart, the whole apparatus of rule would have to be renegotiated, opening the way to civil war.

Osanobu's work was also lost to fire not long after it was completed. However, we have a large cache of preparatory paintings. These are the only concrete evidence of how the interior of Edo Castle looked. But they are so complete that the whole set of buildings can be quite well visualized. We can see, for example, the vast audience room in

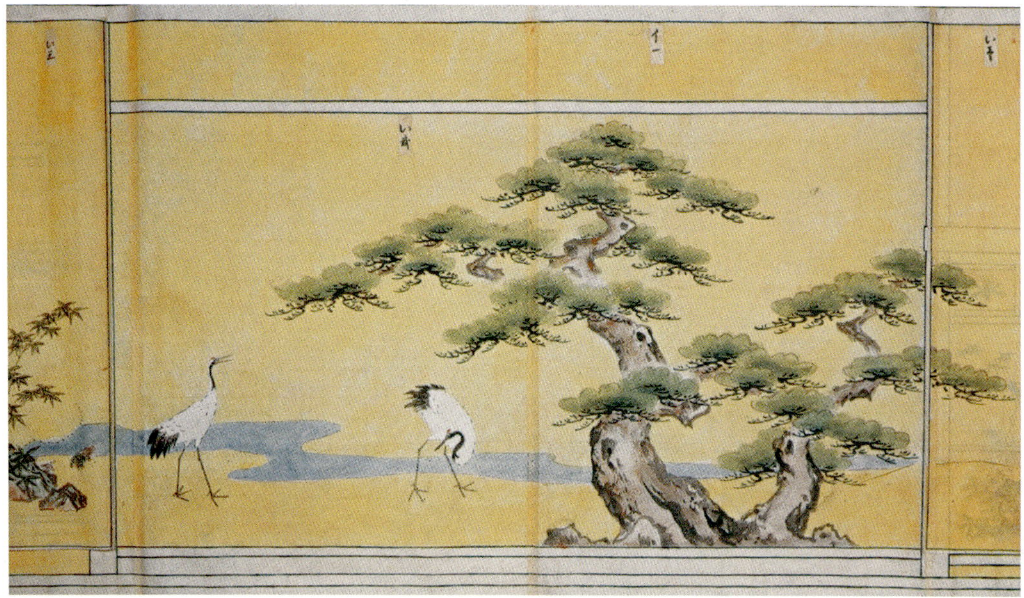

which the Koreans were received and where Kaempfer put on his demonstrations, or at least as Osanobu planned to recreate it. Though much larger than at Nijō, we can see that it seems milder. There are twin pines, with a river running past and a brace of cranes, with more cranes on the side walls. The meaning is no different; perhaps it is even reinforced, as the pines are given a 'supporting double' of cranes, which were said to live for 1,000 years (illus. 85).

85 Kano Osanonu, First Room of Great Rooms Suite at Edo Castle, 1854, preparatory drawing, ink and colour on paper. The decorations of Edo Castle are lost, but can be understood from large and complete preparatory paintings made to replace works lost in the early 19th century. This detail shows part of the most important room of the Tokugawa regime. Pines stand for good government, while cranes were said to live for 1,000 years.

Five

The City's Poetic Presence

Edo's location, by the sea yet in the shallows, ensured that it was accessible but militarily secure. Its huge castle and the Tōkaidō highway allowed for travel in and out that was comfortable, but also watched. Edo was further guarded by the forces of geomancy and Buddhism. The city was made the seat of the shogunate in 1603, because the Tokugawa were already ensconced there, but as a location Edo had its own meanings, which it is the purpose of this chapter to explore.

Far from the capital and from the vestigial institutions of the dairi's authority, Edo was nevertheless not very distant from Kamakura, where Japan's first shogunate had been declared, under the Minamoto family in 1194. That first definitive break with rule by courtiers had taken place to the east of Mount Fuji, where Edo also was. In giving Japan warrior rule, Kamakura demarcated the archipelago from all other Sinospheric lands, which were governed by civil powers. The Tokugawa looked to Kamakura for nomenclature and ritual precedent, far more than they did to the second, Muromachi shogunate, which had operated from the capital and which had been all but assimilated into the court. The Tokugawa did not intend to undergo the same transformation and declared themselves descendants of the Minamoto, promoting Edo for, among other things, its proximity to Kamakura.

Despite the manifest reality of their power, and the historical depth added by these borrowings, the Tokugawa knew that something still was missing. Edo had authority and culture too, but it had no *poetic* presence. The Japanese landscape was dotted with 'famous places' (*meisho* or *nadokoro*), or 'poetic pillows' (*uta-makura*), known from verses written about them in the courtly style of *waka*, composed by poets across the centuries. It was the dairi's job to commission periodically compilations of the best compositions, ensuring that no sublime articulation would be lost. Two collections are relevant to us here, so must be introduced. The first was put together as early as 905 by the great poet Ki no Tsurayuki and was entitled *Anthology of Verses Ancient and Modern* (*Kokin waka-shū*). The second, of three hundred years later, was the work of Fujiwara no Teika in 1205, the *New Anthology of Verses Ancient and Modern* (*Shin kokin waka-shū*) – the verses it contains on Uji and Sano have already been cited. Not all verses were geographical, though anthologies were full of cases where poets used topography to evoke the sentiments they wished to express, whether wonder, sadness, elation, isolation, success or failure. Poets might have visited the places triggering the composition, but some 'poetic pillows' were arbitrary, the location invoked, for example, because of a possible pun in the name. As we saw in a previous chapter, Uji is a real place but its name sounds like the word for 'sadness', so it was a ripe place to 'pillow' a mournful verse, with the poet imaging herself there, whether she had really gone or not. Later poets built on former verses, deepening, as it were, the softness of the 'pillow'. The picking up and developing of an earlier composition was theorized by Fujiwara no Teika as 'taking a root verse', sometimes translated 'allusive variation' (*honka-dori*).[1] By this means, sites became encoded with prescribed sentiments. It was never regarded as a prerequisite for writing to make a personal visit. If a person felt mournful, they could render the expression of their feelings more profound by imagining themselves at Uji, writing as if they were there. It would be grossly ignorant to set a happy verse at Uji.

Japanese verse in all genres is highly seasonal. In *waka*, called 'court poetry', place and season fused from encoding in a first, foundational verse on the place, preferably making a combination that was logical. A place with many cherry trees, for example, would indicate springtime blossoms, so also joy. If such a place also had a name suggesting happiness, via a pun, it was doubly suitable as a 'poetic pillow'. So, of the many sites in Japan with excellent cherry blossoms, Mount Yoshino became the premier 'pillow' because *yoshi* means 'joy' (*no* is a plain). So too would a place with many maple trees indicate autumn leaves, and so be tied to sadness, since that was the assumed emotion of those months. If a place had an evocative name, it would become the 'pillow' for the relevant feeling – one such was the River Tatsuta, since *tatsu* means the greatest of all created beings, a dragon (*ta* is a rice paddy). A major part of Edo period education, whether for elites or commoners, was teaching these matters, imprinting verses on children's minds. The landscapes they might or might not visit; but either way the place could be used to lodge their feelings in future verses of their own.

The *Anthology of Verses* [*waka*] *Ancient and Modern* was entirely court-focused. It contained hardly any 'poetic pillows' from areas far from the capital. Even the *New Anthology*, though assembled after the Kamakura shogunate had come to power, presented the East as nearly devoid of 'pillows'. Where the East was invoked, it was for its barren landscape. In the minds of courtiers, the whole eastern region had just one significant site, and that was the Plains of Musashi (Musashino), a rather loose designation for the area beyond Mount Fuji. Musashi had been used by writers over the ages to denote barbarian nothingness, a site to expound sentiments of desolation. The fact that *musashi* literally means 'military storehouse', while *mu* means 'nothing', made the place stand for alienation bordering on terror.

One such verse appears in Teika's *New Anthology*, written by the Great Minister of the Left, Kujō Yoshitsune. Being a courtier, he never went to Musashi, nor would he have wished to. He felt alienated by the political changes occurring around him and expressed this via the relevant 'pillow', established by prior verses which evoked expanses of uncultivated grassland stretching on for ever – also therefore implying autumn, which was when the grass would be longest, appropriate to

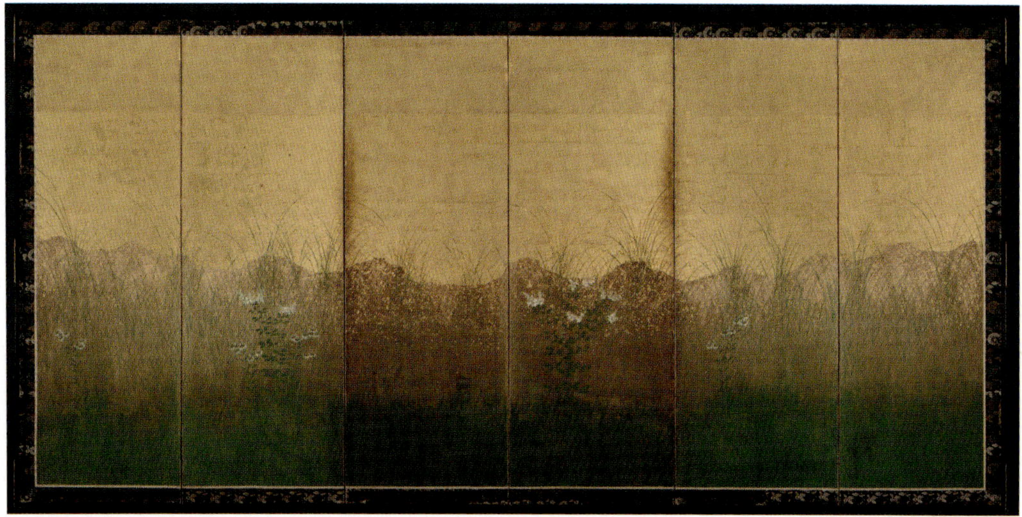

feelings of desolation. Autumn also invited a reference to the moon, hence Yoshitsune wrote,

> At the end of all travels
> The skies are one.
> At Musashino,
> From the grassy plain
> Moon shadows emerge.[2]

The capital is ringed with hills, so no courtier, ensconced at home, ever saw a moon rising through grasses; to them the idea was alienating. On the Musashi Plains, night falls on open, uninhabited fields, leading a civilized person to emotions close to panic.

The next great anthology, *Sequel Anthology of Verses [waka] Ancient and Modern (Zoku kokin waka-shū)*, was compiled in 1265 and included a poem by Yoshitsune's successor as Great Minister of the Left, Minamoto no Michikata. He made the same point:

> The plains of Musashi.
> For the moon to hide,

86 Unknown artist, *Autumn Evening with Full Moon on Musashi Plain*, early 1600s, pair of six-fold screens, ink, colour and gold and silver foil on gilded paper, 170.2 x 346.7 cm each. The Plains of Musashi stood throughout history for wildness and loss of civilization. Yet, from 1590, they became the Tokugawa homelands.

There are no mountaintops.
Yet tips of pampas
Seem covered in white cloud.[3]

Flatness extends, without mountains for the moon to rise from, or sink behind. The loftiest things are grasses, with pampas heads resembling clouds.

Kamakura was not technically in Musashi, but it was close. The shoguns were thus, poetically speaking, outside the orbit of refinement, as the court saw it; indeed, their region actually embodied cultural absence. In a sense, it suited the Kamakura warriors to agree to this characterization since their polity, at least initially, was remote from court norms. That was history, but in the Tokugawa age the matter rose again, because Edo is actually in Musashi.

Paintings of 'poetic pillows' were common, often produced in the form of paired folding screens, which was the most elevated format. An example showing Uji was discussed above (see illus. 26). Where a painting of Musashi was made, it would have to show nothingness, apart from grass, moon and sky, and this is what was done (illus. 86). But after 1603, it was hardly conducive to adumbration of virtuous and

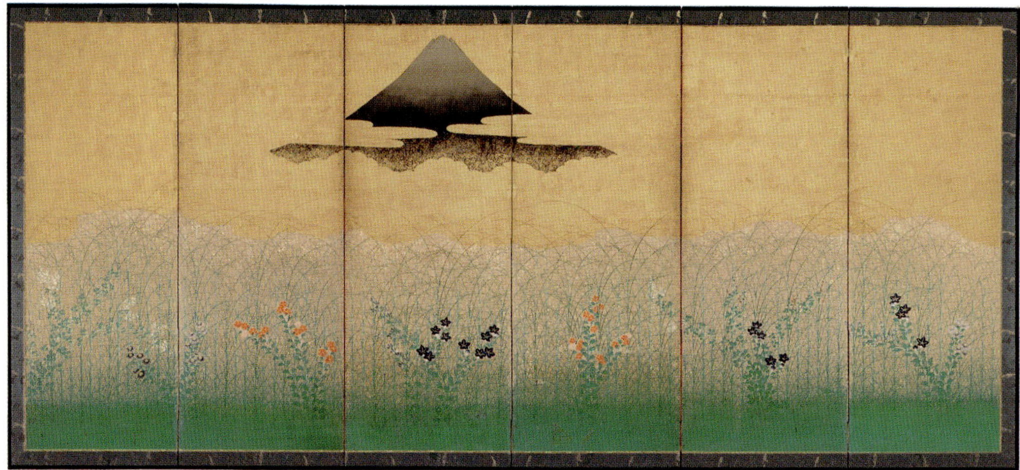

87 Unknown artist, *The Plain of Musashi, Mount Fuji and the Moon*, c. 1760, pair of six-panel screens, colour, gold on paper, 170 x 370 cm each. This pair respects the old association of Musashi with wilderness, but by adding Mt Fuji it renders the location auspicious. Silver pigment has oxidized to black.

cultured shogunal rule in Edo. Steps were taken to remedy this. It was not possible to override what, for centuries, exalted writers had said Musashi was. But, in truth, the region had another established poetic site. It had always been there, even if the court had not taken notice of it, or at least had not coupled it with the Plains of Musashi. The Tokugawa shogunate would make much of this other place. It was, of course, Mount Fuji. It is not in Musashi, but in neighbouring Suruga Province, though Fuji is clearly visible across the plains.

An unknown artist of the early Edo period, or more likely their patron, reconceptualized the Plains of Musashi. The agenda was to be correct within the poetic canon but also to present the Tokugawa land in more positive terms. Since screens come in parts, it was a simple thing to use the right-hand element, the first in order of viewing, for the standard interpretation, with a moon rising through grasses. Then the left-hand side was to depict Mount Fuji, hovering above (illus. 87). The combination is illegitimate insofar as none of the anthologized verses on Musashi spoke of seeing Fuji from the plain. But Fuji was a 'pillow' in its own right, and there was no objection to combinatory formulas. The result was visually harmonious, with a formalistic balance between the circle and the triangle. Fuji's auspiciousness cancels out Musashino's gloom.

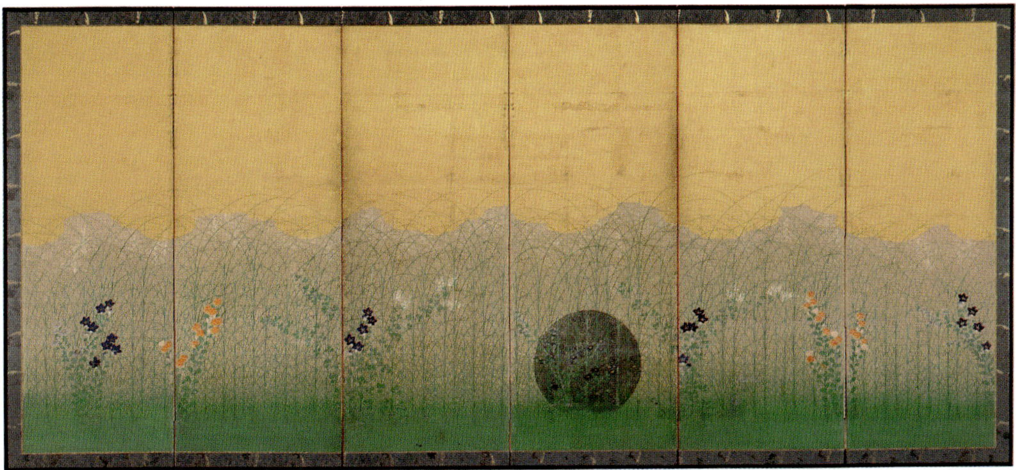

A second avenue was also available to negate Musashi's poetic blankness and to redeem what became the Edo area as a more blissful 'poetic pillow'. In addition to the court anthologies, 'poetic pillows' figured in longer 'verse tales' (*uta-monogatari*); *waka* and *uta* are synonymous, while *monogatari* means 'story'. Reading 'verse tales' was every bit as much a part of formal education as reading poems. Among the oldest was the *Tales of Ise* (*Ise monogatari*), thought to date from about 900. *Ise* is a collection that contains many episodes, but the longest tells of a courtly protagonist, referred to only as 'the Man' (*aru otoko*), who left the capital accompanied by a few close friends and wandered into the countryside. Later tradition identified the Man as Ariwara no Narihira (820–880), a great poet and lover. *Ise* states clearly that the Man left the capital because he had grown tired of it. Very few classical works condemn the capital in this way, much less describe a courier taking the initiative to vacate the odious place. In *Ise*, the Man and his companions head off in an eastward direction, so this key section is known as the 'Descent to the East' (*azuma-kudari*).

The men are described as going past four specific places, and though a touch unclear, they can be traced on a map. At each, they write a compelling verse, set within the narrative. Their first stop is in Mikawa, the province that includes modern Nagoya. Here they sit beside a farmer's wonky bridge and prepare their lunch. The place is referred to as Yatsuhashi ('eight-plank bridge'), though there is no such place in fact. The men see irises in the stream and decide to compose a verse collectively, on the spirit of travel, linked to the early summer flower, which must be the season in which the 'descent' began. The poem is so poignant they weep into their rice, which swells up from their salty tears. Next they come to Suruga, about a week's walk away in reality. They move into hilly country by what the text calls a 'narrow ivy path' (*tsuta no hosomichi*). Here they encounter a monk coming in the other direction, and, recognizing him, they ask the cleric to take letters back to their loved ones in the capital, since they have determined never to return. Pressing on into the uplands, the men see the third spot, Mount Fuji itself, which they have all heard of but never witnessed before. The Man extolls its size and form, noticing, in a verse, that despite the season it is covered with snow. From here they descend the other side of the mountains and enter Musashi proper. They come to a river, which the text identifies as the Sumida. This 'descent', quite literally and also uniquely, put what would later become Edo on the map of classical literature. More than the generic Plains of Musashi, the men cross by Fuji and come down right to the Sumida, or what Edo people called the Great River (Ōgawa), running through their city.

The 'descent' was, accordingly, repeatedly invoked after the creation of the Tokugawa shogunate. It was self-validation, and a final dismissal of Musashi's putative nothingness. The fact that this legitimation even came from a classical work – not some desperate later imposition but from one of the earliest works in the tradition – lent all the more weight. The *Tales of Ise* had always been read, but only in the Edo period was it turned into the paramount literary text, above all others.

A salient, if coincidental, point of significance was that the Tokugawa family hailed from Mikawa. The Man and his companions, having forsworn the capital and moved east, stop first at Yatsuhashi in Mikawa, then go to the Edo region. It was exactly as the shogunal family had done. In fact, the whole 'descent' can be read with a curiously exact Tokugawa coloration, as a mysterious foretelling. From the bridge in Mikawa, they are said to take the Ivy Path in Suruga. Like Yatsuhashi, this path cannot be pinpointed very closely, but the text continues, calling the place where they meet the monk Mount Utsu. Again, no such mountain exists, so the name was either included through ignorance or with poetic licence, because it offered a pun, *utsu* meaning 'awakening' from a dream. The men break out of their befuddlement here. They realize something new, and that must be the content of the letters they send home and the reason they have decided never to return to the capital. They have seen through something, namely the self-centred vanity of their old courtly lives, scornful of everyone beyond, and already irksome to them. It was not legitimate in classical literature to make up false locations. A place called Yatsuhashi must once have existed, or, being no more than an eight-plank bridge, it was perhaps a descriptive name. Mount Utsu, certainly, was not a toponym, but it was actually a dialect term for animal tracks ('sheep-track' in English, though Japan has no sheep), thus Mount Utsu is 'the hill with animal tracks'. This dialect usage was found in the area around Sunpu (modern Shizuoka, then part of Suruga), which was a Tokugawa site too. Ieyasu had been brought up in Sunpu Castle, and from 1605 resided there in retirement, until his death in 1616, after which his glorious mausoleum was built just outside the town (pre-dating his later one at Nikkō).

After Mikawa and Suruga, the Man next sees Fuji. Though not a Tokugawa site as such, the peak was used to denote Edo. It was central to the vista created at Nihon-bashi. The Man then arrives at the Sumida, now below Edo Castle. He traverses the river in a ferry, and it so happens that a very ancient ferry plied the Sumida at Asakusa – not surprisingly, given the Kannon temple was here. The temple is not mentioned in the *Tales of Ise* as it was not yet there, but the Man crosses the river at the place where Ieyasu had prayed to secure the establishment of his regime before the battle of Sekigahara, which he had won. The four points, then, take the Man along a precursive route to Tokugawa greatness.

As the Man and his companions cross the Sumida, they see an unfamiliar bird and enquire from the ferryman its name. He says it is a 'capital-bird' (*miyako-dori*). It is ironic, for they too have fled the capital. They alight from the boat and walk on, ending the section, the capital a thing of the past and the soon-to-be Edo region taking over as centre of their lives.

❧

What we today call 'classical Japanese literature' – including the *waka* anthologies and the verse tales – had been read by members of the court over the centuries. Works had not been accessible to people outside that circle. Texts were not allowed wide distribution, and in any case they were hard to understand without commentaries, which were secret transmissions. The Kamakura shoguns had probably not been exposed to many of them. But five years after establishment of the Edo shogunate, in 1608, cataclysmically, some works of classical literature were published. Court proprietorship of its writings had probably leaked out before, but now it was broken entirely by printed books. Of all the possible titles, the *Tales of Ise* was among the first selected.

Details regarding the motivation for this opening of previously sequestered texts are unclear. The printer Suminokura Sōan had been furnished with nearly unobtainable copies of the works by a courtier named Nakanoin Michikatsu. We cannot know Michikatsu's purpose, but he had spent almost twenty years rusticated, having incurred some great courtier's displeasure for an unknown misdemeanour. It is possible that he was taking revenge. Sōan's business was outside the capital, at Saga, which at least meant he avoided infringing the court's prerogatives on its very doorstep. The several titles he published are known as the Saga Editions (*saga-bon*). All are in large format, with beautiful but fully legible calligraphy, brushed by Sōan himself, who had studied with the admired master Hon'ami Kōetsu. Accessibility was enhanced in some cases with line drawings, by an unnamed hand thought to be a Kano Eitoku student, that is, from a military background.[4] In the

88 Suminokura Sōan (callig.), artist unknown, 'The Eight-plank Bridge', from *Tales of Ise* (*Ise monogatari*, 1608), monochrome published book. The so-called Saga Editions took classical texts into the public realm for the first time. The 10th-century *Tales of Ise* tells of a courtier who grows weary of the capital and wanders east, stopping first at a place called the Eight-plank Bridge.

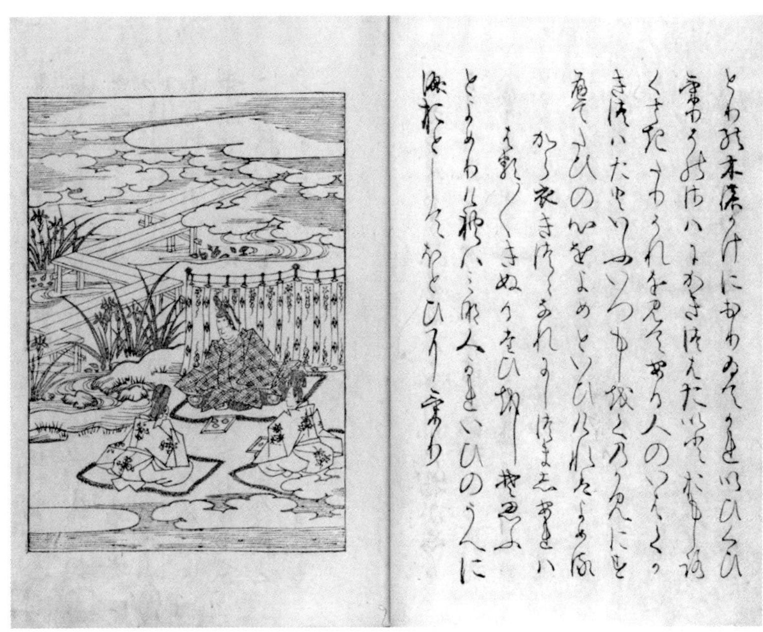

89 Suminokura Sōan (callig.), artist unknown, 'Mount Fuji', from *Tales of Ise* (*Ise monogatari*, 1608), monochrome published book. Further on from the Eight-plank Bridge, the courtier and his companions see Mount Fuji.

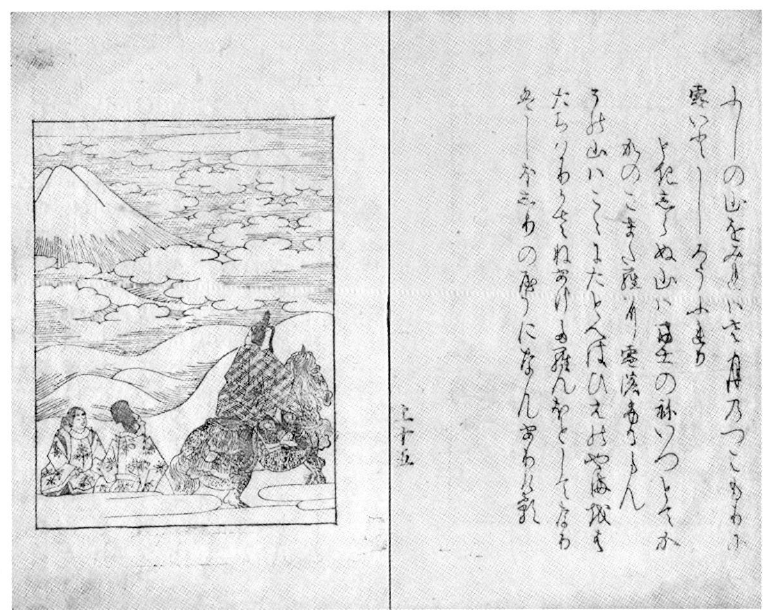

printed *Ise*, the 'descent' alone is given four illustrations, showing the men on their route eastwards (illus. 88 and 89).

By 1610, the Saga *Tales of Ise* had appeared in no fewer than four distinct versions, meaning each set of type had been exhausted, so another had to be made (unusually, Sōan used movable type, not one-page printed blocks). A single set could survive about a thousand impressions, so the book clearly had massive sales, even if perhaps not as many as 4,000. A very large number of readers would have had access to the publication and would have been struck, and surprised, by the 'descent' and how Mikawa-Surugu-Fuji-Sumida were all mentioned, until the Man walks right into what has become central Edo. With the return of peace, many families, not just the Tokugawa, were making their own 'descents', responding to the torque of Edo, with its economic potential. Real travellers took exactly the same road as the Man, which was more or less the Tōkaidō. They could drop by the sites, recalling the Man's experiences as they did so.[5] The Eight-plank Bridge was not clearly determined, but enterprising locals asserted a site; the Ivy Path, too, could be identified, as where the Tōkaidō entered Fuji's foothills. One traveller, for example, Tsuchiya Ayako, was most excited to take the trip and muse on the *Ise*'s 'poetic pillows'. She later much regretted that she had fallen in with a group of philistines having 'no knowledge or taste whatsoever in poetic imagination or a graceful state of mind'.[6]

Before Edo times, classical works might not have been accessible directly, but many were known at one remove, recycled as the bases of nō plays. Nō is a medieval form, and it often picks up on classical texts. It tends to do this by the device of having a contemporary (for the time of writing) visit a poetic site, and muse upon it. In this way, nō paints a classical time already lost. Five or six plays are based on *Ise*, at least two on the 'descent'. One is called *Iris* (*Kakitsubata*), sometimes attributed to the most famous nō playwright Zeami, which would date it to before about 1430. It tells of a monk 'who has visited all the famous places of the capital' and finds himself at Yatsuhashi, centuries after the Man had been there. He encounters the spirit of the iris plants, who explains that the Man, identified in the play as Narihira, was actually a bodhisattva.[7] The other 'descent' play is entitled *River Sumida* (*Sumida-gawa*), and it picks up the ferry crossing episode and the appearance of the capital-bird. The author is Kanze Motomasa, making the text from about the same time as *Iris*. Motomasa tells of a woman of the time of writing who comes to the ferry again, centuries later. She is in distress because her son has been taken by slavers, and she is seeking him. As the ferryman takes her over, they see a capital-bird, provoking a recitation of the Man's experiences and verses. Unlike *Iris*, the second play develops the original story, for on the further bank the woman sees a grave and realizes it is that of her son, murdered there for being too weak to go on further. The tragedy is all the more intense because the boy is named as Umewaka, 'young plum': the beauty of plum blossoms is greater when the tree is old.

The play *River Sumida* was important to Edo people because of the location. The tragedy that Motomasa has projected onto the site – which is absent from the original poem tale – had been dealt with some time after the composition of the play: a temple had been founded across the Sumida from Asakusa, dedicated to the memory of this (fictional) boy. Called the Baijaku-ji ('temple of the young plum'), it was complete with grave mound. Naturally it was heavily patronized by Ieyasu on his arrival into the area, to identify himself with the Man's trajectory and its later reworking.[8] Ieyasu is said to have planted willows beside the grave, the species chosen because its swaying branches were said to resemble a distressed woman's loose and tangled hair. Ieyasu also gave the temple a 'mountain name' in reference to his arboreal addition, Bairyū-zan ('mountain of the plum and willow'). In 1608, just as the Saga Edition *Ise* came off the press, a court calligrapher well disposed to the military, Konoe Nobutada, proposed a revision of the temple name itself. Nobutada felt that Baijaku-ji sounded too sad, and he suggested relieving this by dividing the character 'plum' in half. Since 'plum' is made up of the characters for 'wood' and 'mother' placed side by side, when his change was accepted the place became the 'temple of wood and mother', or Mokubo-ji (illus. 90). The temple is still there, with the same name, though as rebuilt in the 1960s.

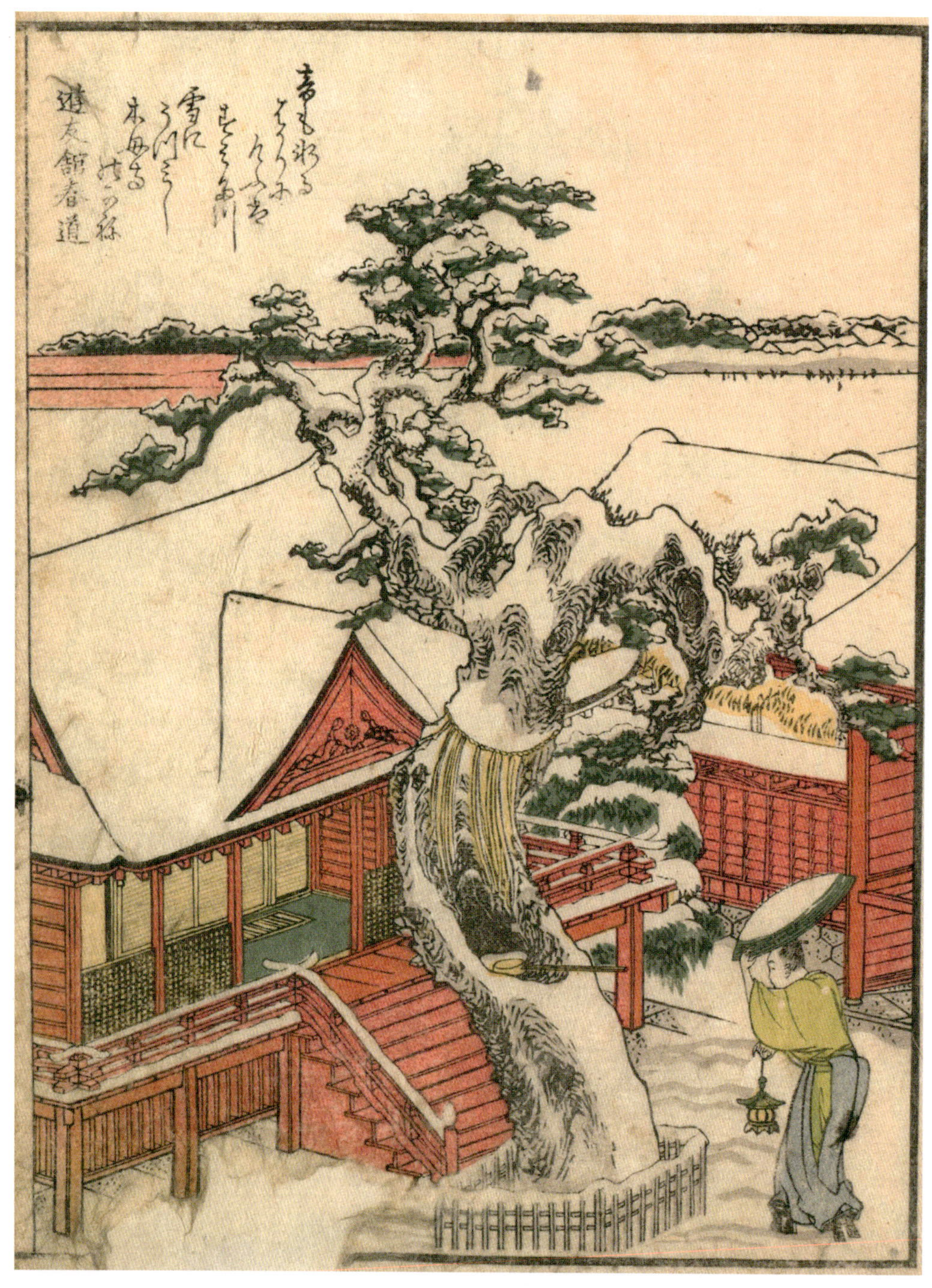

90 Katsushika Hokusai, 'Bell and Drum of the Mokubo-ji', from *Pictures of Both Banks of the Sumida River* (*Ehon Sumidagawa Ryōgan ichiran*, c. 1804), colour printed book. The Mokubo-ji was a sad place, so was always shown in winter. Pilgrims honour the spirit of Umewaka-maru, killed here by slave-drivers.

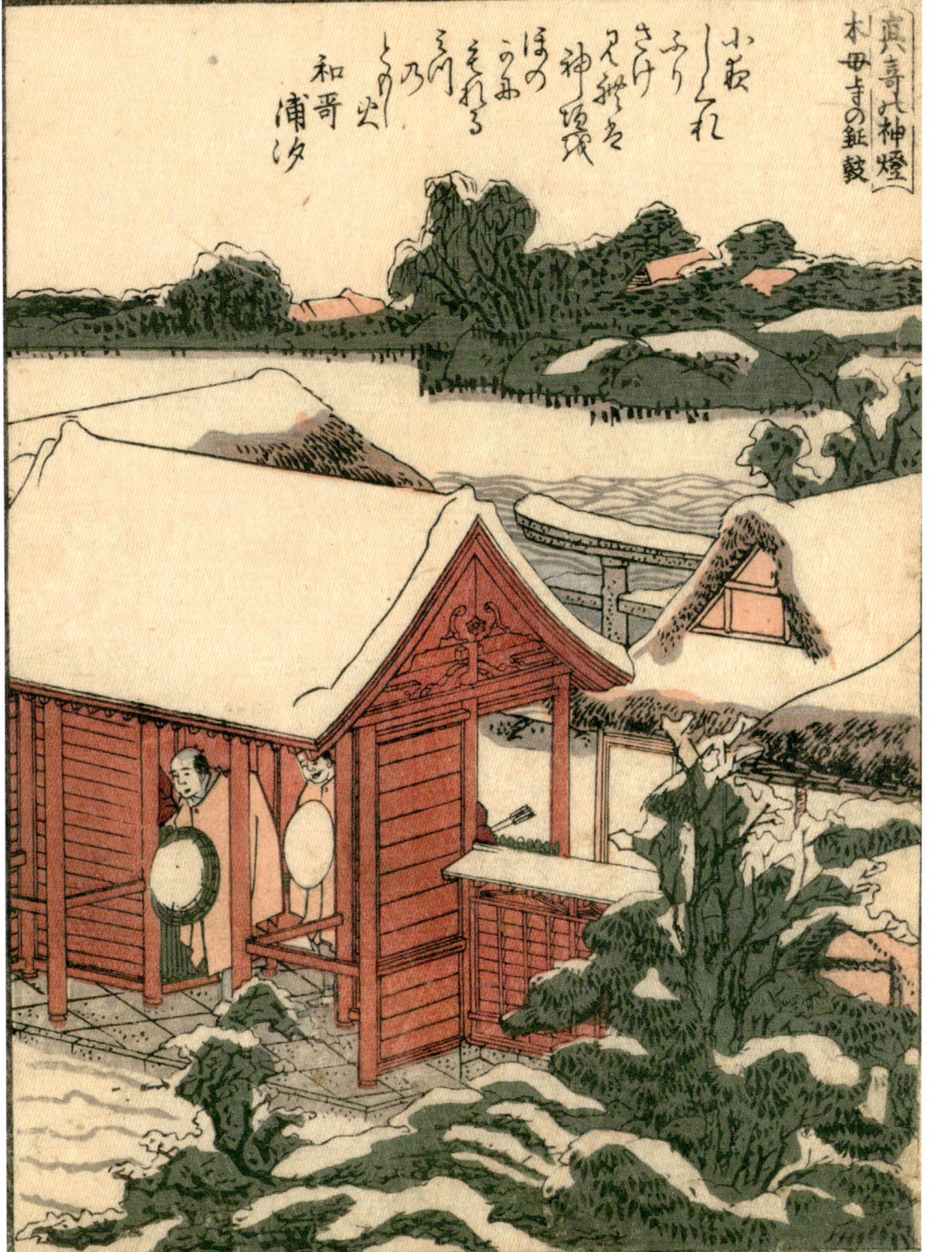
眞壽八神煙
村田まの鉦鼓
小萩
しくれ
ふり
さけ
又秘名
神頃袋
ほの
のうみ
それる
高乃
とり火
和哥
浦汐

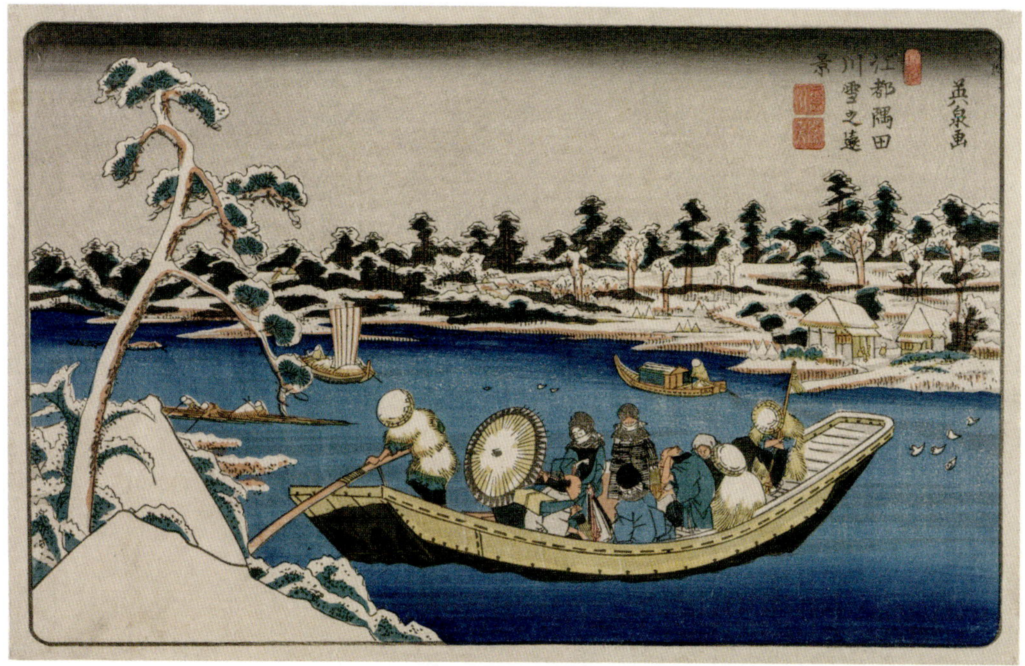

At some point, Edo acquired one of its best restaurants here, right next to the Mokubo-ji. Real and poetic urban topography merged. Visitors in winter would see the migratory birds that congregated in these reaches in the cold months, and they could call them 'capital-birds'. Tourist pictures of the site always show it in winter, when the birds are about. Winter also suited the bitterness of the nō story, and it was also the season when the plum blossoms bloomed (illus. 91).

ℰℐ

The 'Descent to the East' grew into a major painting theme. Foremost among those who developed it was an early eighteenth-century artist named Ogata Kōrin. Living in the capital, he took up his brush only late in life, seemingly as a result of a collapse into poverty. Kōrin was the great-nephew of a celebrated calligrapher associated with the Saga Editions, Hon'ami Kōetsu, and it was to proclaim this that Kōrin borrowed the kō in his ancestor's studio name (rin means 'solitary'). Kōrin

91 Keisai Eisen, *Distant View of Snow on the River Sumida in Edo*, c. 1840–44, multicoloured woodblock print. The ferry mentioned in the *Tales of Ise* still ran in Edo times, as shown here. The season is winter and 'capital-birds' are visible in the stream.

probably trained with the Kano school, since most aspiring artists did, but he also spent time learning by copying old works in temple collections. Then, almost exactly a century after the Saga Editions came out, perhaps in the year 1708 itself, Kōrin gave up on the capital too. Emulating the Man, he took the road eastwards. He had already done well, but hoped his career would flourish better among the shogunal elite, and to appeal to them, as a disaffected man of the capital, Kōrin painted the 'descent' repeatedly. It became his signature theme. Records state that just before his departure for Edo, Kōrin dreamed about crossing Mount Fuji, and on waking he painted the peak, producing his first rendition of the peerless mountain he had not yet seen. The work is lost, but he showed it to an admirer, a learned abbot named Jakunyo, of the Nishi-Hongan-ji ('western temple of the original vow'), a temple lavishly supported by Ieyasu and subsequent shoguns. The abbot wrote an inscription on the painting.[9] Jakunyo's temple came into possession of a pair of screens by Kōrin showing irises, without any bridge but clearly a depiction of Yatsuhashi and the first leg of the 'descent'. When this work was painted is uncertain, but it might have been given to the temple by Kōrin in thanks for Jakunyo's contacts that ensured his astounding success in the shogunal city. Kōrin worked in Edo extensively for the shogunal elite, and perhaps for top-flight merchants. Another *Iris* screen, this time with bridge, is recorded in the possession of a rich lumber wholesaler, either commissioned by him or given by a senior military figure in lieu of repaying a loan (a common event). He also often painted the theme on more modestly priced hanging scrolls (illus. 92).

Kōrin had three long stints in Edo. On the second and third he was invited to become in-house painter to the Sakai family, who, like the Tokugawa, came from Mikawa. Sakai Tadataka, a member of the ruling shogunal body, the Council of Elders, was one of the most powerful men in the land. He secured Kōrin a pension and household staff. When Kōrin left Edo for good, opening a workshop back in the capital, he still undertook work for senior Edo clients, sending the finished pictures up to the shogunal city. Kōrin also engaged in a range

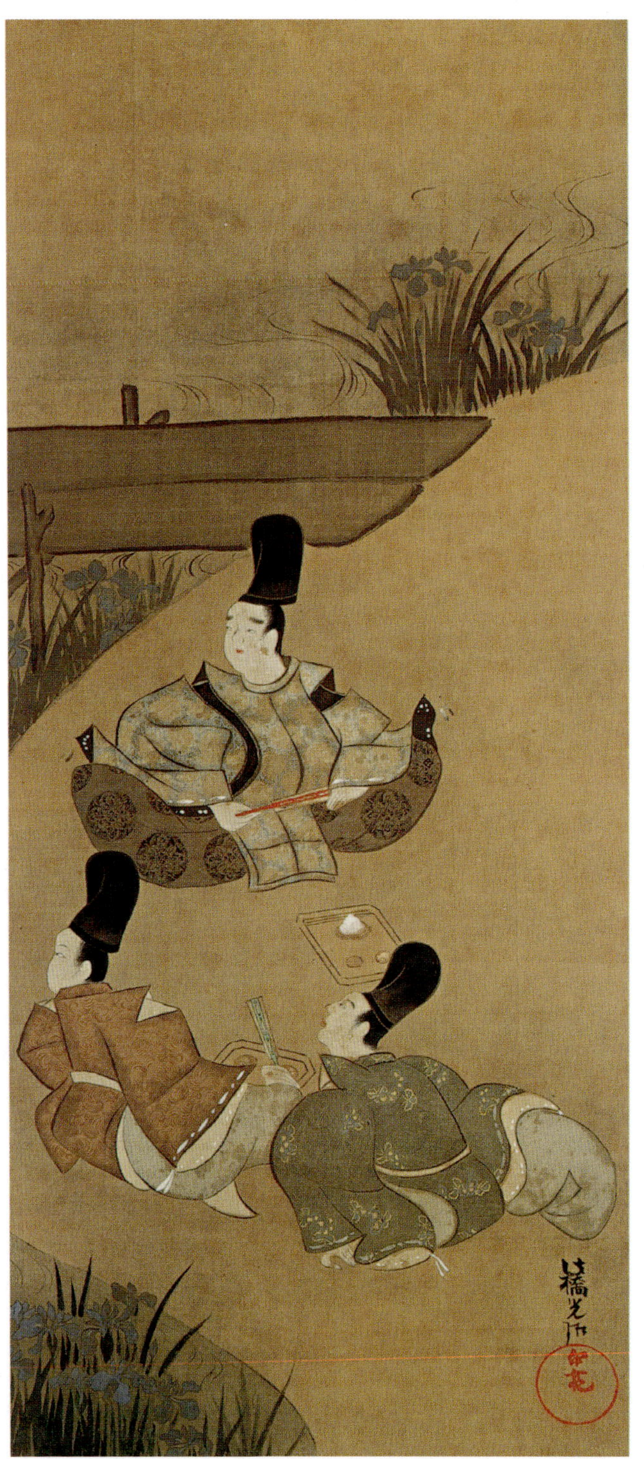

92 Ogata Kōrin, *Eight-plank Bridge*, c. 1710, hanging scroll, ink and colour on paper. The Eight-plank bridge was said to be in the province of Mikawa. It was long gone, and the exact place uncertain, but to Edo viewers, it stood both for the courtiers' frustration with the capital and for the Tokugawa family's departure from Mikawa for Edo. Kōrin was greatly admired for his many interpretations of the topic.

93 Sakai Hōitsu, *The Ivy Path (Mount Utsu)*, early 19th century, hanging scroll, colour on paper. In the *Tales of Ise*, after the Eight-plank Bridge, the courtiers take an ivy-clogged path over the imaginary Mount Utsu ('mountain of awakening'), where they pass a monk heading back to the capital.

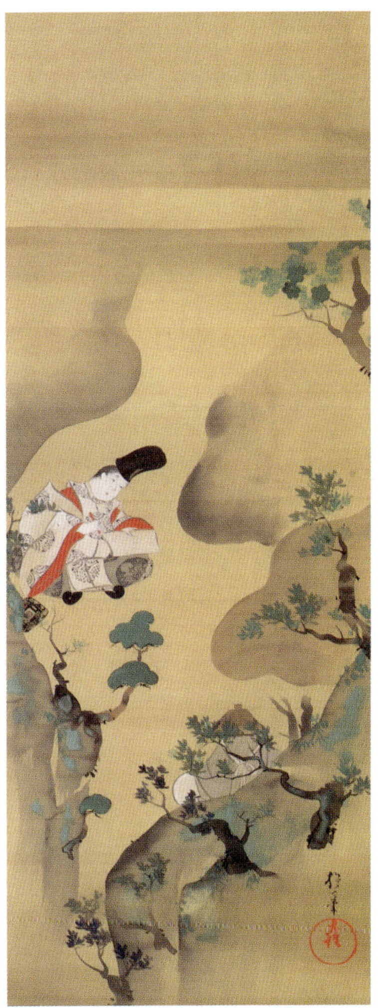

of aestheticized, spendthrift activities, calculated to recall feckless ancient courtiers, which suited his patrons too, as they imagined him a leftover classical man, painting themes about the demise of the capital and the rise of Edo, for his more gritty Edo buyers.

In about 1800, a descendant of Sakai Tadataka, Sakai Tadanao, found in his family collection a quantity of Kōrin's works. He was already an accomplished painter in another mode, but he took to emulating his new discoveries. Tadanao painted copies of Kōrin's pieces, as well as Kōrin-style work of his own invention, using the name Hōitsu ('embracing one idea'). When the centenary of Kōrin's death came in 1816, Hōitsu published *One Hundred Pictures by Kōrin* (*Kōrin hakuzu*), perhaps the first single-artist catalogue produced in Japan. In parallel to Kōrin's adoption of the Eight-plank Bridge as his signature theme, Hōitsu adopted the second part of the 'descent', the Ivy Path (illus. 93). He followed Kōrin sequentially, in time and in narrative, as deferential homage. But as a daimyo's son, Hōitsu also showed more direct reference to Tokugawa power, since the Ivy Path was an oblique refence to Sunpu Castle, where the early Edo founder of the Sakai line, Sakai Tadayo, had spent much time with Icyasu, and had been highly rewarded. By Hōitsu's day, the Sakai family had been allocated even more lucrative lands and resided in the country's most beautiful castle, still on every tourist's trail, at Himeji. The colourful, abbreviated manner that Hōitsu took from Kōrin is now dubbed Rinpa, that is, the school (*ha*, or *pa*) of [Kō]rin.

Hōitsu was too elite to think of training pupils. Instead he engaged a younger secretary, Kiitsu, to follow him and continue his, or rather Kōrin's, manner. Kiitsu duly took the third leg of the 'descent' as his signature. Over and over again he painted the Man and his companions passing Mount Fuji. It was customary for Edo residents to put out

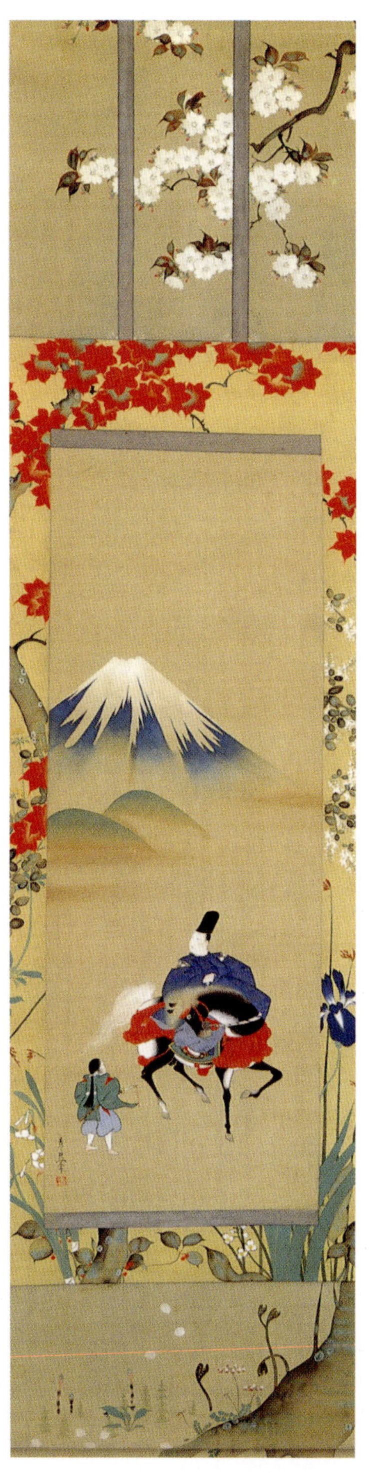

94 Suzuki Kiitsu, *Mount Fuji and the Descent to the East*, c. 1820, hanging scroll, colour on paper. The courtiers from the *Tales of Ise* see Mount Fuji. Kiitsu has also painted the mountain so as to include all four seasons.

paintings of Fuji at the New Year. To display not a generic Fuji, but an image of the Man passing before the mountain, would be a way of coupling the expected seasonal theme with a specific endorsement of the translation of authority from the capital to the Edo region (illus. 94). Kiitsu died in 1858, just as the shogunate began to topple. He had no successor, but had there been one, that person would no doubt have adopted the next episode from the 'descent', and repeatedly painted the ferry and the capital-bird.

The Kano school, being officials, also painted themes related to the valorization of the East. It was an added bonus that they hailed from Suruga (where Kano is a place name). Once the Kano school became imbricated in the Tokugawa regime from 1617, Tan'yū look the lead in developing appropriate topics, and he painted Mount Fuji very often. One might call it his signature subject. If so, there was a precedent he could not ignore. The greatest Japanese painter of all time, as was universally agreed, was Sesshū, a Zen monk from the fifteenth century. He favoured monochrome ink-wash work and sometimes used it to depict local landscapes with great accuracy. Sesshū was based in the capital, but he travelled, and is likely to have visited Kamakura, where many Zen temples founded by the Minamoto family flourished. Whether or not Sesshū saw Mount Fuji, he certainly painted it, with the sea to the right and the pine-covered spit of Miho no Matsubara counterpoising

95 Sesshū (attrib.), inscription by Zhan Zhonghe, *Mount Fuji and Miho no Matsubara*, c. 1500, hanging scroll, ink on paper. Sesshū was perhaps the greatest name in the entire history of Japanese painting. He worked in the international monochrome style, and once used it to depict Mount Fuji and the Seiken-ji, with the pine-covered spit of Miho to the right. This original was one of the most venerated of all works of art, and often reproduced.

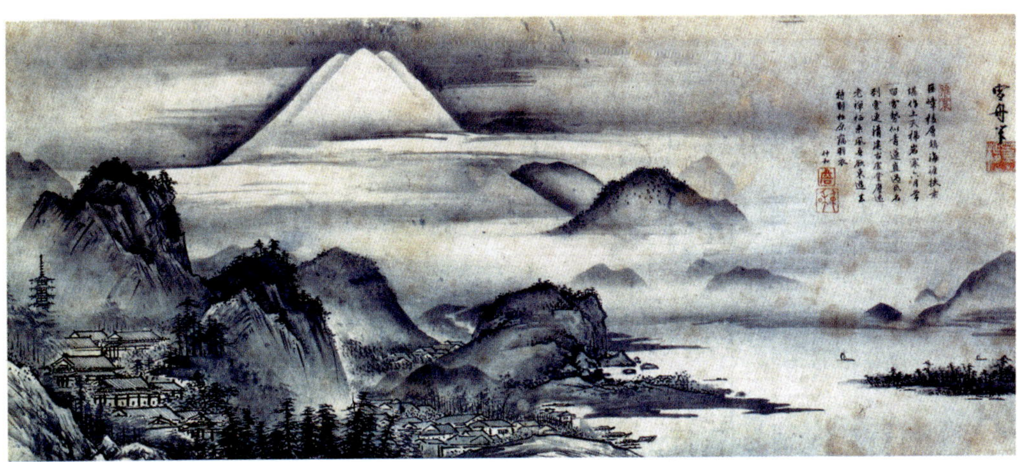

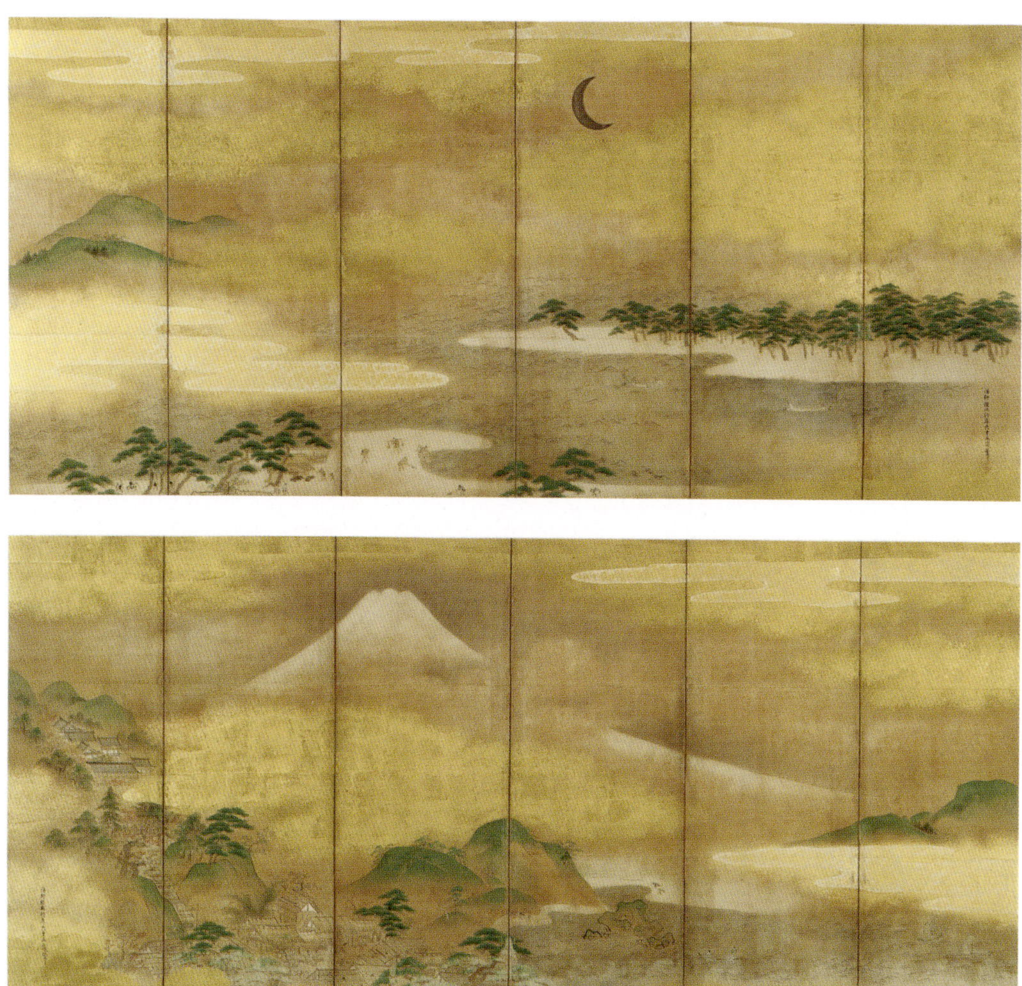

96 Kano Tan'yū, *The Beach at Miho* and *Mount Fuji*, 1666, pair of screens, ink, colours and gold on paper, 182.2 cm x 378.5 cm each. Tan'yū takes Sesshū's formula of two hundred years before and transposes it onto the Edo elite format of paired gold screens. The image above is the right-hand screen and that below the left-hand screen.

the mountain (illus. 95). Below Fuji nestles the Seiken-ji ('temple of the clear view'), a Zen temple founded in about 1260. Sesshū may have made several versions, and in Edo times all and sundry wanted one, since the scene depicted Mount Fuji, the sign of Edo, made by the greatest hand. Kōrin claimed that while in Edo he was endlessly brought so-called Sesshūs to appraise, and although he did not state the topics, very plausibly many were this same Fuji view.[10] Sesshū had painted a hanging scroll, but paired screens were the preferred Edo format, and Tan'yū therefore devised a template that split Sesshū's composition across the two surfaces, giving the sea and pine bank on the right-hand screen and the mountain on the left (illus. 96). He updated Sesshū's model, and his studio made it widely available.

As an artist, Sesshū had enjoyed the rare privilege of making a trip to the Ming (China). It was even reported that he was commended by the court there. Zen was a Chinese school, and Sesshū's monochrome ink-wash painting was regarded as being in the 'continental' mode. His depiction of Fuji, accordingly, showed the Japanese mountain in a foreign style. The Chinese would surely wish to see it and it would be conciliatory to show the mountain in 'their' mode. To paint Fuji in the 'continental' manner was a means to suggest Fuji's international reach, which to Edo viewers conveyed shogunal prestige.

Tan'yū made many works that nod deferentially to Sesshū's foundational rendition of Fuji. But he also went further. He grafted Sesshū's iconic 'continental' rendition onto the 'Japanese', indigenous mode. This he achieved by inserting into Sesshū's vista elements from the *Tales of Ise*, which had unfolded in the very same place. It could be quite simply done, for Sesshū's image was so accurate it suggested a pathway leading into the foothills, which could be turned into the Ivy Path; indeed, it *was* the Ivy Path, forebear of Edo's Tōkaidō, for there was no other track over the mountains to Musashi. All Tan'yū needed to do was add a few red dots to suggest ivy (it was acceptable to add minor pigment elements to monochrome painting). The *Ise* story did not mention the pine-covered spit, which was a distraction, as was the Seiken-ji, so Tan'yū removed the one and turned the other into a

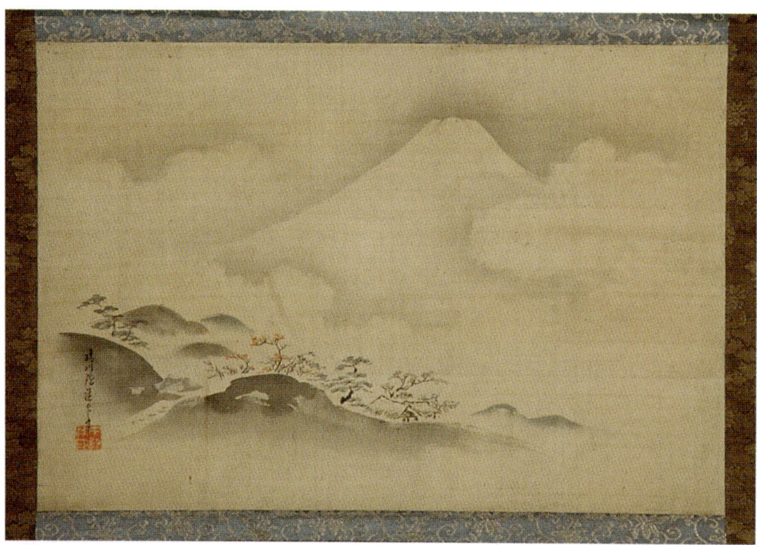

97 Kano Seisen'in Osanobu, *Mount Fuji and Miho no Matsubara*, c. 1834–46, hanging scroll, ink and colour on silk. This is a late Edo rendition of Kano Tan'yū's composite work fusing Sesshū's formula of Mount Fuji with the Ivy Path from the *Tales of Ise*.

peasant cottage. This formulation became a Kano trope and was used by members of the school throughout the Edo period (illus. 97). To hybridize Fuji as both international and indigenous at the same time, both continental and Japanese, was to cover all options. Furthermore, although no one could tell for sure where Sesshū had stood to paint this vista, there was an upland level that must have been pretty close and which does indeed offer a very similar prospect. In Tan'yū's time, right behind this stood Ieyasu's mausoleum. Today the place has acquired the rather nationalistic name of Nihon-daira ('Japanese levels').

The 'Descent to the East' began at the hard-to-locate Eight-plank Bridge. The Tokugawa origins were better left misty, too. But the Ivy Path went past Ieyasu's place of upbringing and death and was a major shogunal highway. Mount Fuji was admired throughout the world. Beyond this, as Sesshū never knew, though as foretold by the *Tales of Ise*, was the shogunal city of Edo, where capital-birds sang of the loss of courtly authority.

Six

A Trip to the Yoshiwara

As Edo grew, the population of townspeople expanded, but they were forced to live within a restricted zone by the waterfront, and later also across the bridge in the newly built areas. Vast numbers of women entered the city from the countryside on a temporary basis to work as maids and domestic servants, while daimyo retinues brought huge numbers of regional males. The authorities understood the need for spaces of social relaxation for residents and transitory single women, and, most numerous of all, temporarily single, military-class men.

Sites of distraction were many, from temple grounds to restaurants and drinking establishments. Edo was filled with cultural and literary coteries, who liked to meet in teahouses and shops. This chapter addresses a more formalized site of recreation, part of what came to be known as the 'floating world' (*ukiyo*). This stood in contradistinction to the 'fixed' worlds of propriety, elegant endeavour, bourgeois civility, warrior loyalty and religious life. Today it is sometimes called the 'pleasure district', though it should not be imagined it was pleasurable for all involved. At first, the main floating world was located near Nihon-bashi behind the fish market, so it was accessible to all residents of Edo. The collective floating world, in essence, was two; or, one might say, like the two sides of a coin. First was the kabuki theatre, second the red-light district, or what was then termed the 'stockade' (*kuruwa*). Both worlds allowed for a range of non-conforming socialization, but they also over time acquired normative codes, with rank debauchery eschewed. The floating worlds were Edo's official sites of alterity and licensed by shogunal decree.

The theatres were spread over two town blocks, named Sakae-chō and Yoshi-chō (*chō* being a street or block), while the red-light district was close by, at Yoshiwara-chō. The theatres enacted urban wish-fulfilment in plays about modern life, while the red-light district was a space for males to enact fantasies themselves. Both offered a range of performance genres, but they were also brothel areas. The actors, who from 1629 were all male, were available for before- or after-performance private assignments, and a host of theatrical hangers-on were effectively boy sex-workers. In the 'stockade', the line between meal service and sexual service was not always clear, and a class of 'courtesans' (*yūjo*) could be summoned for paid encounters. Women and even military ladies were able to attend kabuki, see the shows and also avail themselves of the actors' additional skills, as, of course, could men. But only men could enter the Yoshiwara – that is, apart from the women who worked there, who could not leave.

The devastating fire of 1657, which erased the entire central area of Edo, also destroyed the floating world districts. In response, the shogunate undertook several measures. One was to build a bridge over the Great River, as a means of escape in times of disaster and to lower density in the commoner residential areas, by opening up new ground. The second was to relocate the 'stockade'. The theatres were left as they were, likely so as to keep them accessible for women, who could not easily be allowed to wander through the city. But the red-light district was forced to relocate. It had not been responsible for the fire but was nevertheless a place of oil lamps, braziers and stoves operating at night, with visitors impassioned or drunk. Managers of the establishments were given the option of moving across the bridge into the new area, or else to the northeast, beyond the band of protector temples at Asakusa and Ueno. They chose the latter, and the Yoshiwara opened there as the Shin (new) Yoshiwara. It would be Edo's main place of libidinous male fantasy for the next two centuries. There were other, unofficial locales for drinking and commercial sex with women, called the *oka-basho* ('hill places'), perhaps a corruption of *hoka-basho*, meaning 'other places', while boys continued to be available around the theatres. But only the Yoshiwara, then the New Yoshiwara, was licensed and deemed a legal entity for women to engage in heterosexual sex work. As such it generated a presence that enthralled male and female Edo residents alike; and the arising visual culture of paintings and prints has intrigued Japanese ever since, and also foreigners once the Impressionists in Paris first encountered 'pictures of the floating world' (*ukiyo-e*).

After its removal, the Yoshiwara ('New' was soon dropped) joined those places behind the northeastern temples that the authorities regarded as unpleasant but necessary, like the execution grounds and leatherworking ateliers – known as the 'vile places' (*akusho*). Spiritual force, *ki*, moving from northeast to southwest entered the city here and would become polluted by such odiousness, but would then be purified by the temples before entering Edo proper. The Yoshiwara, however, was not vile for sexual reasons. As mentioned before, its problematic nature came from its extravagance and from being a place of falsity and lies. Women and men swore commitments that meant nothing the next morning. The shogunate had few quibbles with sex, but intensely disliked deficiencies of 'sincerity' (*makoto*). The Yoshiwara encapsulated financial and verbal waste, and unlike in the theatres false acts were performed by real people – legally, actors were categorized as outcast, or 'non-people' (*hinin*).

Once the Yoshiwara had moved from its old quarter in the city centre, going there was quite a trek. Previous books have addressed the district – what went on there and what was produced – but few have addressed the phenomenon of the journey people had to make to the Yoshiwara.[1] Such is the purpose of this chapter, to set the 'stockade' within the Edo shogunal city. An upstanding male left Edo as a 'fixed' person, but about 4 kilometres later he arrived at the Yoshiwara in a different state of mind, 'floating'. The route involved a spatio-cognitive transition. Access was gained by a sequence of nodes effecting a psychological shift. They displaced the Yoshiwara and made a *cordon sanitaire* separating the quarter from the shogun's demesne.

The Yoshiwara had a cold reality, in matters such as its financing, contracts (the women were indentured) and sexual health. But the documentation adduced here is the Yoshiwara *myth* that called men to it. Owners and promoters of the quarter put out self-serving pictures and reports to be consumed in Edo, sugar-coating the real destination. The Yoshiwara was just five city blocks, so much too small for large numbers to visit in fact. For the vast majority of men, and for all women other than those working there, it was a site of the imagination. Pictures of the floating world and stories about it (*sharebon*) were sold to fabricate auras for the place, inducing a sense of relish, predetermining the experience of any visitor and deluding those who never had the chance to see its realities. The lives of the women working there, or even of the clients, were not the main subject of these genres, or rather, smothering them was the point. Pictures and stories were floating world celebrations.

⌘

There were several ways to go to the Yoshiwara. Paths led from the city to Asakusa and beyond, but most visitors went via the Willow Bridge (Yanagi-bashi) in central Edo, where the River Kanda entered the Great River. Boats gathered here at nightfall to take revellers upstream. People would go by water as far as San'ya, a journey of some ninety minutes, then alight and walk the last fifteen minutes to the district itself. Both parts of the route, over the course of more than two centuries, acquired a paper trail of comment and imagery.

There had been a bridge here for a long time, but it acquired the name of Willow Bridge in the mid-eighteenth century, when a stand of trees was planted along the end of the Kanda. Boats departed for many places, but at night, when the Yoshiwara operated, there would be no

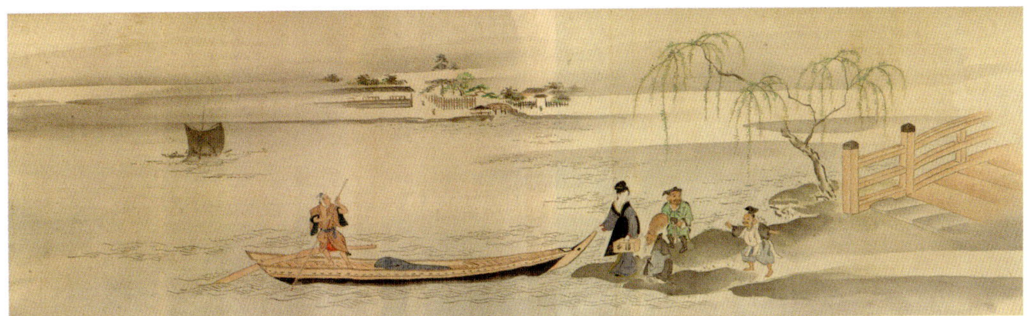

98 Chōbunsai Eishi, 'Willow Bridge', from *Three Gods of Good Fortune Visit the Yoshiwara* or 'Scenes of Pleasure at the Height of Spring', early 19th century, section of handscroll, ink and colour on silk. Eshi took the established theme of handscrolls showing landscapes along the river, and turned it into a continuous view of the trip to the Yoshiwara. Three men meet at the bridge where boats are available to take them upstream.

customers apart from those going there – other than those bound for the nearer 'hill place' at Fukagawa. Some seven hundred boats might be tied up, awaiting custom, with female agents who accosted men and escorted them to the boats (illus. 98).

The boats were of a special type, thin, with raised prows for quickness. Some people said poetically that they looked like leaves floating in the water. Generally they were called 'boar's tusk boats' (*choki-bune*), from the low-hulled shape. It was common enough to take a ferry in Edo, to cross the moats, but those vessels were noisy and lumbering, and filled with a random group. 'Boar's-tusk boats', in contrast, were for private hire. Their maximum load was three people, plus the waterman, but for increased speed most men rode alone. The passenger faced forwards, with the waterman invisibly behind, giving one of the most solitary experiences a man ever knew. Edo's poor people rarely found themselves far from the street, while the rich were seldom free of servants. Darkness increased the sense of waterborne isolation and initiated a mood of dislocation that would gain emphasis as the journey progressed.

The narrow boats were unstable, so it was necessary to keep quite still. The man adopted the *agura*, a relaxed version of the lotus position seen on Buddhist images. It was a common pose, but men remarked how Yoshiwara visitors began the trip in the Buddha's bodily hexis. Transit was meditational.

The invocation of Buddhahood at the outset was decidedly relevant. The Yoshiwara was where men sought pleasure, knowing it to be false. This was the root of its 'vileness'. Yet the notion that what

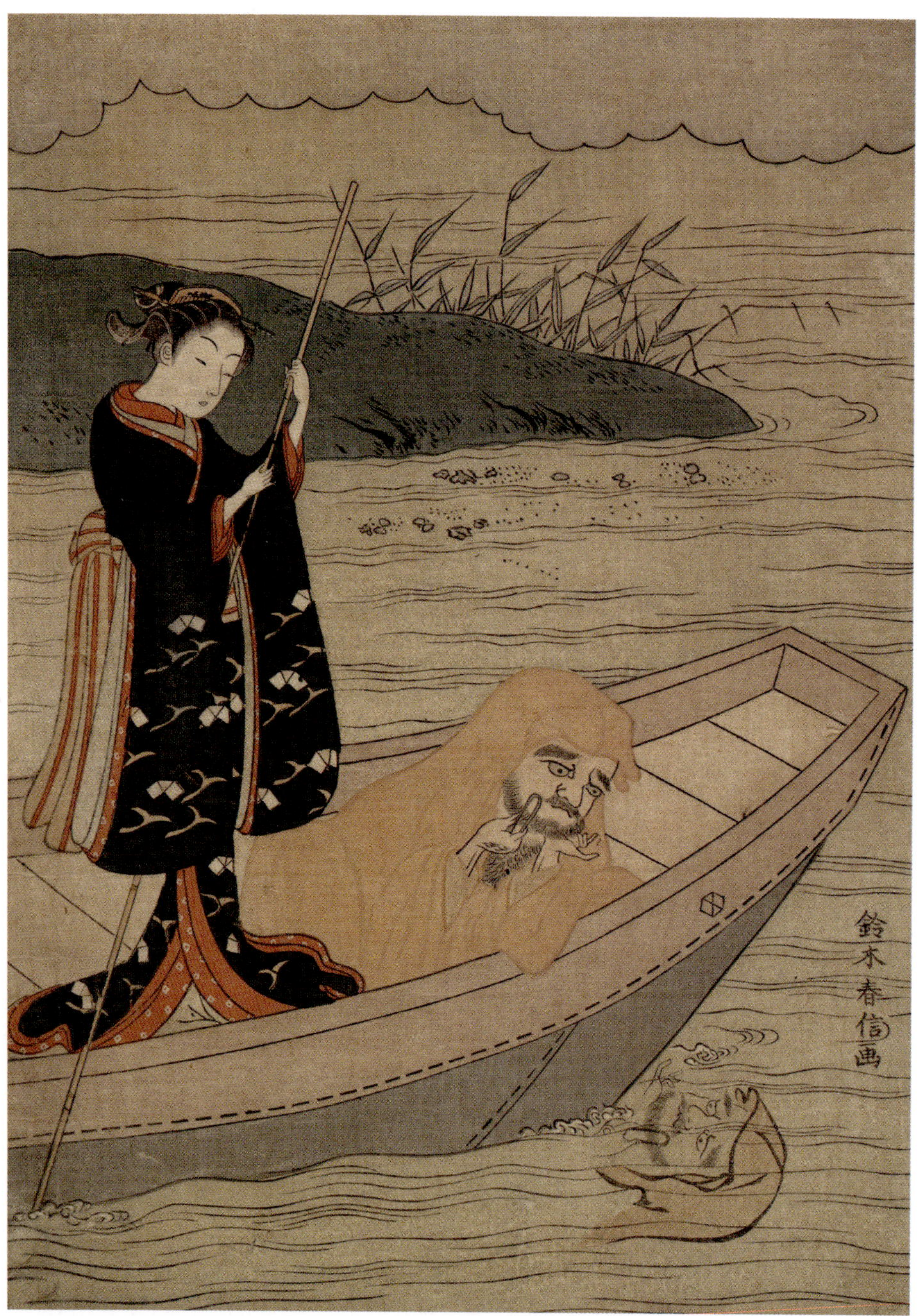

99 Suzuki Harunobu, *Daruma in a Boat with an Attendant*, c. 1767, multicoloured woodblock print. This humorous work turns the crusty boatman into a young woman, and the pleasure-seeking passenger into the founder of Zen, Bodhidharma (Daruma in Japanese) – who preens himself as he is poled up to the 'floating world' district.

is called pleasure is actually vanity is an axiom of Buddhism. The 'floating world', by its label, recognized a lack of durability that was, in fact, concordant with serious religious thought. As the man went on his journey against the current, he would think how time spent with courtesans was an affirmation, not a denial, of the claim that what we call pleasure is actually meaningless. Parallels, not antinomies, joined the Yoshiwara and the world of Enlightenment. It was normal urban life, with its erroneous craving for fixity, that was in error. In a way, a courtesan and a Buddha were alike. Both were unhoused, untied, without karmic links. Neither had home, parents, children or careers. Floating-world pictures were produced to support this parallel. Suzuki Harunobu, from 1765 the first commercial multicoloured printmaker, showed a boar's-tusk boat on its way to the Yoshiwara. It is poled not by a crusty waterman but by a beautiful townswoman. The client is not a typical pleasure-seeker, either, but Bodhidharma (Daruma), the founder of Zen, whose Enlightenment exceeded that of all other human beings (illus. 99). Bodhidharma views his face in flowing water, a long-standing metaphor for the contemplation of vanity, but now using the reflection to preen for the night ahead. Naturally, this argument was self-serving and tongue-in-cheek, but it did also have its serious side. Buddhist clerics had long argued that 'emptiness lies within pleasure and pleasure within emptiness'. There was no need to shun pleasure once its fleetingness was accepted – in fact, clinging to fixity was the graver error.

As the boat moved off, the man pondering these conundrums, the trees faded from view. Willows were established symbols, and relevant to his objective. Their tangled branches were compared to the unkempt tresses of disquiet women. In Edo lore, disquiet women were those deranged through sexual insult and lecherous, cruel treatment. They died with passions that they could not shed, and so were propelled back as ghosts. Willows were the abode of cheated women. As such this was a final warning to the pleasure-seeker, who was invariably someone's intended, if not already someone's husband. Willow symbolism would resurface again before the Yoshiwara was gained.

The Willow Bridge over the Kanda was just above the much bigger bridge built after the fire of 1657. This bridge has been mentioned before, but not named. It was called the Bridge of Two States (Ryōgoku-bashi), because it joined Edo's province of Musashi with Shimōsa province beyond. The boat, turning away from the bridge and heading upstream, ran along an interstice between the two entities. The trip followed a seam that was detached and judicially unaccounted for. As a verse in the comic urban *senryū* genre put it,

Two States,
Moving between them –
Such speed![2]

Having pulled into the Great River, the man's eyes grew used to darkness and he made out features on the bank. Soon the shogunal rice storehouses came into view. This district, known as Kuramae ('in front of the storehouses') or Mikura ('august storehouses'), by day was alive with longshoremen loading and unloading sacks, but at night it was quiet. The Yoshiwara visitor could note how the castle was well provided for, and that its providers had now been allowed to take their well-earned rest. The man, wide awake, was out of kilter, and his night would have no respite.

The concept of 'awe' (*osore*) meant that government sites were hardly ever depicted, and even the shogunal storehouses had to be treated with circumspection. Pictures offer only vague shapes concealed by haze (illus. 100). Where possible, the shogunate actually did hide its structures, behind gates or with evergreen trees. The Kuramae wharves were all but invisible from the city. But they could be viewed from the river. Planted in the middle of the rice wharves was an evergreen tree. The shogunate mostly used pines, being robust and long-living and since they also imparted the figurative meanings of fortitude and permanence – governmental ideals. Just one pine was planted centrally at the wharves, since more would impede business. This tree was peculiar: it was upside down. Popularly known as the

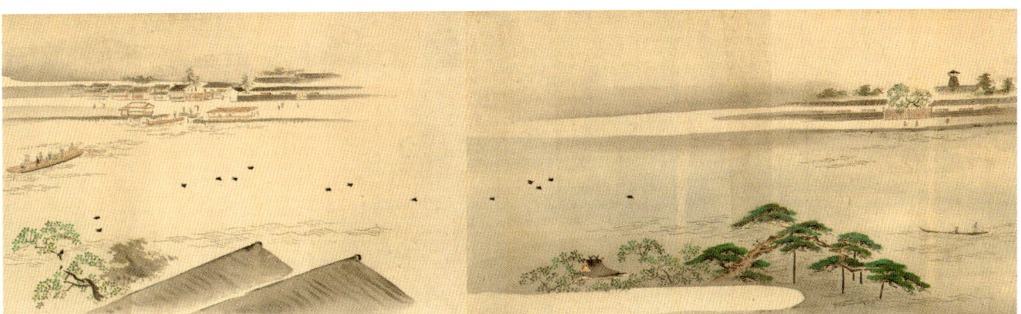

'top and tail pine', or, to paraphrase, 'topsy-turvy pine' (*shubi no matsu*), its branches bent out across the water and leaned downwards. Its head was truly below its heels. It might even have somersaulted had stakes not been placed in the water to restrain it. A more perfect icon of inversion could not have been hoped for. The man was on his upside-down way to sexual excitement and improper behaviour. But the shogunate accepted this and had licensed the Yoshiwara. Those who passed in darkness might wonder if the tree would right itself in the morning, when the workforce was back and proper norms reasserted. There was a pun in the tree, for *shubi* also meant '[amorous] success'.[3]

Slightly further on, on the opposite bank, was another tree, a sweet acorn (*shii*). It graced the mansion of a very old warrior family, the Matsura. Boar's-tusk boats took night-time bearings from the tree and 'dashed like an arrow towards it'.[4] The tree 'was even higher than the fame of the daimyo', and it was 'definitely more fun to see on the right than on the left', that is, when heading upstream to the quarter, rather than heading home.[5] The pine was bent, but the sweet acorn was tall and erect. Sweet acorns have symbolism too, based on a pun. When the medieval general Minamoto no Yorimasa was promoted to the third court rank, he wrote a commemorative verse, punning his old grade of 'fourth rank' on its homophone 'sweet acorn' (*shii*). The poem expressed Yoshimasa's decision to defer fleeing the world, as he had wished to do, because of this attainment:

The tidings of my elevation –
Were it not for them,
Just staying at fourth rank
Just gathering sweet acorns
Beneath trees,
Is how I would pass through the world.[6]

An anonymous senryū referred to Yoshimasa's verse, producing the following:

That sweet acorn!
Fourth rank indeed!
I am now heading to
A hidden village.[7]

Yoshimasa had sought the obscure life, but renounced it. Yet the Yoshiwara visitor is going precisely there, since the 'stockade' was known as the 'hidden village' (*kakure-zato*), and that is where the Edo person is going.

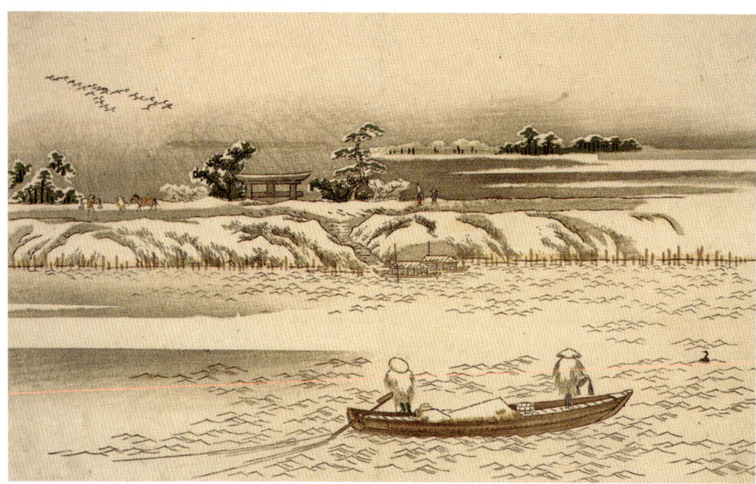

101 Kitagawa Utamaro, 'The Banks of Sumida River in Snow', from *The Silver World* (*Gin sekai*), 1790, colour printed book. The gate of the Mimeguri shrine seems to have dropped down behind the embankment. This part of the river was almost always shown in winter.

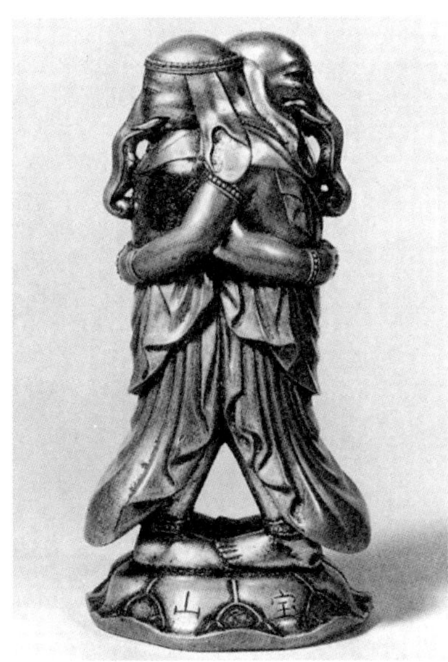

102 Hōzan Tankai, *Shōden (Kankiten and his Consort Embracing)*, 1686, gilt brass. The divinity of matrimonial love was depicted as two elephants (signifying capaciousness) in tight embrace with another. The icon of the Edo temple was (and remains) secret, and cannot be shown, but it probably resembles that reproduced here.

The next pertinent markers were some distance on, when the boat came to the Buddhist institutions in the north-east. Just beyond the Asakusa Kannon (Sensō-ji) were two smaller precincts. Having travelled the seam of the Two States and gone between the two trees, the traveller now ran a gauntlet of Buddhist temple and Shinto shrine. On the right-hand side of the river was Mimeguri Shrine ('three turns', or ritual circumambulations). Its principal icon was the fox-god, Inari; importantly, foxes were thought capable of metamorphosis. They entered the human world, plain to see, but also disappeared into other worlds. Mimeguri was a confused and confusing place. Like foxes, the shrine itself seemed to come and go. Its structure was normal, but an earthen bank had been raised in front to prevent flooding. Viewed from the water, only the crossbars of the shrine gate could be seen (illus. 101). One senryū verse put it like this:

You'd think
The gate had
Sunk into the embankment.[8]

Back on the left-hand side, of the many temples depending on the Asakusa Kannon, only one was right on the waterfront, and this was dedicated to Shōden, divinity of matrimonial felicity, whose iconography fused male and female forms, not humans, but elephants (denoting capaciousness) (illus. 102). This was consequential for the Yoshiwara visitor, whose marriage bonds or future wedding vows were inevitably loosening. The traveller would recall with anxiety how his trip began under trailing willows. The Shōden hall was on an eminence, Matsuchi Hill, which had once been taller but had been partially levelled to provide earthen flood embankments. As with the shrine gate, this temple seemed to be dropping out of view. To the denizen of the night, religious demands made by the 'fixed' world were slipping away.

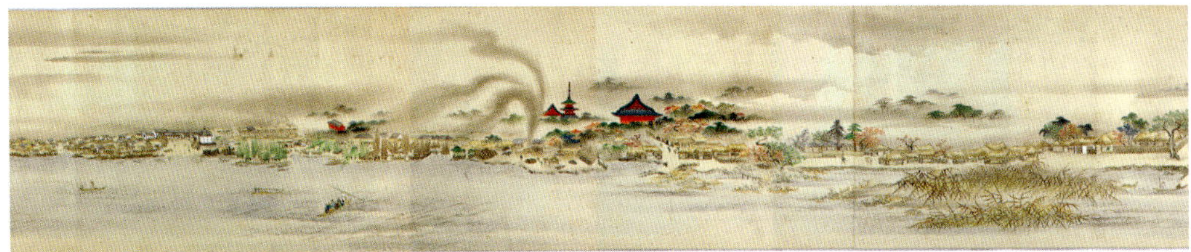

Something mysterious happened to the traveller here. Having become unpicked and inverted along the route, he died. Asakusa was where most Edo families had their graves, and many people made trips here to tend the tombs on designated days. Just beyond the temple were Edo's tile kilns. By shogunal command, all buildings had tiled roofs as a fire precaution. Making them was dangerous, so production was confined to outside the city centre, where water was plentiful and clay and finished tiles could be moved by boat. On holidays, the area was quiet, but on workday evenings, the furnaces were still alight, with billows of smoke filling the air and sparks visible. When combined with the graves, where tonight's visitor would in due course go, it might seem that he had come to the gaping mouth of hell (illus. 103). An anonymous floating-world writer noted in 1678, 'As it will be in the next world, the smoke of evanescence billows. But what of that? You don't think it impinges on you . . . you tremble with expectation . . . what folly!'[9]

A medieval literary genre known as 'taking the road' (*michiyuki*) recounted the capture of a great warrior and his conveyance to a place of execution. Such stories had protagonists pass a sequence of famous places along a road that was not geographically possible but which encompassed sites that invoked his tragic plight. The genre ends with death. A trip to the Yoshiwara was a parody *michiyuki*, part humorous but part deadly serious. The points along the trip were like 'poetic pillows', carrying salient meanings, the dark boat ride linking them in a non-geographical way. And now he was dead.

Asakusa was also the site of an ancient ferry that crossed the River Sumida, as mentioned in the tenth-century *Tales of Ise* discussed in

103 Kano Kyūei, 'Asakusa Kannon and the Tile Furnesses', from *Views along the Length of the Sumida River* (*Sumida-gawa chōryū zukan*), c. 1750–72, set of three handscrolls, ink and colours on paper. As an official Kano artist, Kyūei would not depict 'floating world' topics, but he could show wholesome river views, as here. Asakusa had the main commoner temple, and nearby was the production centre for the all-important roof tiles, seen here in smoke rising from the furnaces.

Chapter Five. It was probably plying as the traveller's 'boar's-tusk boat' drew close. There were various theories why the protagonist of the *Ise* stories came to be here, so far from his home in the capital. An authoritative commentarial tradition asserted that he was in exile. It was not stated in the text, but exegetes said he had engaged in an inappropriate sexual liaison. This theory derived from verses purporting to be from the man and his lover contained in the *Anthology of Verses Ancient and Modern* (*Kokin waka-shū*) of 905. The woman's verse reads,

> Did you come,
> Or did I go?
> I cannot tell.
> Was it a dream or not
> Did I wake or sleep?[10]

The man responds with similar equivocation,

> I have strayed
> In the darkness
> Of a gloomy heart.
> Whether it was dream or waking,
> People of the world decide.[11]

The significance of this spot on the Great River, the only place where classical literature said anything about what was later to become the Edo area, was generated from a lustful impropriety, which the verses interrogate but conclude with utterly self-serving responses. The Edo traveller, too, now 'dead', has no one to answer to as his own boat pressed on athwart the ferry's path.

The ferry left the Shōden hall and arrived by the Mokubo-ji, a temple that had grown up around a grave widely known because it featured in the medieval nō play *Sumida-gawa*, also mentioned in the previous chapter. The play tells of a woman who came here, mad and distracted because her son had been taken away as a slave. As the boatman rows her over, the women sees a grave and realizes it is her son's, killed by slave-drivers. The ferry plied between Asakusa, a place of modern death, spouting ash and flames, and the Mokubo-ji, with its antique, literary death associations. To capture this sense, depictions of the river at this point often show it in winter, with thick snow (illus. 90 and 91). Migrating birds were known to gather in winter, so there was a legitimacy to the associations. In *Ise*, the man had seen 'capital-birds' here, as also recalled in the play. A senryū ties this all together:

The tile makers,
Making out as if they know
The capital-bird![12]

Hokusai brought the two together too, with a two-page illustration in a guidebook to the Sumida (illus. 104). Here was the sequence: the Willow Bridge alerted the visitor to the fearsomeness of slighted female passion, and the Shōden to regulated marital ties; the sites mentioned in the *Tales of Ise*, and their associated verses, pointed to the bitter fruits of broken codes, and then the Mokubo-ji invoked the tenacity of women. Lest this seem frightening, we recall that the shrine and temple were sinking underground, and the Yoshiwara visitor was also 'dead', no longer a 'person of this world'. In his posthumous darkness, fixed rules recede.

The boat pulled in to the shore for the man to alight at San'ya, where an inlet allowed protection from the current. A bridge over it led back to the tile furnaces, and there was a teashop here called The Capital Bird. He got out of the bobbing boat, no longer an Edo man, but a person in suspension.

❧

If the river journey displaced civic norms, then progression along the next leg, from San'ya to the Yoshiwara, afforded a realignment. Because of flooding, a raised path had been built from the river to the 'stockade'. It crossed over a marshy territory, an in-between zone of neither land nor water. The path was wide, allowing for movement in two directions, and so was known as the *nihon-zutsumi*, or 'Two-track Embankment', in exactly the same pun as at Nihon-bashi.[13] However, while Edo's core was both 'two carriageways' and 'Japan', binding the land together, this path was a curious analogy: it bound death, at the riverside, to a rebirth that was about to come. 'Japan' because the access road to the joys of the Yoshiwara was constructed by order of the shogunate.

The distance was short enough to walk, but it was preferable to hire a palanquin. Hundreds waited at San'ya, and boar's-tusk boats and palanquins were the twin vehicles of this passage. Both kinds of vehicle were peculiar to the Yoshiwara trip. Boar's-tusks were scarcely used other than for coming here, and the palanquins, too, were of a special type not found in town. The common Edo chair was an open platform slung from a pole; important personages had enclosed ones to prevent them being seen. But because of cold and embarrassment, Yoshiwara palanquins alone were provided with sides. The boat had been isolating and silencing, but the palanquin effected another kind of removal. The person was shut up within it as they never were in town, swinging towards somewhere they could not see. This was exactly what happens after death. The deceased is greeted by Kannon, the same divinity worshipped at Asakusa, who will proffer a lotus in which to enclose them, and take them away for rebirth in the Pure Land. The Yoshiwara would be that paradise. Another senryū pairs this with the tile furnaces:

> The roads to paradise
> And hell
> Divide at San'ya Bridge.[14]

The Two-track Embankment also had a nickname, the 'Road of Transformations' (*bakemono no michi*).[15] At the end of it, a man was not the same man he had been before. But more precisely, Edo's most

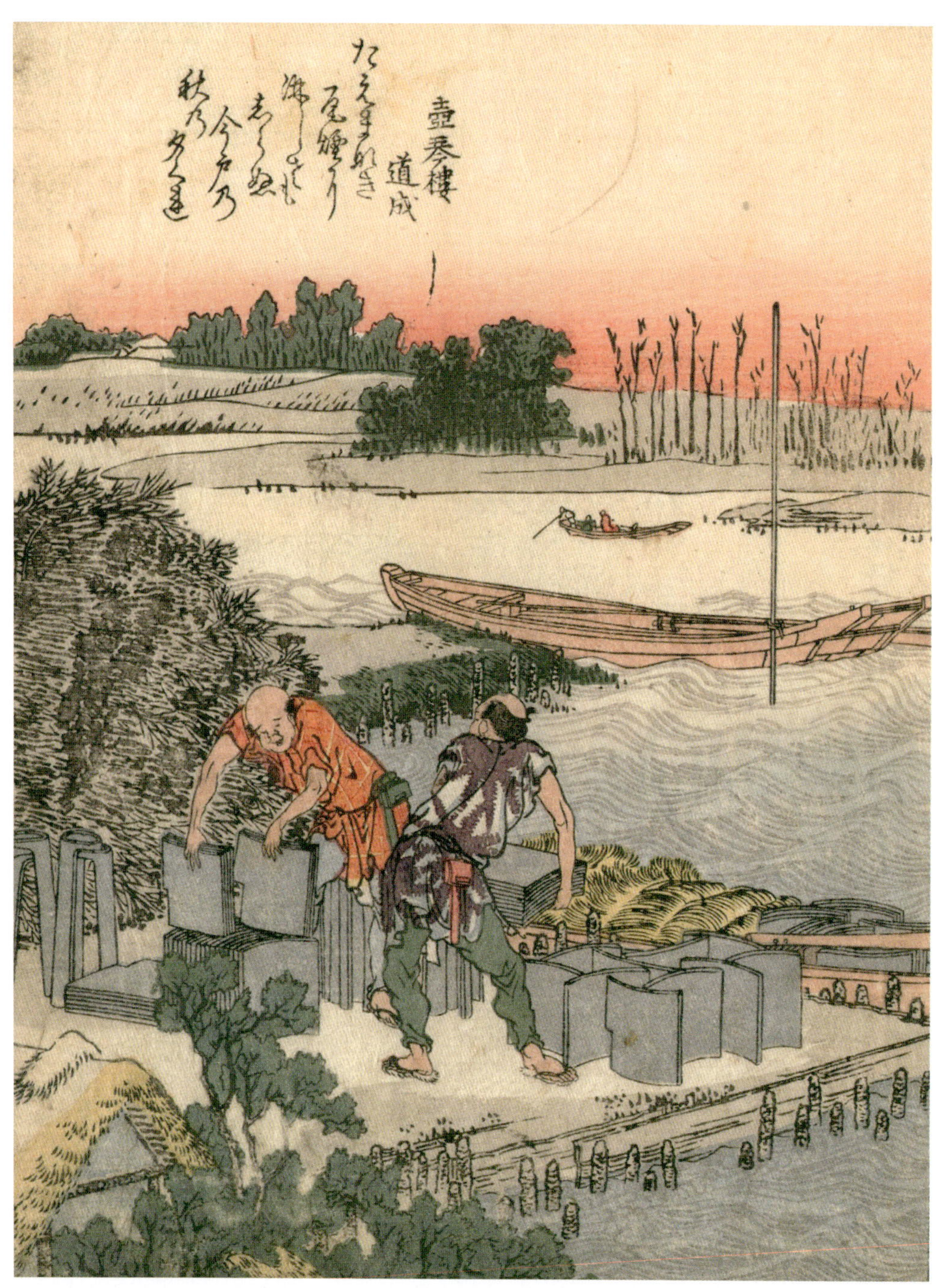

104 Katsushika Hokusai, 'Evening Smoke at Imado', from *Pictures of Both Banks of the Sumida River* (*Ehon Sumidagawa Ryōgan ichiran*, c. 1804), colour printed book. The tile furnaces operate late into the evening, while a 'capital-bird' is about to drop into the river.

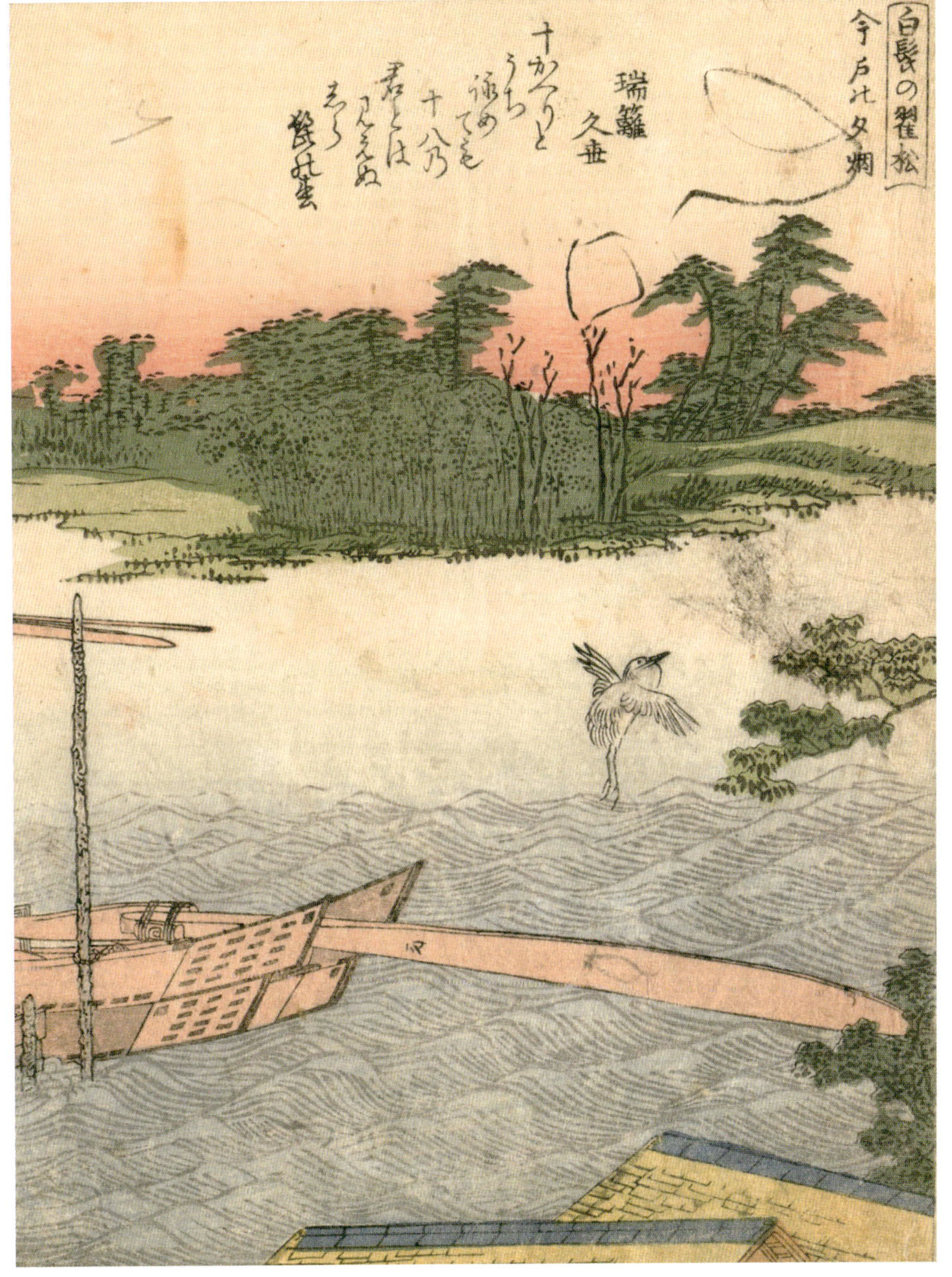

白髭の雛松
今戸ゟ夕烱
瑞籬
久壺
十かつりと
うち
詠めても
十分乃
君とは
つきえぬ
もう
鶯氏生

concrete system of human classification had fallen away. The danger of brawls meant that military hardware was banned from the Yoshiwara. Along the embankment were huts serving as left-luggage offices. A military-class man had to deposit his weapons, to be collected in the morning. Men left their boats as members of prescribed, inherited-status groups. On the embankment they lost this and became just *people*.

The military/commoner division was the primary definition of Tokugawa social existence. The second division was between clerical and lay. Monks were seen all over cities, recognizable by their vestments and shaven heads. They were banned from the Yoshiwara (male–male sex was permitted, but intercourse with women was thought to foster karmic links). Yet with so many temples in this part of town, inevitably some monks sought ways to enter. Vestments could therefore be checked in at the huts too. A monk's absence of hair was less easily concealed, but since physicians also shaved their heads, monks swapped their cassocks for medical gowns. Ribald comments are not hard to find on the furtively unfrocked.[16] One takes the form of a parody of a well-known verse by Bashō. The poet had written of lying in bed between the Asakusa Kannon and the Kan'ei-ji, and of hearing a temple bell. He had wondered,

> In a cloud of blossoms
> A sounding bell – is it from Ueno?
> Is it from Asakusa?[17]

The parody had it:

> Along the Embankment
> A walking physician – is he from Ueno?
> Is he from Asakusa?[18]

He was in reality a monk from the Kannon or Kan'ei-ji temples.

A more sustained parody on the warping effects of the Nihon Embankment was offered by Sharaku-sai Manri in a novella of 1771,

Modern Foibles (*Tōsei anabanashi*). Manri sets the transformations in an absurdist entomological context:

> Consider the transformations taking place in the world today. We find larvae sprouting wings and flying off as mosquitoes, or maggots growing wings and taking off as flies. Also, caterpillars change into butterflies. Courtesans transform into ordinary women [allowing them to exit the Yoshiwara] and head off for a spree. Men transform into women and get known as 'female role experts' [at kabuki]. Military people drop off their two swords at a boatmen's hut and transform into normal townsmen. Monks change into physicians.[19]

A butterfly may be freer than a larva, but once the larva has lost its carapace, it does not live long. The Yoshiwara, as an inversion of reality, is not an alternative to it, and its patterns of pleasure are not sustainable in the long term.

Hiroshige depicted the embankment in his series *One Hundred Famous Views of Edo* (*Edo meisho hyakkei*) of 1856–9. Men scurry on foot or are conveyed in palanquins between a row of huts (illus. 105). The embankment runs in a liminal way, through neither water nor land, while geese fly overhead across a bright moon, indicating autumn, which is the season of change. Just as pictures of Asakusa to San'ya almost always show the place in winter, the embankment is almost always shown in autumn. Although Hiroshige does not do so, many depictions include rain, drenching the male (yang) travellers with the female (yin) element.

Autumn is associated with maple leaves, and along the embankment was a noted temple, the Shōtō-ji ('temple of the true lamp'). It had a number of maple trees in its precinct, which attracted many tourists when the foliage turned red. Again, there was a logic to the convention, a senryū suggesting how the embankment was best conceptualized as a place of autumn, and cannot be condoned out of season:

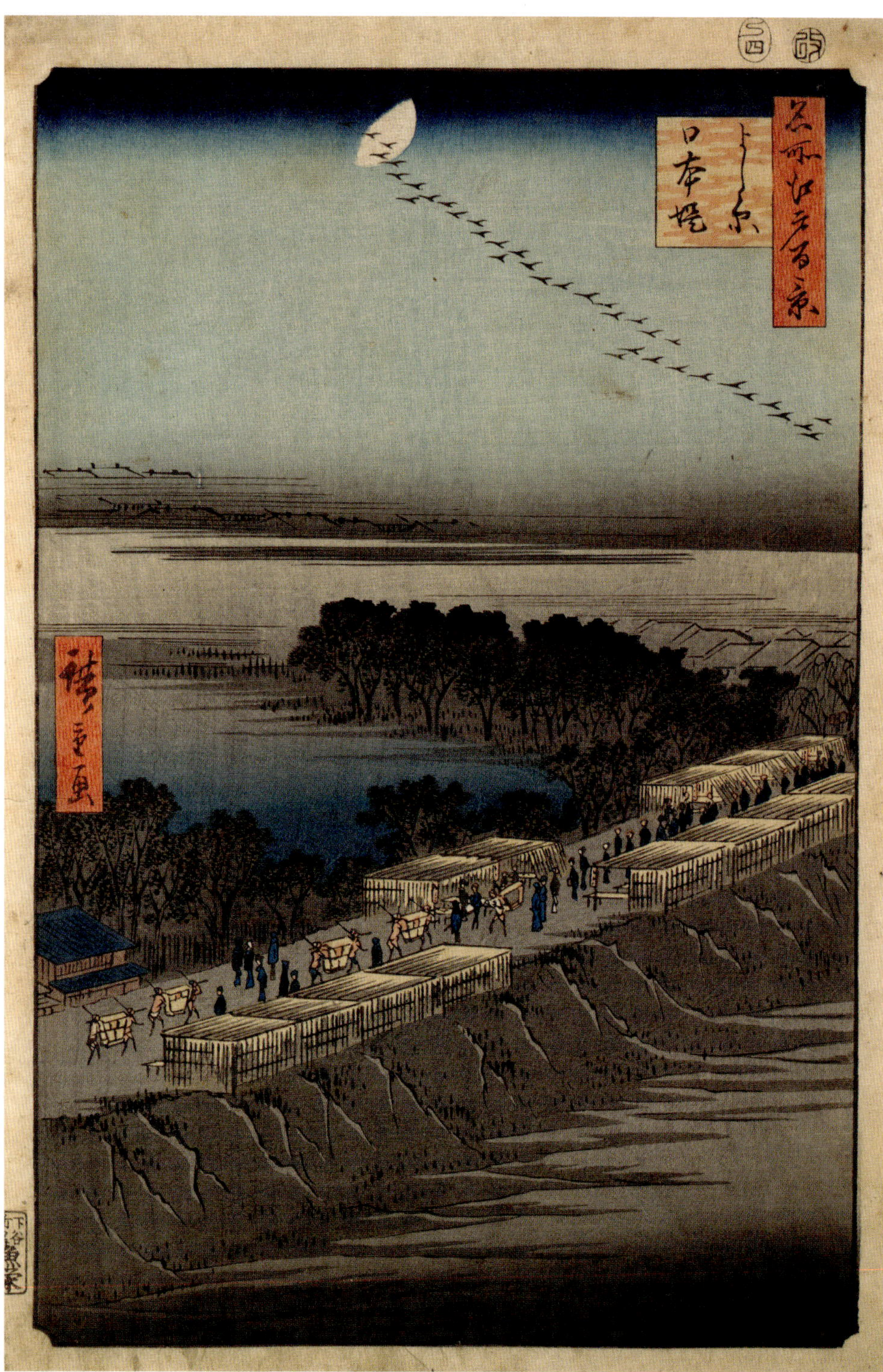

The Shōtō-ji
What, dead leaves?
You pass straight on.[20]

A path known as 'Clothing Slope' (*emon-zaka*) descended from the embankment to the left. Sumptuary laws forbade luxurious garments in Edo, but these were tolerated in the Yoshiwara. Here a traveller might pull out a fancy tunic, or reverse what he was wearing to reveal a gorgeous lining. People entered the quarter in their own preferred apparel, not what the authorities stipulated for them. They might literally be their formal self turned inside out.

Clothing Slope traced the form of a chevron or dogleg. This replicated entrances to government checkpoints found on major highways, where barrier approaches were designed to prevent them being stormed. The dogleg was an indication of progression from open space to something overseen, or from freedom to surveillance. The person arriving at the Yoshiwara felt the weight of an impending bureaucratic nightmare, and the sensation was accentuated by the Yoshiwara's Great Gate, with a fence around it, which did rather resemble a checkpoint. The Yoshiwara operated on sufferance, and it could be closed down. But once inside, this flipped, and instead of a place of special severity, the man found a space of special permission.

Clothing Slope and the ground that led up to the gate was 50 *ken* (0.5 km) in length and known as Fifty-*ken* Street. Proverbially, the distance from earth to paradise was said to be 'fifty times one million leagues'.[21] Here a man made his ultimate transformation in a much-truncated way. As it was forbidden to ride a palanquin through the Yoshiwara gate, this was where he descended. His lotus bud had opened and he found himself in paradise.

To the right of the entrance was a signboard, like many about town, detailing regulations and directives. This one posted the bylaws of the quarter. It was the final reminder that the Yoshiwara operated subject to conditions and that its licence could be revoked. Opposite this, on the left, was a single willow. It bore the name Looking-backwards Willow

105 Utagawa Hiroshige, 'Nihon Embankment at Yoshiwara', from the series *One Hundred Famous Views of Edo* (*Meisho Edo hyakkei, Yoshiwara, Nihonzutsumi*), 1857, multicoloured woodblock print. The embankment led to the red-light district, and Hiroshige shows it with geese flying across an autumn moon, accentuating its nickname of 'path of transformations'. Pleasure-seekers walk or are carried, while booths are set up to look after their possessions. The Yoshiwara is seen in the middle ground.

(*migaeri yanagi*). In the morning, visitors would turn repeatedly back as they wended their way to San'ya. The trip, which had begun under willows, ended with one too, though this took its relevance from the return trip. It reminded the man even before he entered the quarter that he would have to leave it and return to a place where women were more 'sincere'.

The flat stretch between the slope and the Great Gate accommodated a row of shops, about a dozen on either side. In the middle on the left was Edo's foremost dealer in floating-world books and prints, Tsutaya Jūzaburō, an innovative newcomer whose publications were industry benchmarks. Tsuta-jū, as he was known, operated here from the mid-1770s, and in 1782 he bought the rights to a biannual compendium of the Yoshiwara, published since 1718, the *Yoshiwara saiken* (Yoshiwara Guide). Acquisition of this made Tsuta-jū the chief circulator of the quarter's information and mythology. Visitors leafed through his latest volume, consuming its data, before passing through the gate and taking in the surroundings empirically. The location had limitations, for not all men came here, and no women did. Tsuta-jū therefore secured a shop in Edo proper, greatly expanding access. This had the effect of breaking the cordon between the floating world and the fixed. The shogunate had expelled the quarter, but now it swept back, through printed books and images. No little consternation was caused to the authorities, especially by the thought that their sanctions should so easily be collapsed. One senior official objected that it had become the norm for mothers to dress their daughters in Yoshiwara fashions which, 'though pretty, make the girls look like trainee courtesans from the pleasure district'.[22]

However, finally, the visitor was at the Great Gate. With Asakusa and San'ya set always in winter and the embankment in autumn, the Yoshiwara was shown always in spring (illus. 106). This was the best season (summer was too hot), and also the time of cherry blossoms. The Yoshiwara was quintessentially represented by that flower, the icon of female beauty. Among the myriad pictures of the Yoshiwara, hardly any are set in a season other than spring, or without cherry

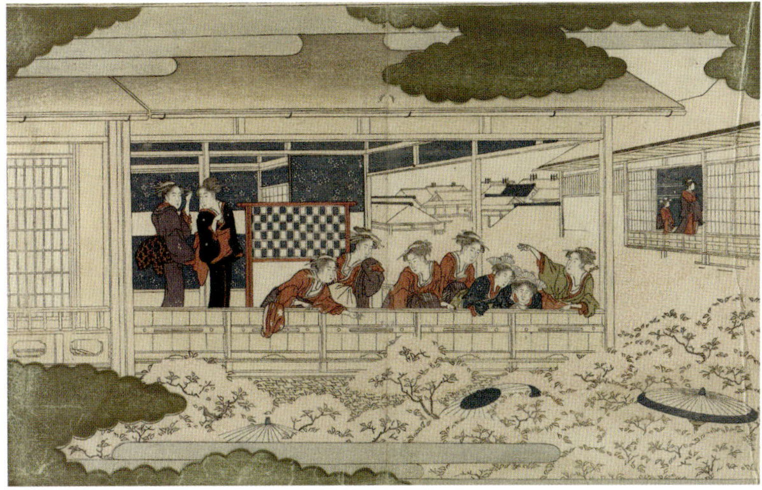

106 Kitagawa Utamaro, 'Viewing the Parade Down the Main Street, Nakanochō, in the Yoshiwara Pleasure Quarter', from *Statue of Fugen* (*Fugen-zu*), 1790, colour printed book. Although not fun for people employed there, the Yoshiwara was projected as a place of universal happiness, and as such was always shown at the best time of year, with cherry blossoms out.

blossoms. Pictures can take liberties with fact. But nature copies art. The main street of the Yoshiwara was planted with cherry trees, but only in springtime. They were dug up and removed when the blossoms had gone, to be brought back the next year. People within the quarter never had to see a cherry tree out of season, even in reality. Hence,

Year on year, age on age,
To pull the custom in,
They plant them out.[23]

In the 1780s, a floating-world artist, Chōbunsai Eishi, who was prominent in Tsuta-jū's circle, thought up the idea of handscrolls showing the route to the Yoshiwara as a continuous composition. Images of the Great River, with its sites and diversions, had been made before, but those were for general audiences. Eishi made these too, but he also produced a subsection showing the Willow Bridge to San'ya, then the Nihon Embankment to Clothing Slope and the Great Gate, right up to the Yoshiwara boudoirs. (Some details have been shown above (see illus. 98 and 100).)

The figures making the transit in Eishi's pictures are often not human, but so-called Lucky Gods (*fukujin*). These divinities featured as

New Year ornaments, so Eishi may have intended his works as presents, to be exchanged between bordellos and clients or between spendthrift male friends in that season. Alternatively, his point may have been to make pictures equally enjoyable to either status group, since military and townspeople, visibly different until they got to the quarter itself, might not identify with a mismatched picture.

The trip from a person's home or place of work in Edo to the Great Gate must have taken some two hours. In Edo time-telling, the main division was a *koku* (also called a *toki*). One koku lasted about two modern hours, so a day and night were made up of twelve koku, rather than 24 hours. Six koku were allotted to daylight and six to night, each announced by a bell sounding the koku number, taking the lead from Nihon-bashi. Koku were subdivided into sixths, with clappers struck roughly every twenty minutes.

A visitor to the Yoshiwara would leave central Edo during the last daylight koku, or 9 p.m. to 11 p.m. They had to arrive before the Great Gate closed, at the beginning of the first night-time koku, at 11 p.m., as it would not do to be shut out (though in practice a postern was kept open for the tardy). So that men were not tempted to abscond from the city too early, the Yoshiwara, which twisted everything, also twisted time.[24] The last daylight koku began in the normal way, but its four internal clappers were omitted, making time seem elastic. This long stretch of silence was broken only at the end of the koku, when the bell rang. But it did not sound the number for the next koku (the first of darkness), but rather sounded the last koku of daylight a second time. In modern terms, 9 p.m. to 11 p.m. felt loose, its subdivisions removed, and then it replayed, occupying what should have been the period from 11 p.m. to 1 a.m. The omitted period was made up for by leaping a koku forward deep in the night – one reason why men felt nights in the quarter were too short. Cogently for our purposes, since the typical trip to the Yoshiwara took two modern hours, a person would leave home or work with the bells sounding, and arrive with them sounding the same time. The journey above, so replete with meaning, thus occurred in no time at all. Then the

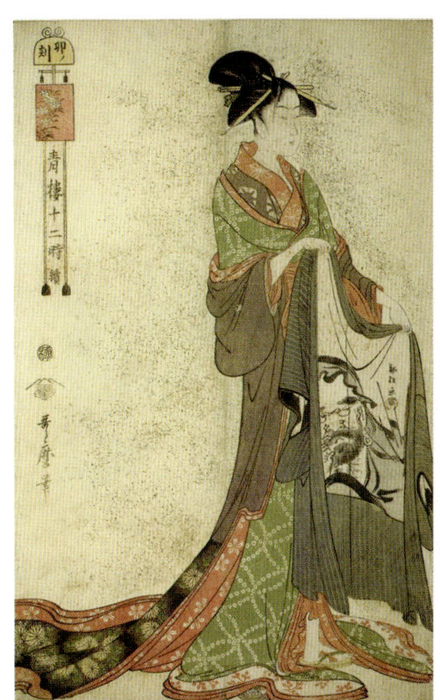

107 Kitagawa Utamaro, 'Hour of the Hare [5 a.m. to 7 a.m.]', from the series *The Twelve Hours in Yoshiwara* (*Seirō jūni toki*), c. 1794, multicoloured woodblock print. It is morning and an exhausted sex worker hands her client back his tunic. Inside is a depiction of Daruma, the founder of Zen. The print proposes that a night in the quarter imparts a kind of Enlightenment.

gate was locked, severing contact between the floating world and the fixed.

Through the gate, within the Yoshiwara, life took on new forms, but pleasures were still ordered. Civic laws might be suspended and hierarchies obscured, but self-generated codes were firmly in place. No one wished to be branded an ignoramus, or lout (*yabo*). To become knowledgeable in the mores required frequent visits, and those who attained this were called *tsūjin* ('those who made the trip'). Though tsūjin might not have expressed it in the same way, they knew all the details of what has been discussed above, and also what went on inside the gate, which some called the Land of Yoshiwara (Yoshiwara-koku), as if it were an autonomous region in the shogun's realm, like a daimyo domain. It was Japan nonetheless, only under distortion. Legislation required Yoshiwara architecture to be of a standard kind, and its streets looked little different from those of Edo proper.[25] But to aficionados, and to those who consumed its visual and textual fantasies, the Yoshiwara was a place unto itself. Maps were even printed plotting it over a delineation of Japan.[26] Such a topography was useless to orient the visitor, but it postulated the courtesan district as a distinct type of reality.

☙

In about 1795, Tsuta-jū published a set of prints by the great floating-world master Kitagawa Utamaro entitled *Twelve Toki* [hours] *in the Blue Towers* (*Seiryō jūni toki*). 'Blue towers' was a poetic term for courtesan districts, here the Yoshiwara. The prints span a day and a night, and of interest is the image for the last koku of darkness (5 a.m. to 7 a.m.), which Utamaro names from the zodiac as the toki of the rabbit (illus. 107). It depicts next-morning home-goings.

No customer is shown in the picture, and so the (male) print buyer can imagine himself in that role. A courtesan hands back his tunic.

Utamaro's women are always impeccable, but this one has a lock of hair falling forwards, which is as far as Utamaro will go in showing her exhausted state. The man's garment reveals a luxurious lining painted with the figure of Bodhidharma (called Daruma in Japanese, founder of Zen, already encountered in Harunobu's print, see illus. 99). After a night in the Yoshiwara, Utamaro suggests, visitors reach a state of detachment from this-worldly cares akin to Enlightenment, even to the degree that Bodhidharma attained. This realization is internalized, as it were, and the man hides the knowledge that 'floating' has taught him, returning to the city and the world of work.

The visitor going home would walk up Clothing Slope, looking back at the willow. He found San'ya's furnaces in full operation as he boarded a boar's-tusk boat and lay down, to sleep his way back to Edo. The trip upstream so full of meaning would be unseen on return. He would be unable to check if the topsy-turvy pine now stood upright.

> The morning boar's-tusk:
> Bodhidharma,
> And a *parinirvana* too.[27]

The man had travelled up in the *agura* posture of Buddhist meditation, but in the quarter he had learned the meaning of impermanence, as Bodhidharma had, but even more, he now adopts the pose of the Buddha, who is said to have been recumbent when he entered 'complete extinction' (*parinirvana*). Again, another senryu:

> The out-going boar's-tusk carried an aspirant;
> The returning one has
> The Buddha in Nirvana![28]

When the boat arrived in central Edo, the man would be awakened by the waterman. He opened his eyes beneath gently drooping willow branches.

Epilogue
From Edo to Tokyo

In 1867 Tokugawa Yoshinobu left Edo, no longer shogun. In November he had travelled to the capital, using Nijō Castle for the first time in two hundred years, and surrendered his office to the dairi. A powerful faction in Japan wanted a Western-style king, sitting on a Western-style throne, thinking this the best way to deal with the menaces and challenges of modernity. Similar revisions were afoot elsewhere. The British had just deposed the king of Burma, stripping Mindon of half of his lands and in 1852 consigning him to a rump of his country as 'king of Ava'. In Siam, King Mongkut was playing his cards better, offering a template of possible shift. Modernity was not only transforming politics east of Suez. In Europe, too, elites were reinventing themselves. The first king of Italy was crowned in 1861. A kingdom of Germany (called an Empire) was realized a decade later, in 1871. Japan was following an internationally set practice. For non-European nations, the issue was very urgent. Without change, there was the threat of colonization, even annexation.

The Tokugawa had been fully aware of this threat from the early 1840s. The shogun was well placed to become a new-style Japanese king, not least as Westerners translated 'shogun' as 'Emperor of Japan', and had done so for centuries. Yoshinobu, and his predecessor,

Iemochi, had made singular efforts to meet international expectations and adapt the country to what a modern state should be, but there were objections. The Tokugawa had been in office for 254 years and 15 incumbencies. This almost exactly mirrored the previous, Muromachi shogunate, which had lasted 240 years and also 15 generations, and well exceeded the first, Kamakura shogunate, which had lasted 148 years and 9 incumbencies. Was it not time for the Tokugawa to withdraw from the field? They had many enemies. The daimyo in the western regions, who had never been fully accepted and were mistrusted as 'outer lords' (*tozama*), argued against shogunal continuity and for something more radical. These daimyo controlled precisely the regions where the European ships were now arriving. The most powerful state in those waters, the United Kingdom, was neutral, but British traders in Shanghai and elsewhere began running guns to the anti-Tokugawa factions. Yoshinobu, seeing how matters were lining up, and not wanting to start a civil war – the whole point of shoguns was to prevent them – with surprising grace, resigned. No shogunate lasts forever: history had made this plain. They knew themselves to operate within a limited timeframe. Yoshinobu simply bowed out.

The 'outer lords' had already selected who was to be their new king instead. It was to be none other than the dairi. But the 36-year-old Osahito, living his life of ritual and poetry in the capital, was not sure that he was able to take this on. It is generally assumed that he was gently euthanized, making way for his more pliant son, the fifteen-year-old Mutsuhito.

In 1868 Mutsuhito became king. However, as the shogun had been known as 'Emperor', the title was carried across. Any lesser rank would look like a degradation. (Queen Victoria was pressing to be allowed to use the title Empress, against the will of Parliament, who in 1877 conceded that she might be Empress of India, but not of the United Kingdom. The German king could be Emperor (*Kaiser*) too, and there were emperors in Ethiopia, Brazil, Russia and elsewhere.) To the Japanese themselves, he had been termed the dairi, but that was a medieval label, used after the shoguns had assumed real control.

The classical title was *tennō*, and this was revived, though it had been unused for well over a millennium. Foreigners found it hard to pronounce (there may have been other reasons too), so the tennō was also called by another, even more obscure ancient term, but one that rolled off the tongue well, *mikado*. It was euphonic and memorable, so left untranslated, used alongside 'emperor'. The title also fitted the British Imperial preference for retaining romantic, exotic terms for foreign rulers. Mikados could colourfully join the list of emirs, khans, shahs, nizams and rajas.

By convention, Japanese rulers are not known by their given names. The shoguns named in this book would not have been addressed in so bald a way at the time. More lofty designations were used, or posthumous titles. This was the same for the dairis. Osahito, now deceased, was called Kōmei, and as 'tennō' replaced 'dairi', it also came to be used as a suffix (dairi had the suffix *-in*). Dead Osahito became Kōmei-tennō. On the succession of his son, Mutsuhito, it was decided that a system of regal names should be introduced (also a lapsed antique practice). The emperor would have a designation while alive, which would be co-terminous with his period in office, and also his posthumous name. Mutsuhito's designation was Meiji, literally 'bright government'. He was the Meiji Emperor – note, not the Emperor Meiji, as it was never his name. The lustrous label was also calculated to make Edo a dark age.

Thus 1868 became the first year of Meiji. Some shogunal diehards would not accept the start of a new reign. They began to organize resistance, holing themselves up in Ueno by the great Tokugawa mortuary temple of Kan'ei-ji. The Meiji troops shelled it. Defence was hopeless, and some three hundred people died. The main result of what is now known as the Bōshin War was to incinerate the Kan'ei-ji utterly and to destroy the shogunal graves, the preservation of which was one of the Tokugawa loyalists' goals. In the now vacant space of the Kan'ei-ji precincts, the Meiji regime erected a national museum as a repository of the glorious and beautiful artefacts of the past. Items that had remained in use shortly before were now categorized as patrimony, or 'heritage', without further utilitarian value. A line was drawn across history. A large part of these aesthetic materials was Buddhist. The Meiji regime saw Buddhism as an impediment. About 40,000 temples were forcibly closed, with most of their possessions destroyed, generally in ways intended to be offensive. But where quality or antiquity could not be denied, pieces were removed to the museum. Also kept for display were items that might evince a historical role for what was now called the Imperial House (*kōshitsu*), as patrons. Whereas much of the European past was indeed the result of royal or aristocratic commissions, that of Japan was almost entirely shogunal, which compromised the Meiji narrative of a mikado who had been installed in 1868 but who had always been there, directing the nation, and was now 'restored' under modernism.

The Meiji Emperor left the capital and moved to Edo, now called Tokyo (properly Tōkyō), the 'eastern capital'. For a residence he took over the shogunal castle, which had suffered a conflagration some decades before and so did not reek too much of the two and a half centuries of the Tokugawa realm. The population of the city promptly halved. The shogunal entourage returned to its country towns, and migrant workers to the countryside. Open spaces once occupied by daimyo residences, in central locations, were readily available for institutions required of the new age, like railway stations, post offices, government ministries and embassies.

Grand buildings were now put up across Tokyo to meet modern expectations. Parts of the city came to resemble Yokohama, Shanghai, Rangoon (Yangon) and other colonized or annexed port cities. In Europe too, new cities were analogously being built as displays of change – in Britain, for example, Liverpool. It was Berlin that came closest, however, as a fast-developing capital. The German architectural practice Ende & Böckmann were invited to Japan to undertake a series of projects, their Landeshaus for West Prussia having been regarded as a masterpiece. Of their many designs for Tokyo, several were realized, using the same so-called German Neo-Renaissance style (illus. 108).

It was crucial for the Meiji state to create an environment that carried worldwide conviction. This could be done with Western-style

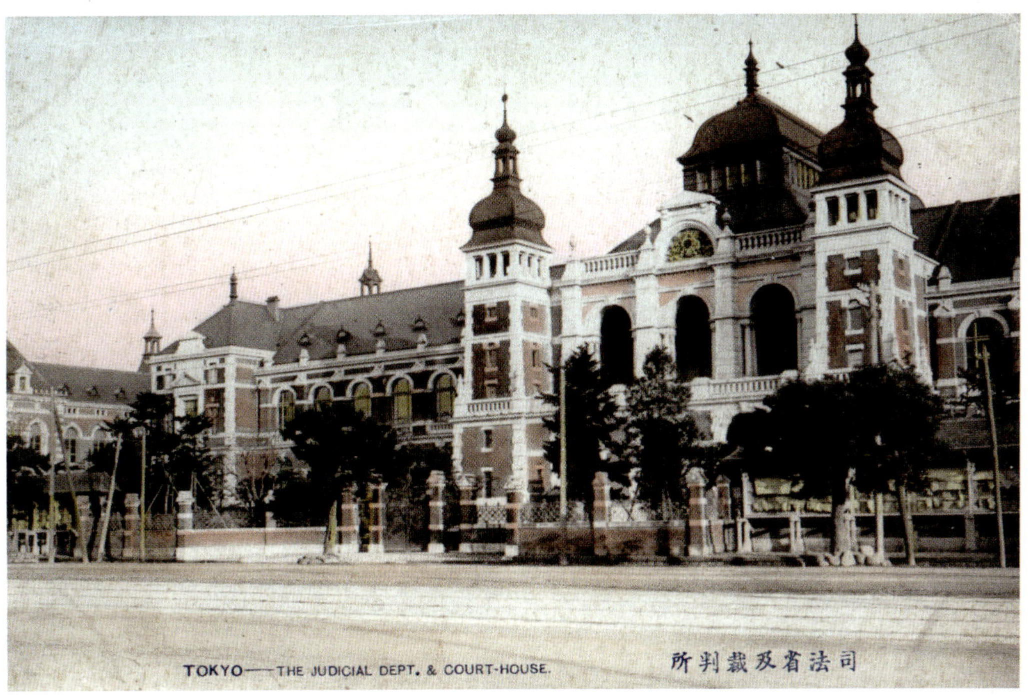

108 Ende & Böckmann, 'The Judicial Dept. & Court-House', Taishin-in, Kasumigaseki, c. 1910, postcard. One of many buildings required by the new Meiji government, constructed in the Western style (and here designed by German architects). These were erected over old shogunal compounds to expunge Tokugawa space.

buildings, but not necessarily with them alone. A certain Japanese character, however inflected, was understood to be part of the hue. This also fitted with prevailing norms. In many countries, the international mode was accompanied by pastiched elements derived from local architecture. German Neo-Renaissance was one example. The British and French had their equivalent in Neo-Gothic. One young specialist in this, named Josiah Conder, arrived in Japan in 1877, before Ende & Böckmann. He deployed a style devised by the British for colonial places – a sort of Neo-Gothic for foreign parts, called Indo-Saracenic. It had generic Islamic features appended to modern buildings. Japanese architecture was able to supply analogous motifs, though Conder claimed he could not find any, so he added Indo-Saracenic ornaments there too. His national museum, opened in 1882, had Mughal turrets over the entrance.

The Meiji regime was a forceful one, and it needed to be. But it arrived in tandem with a notion that few would find fault with.

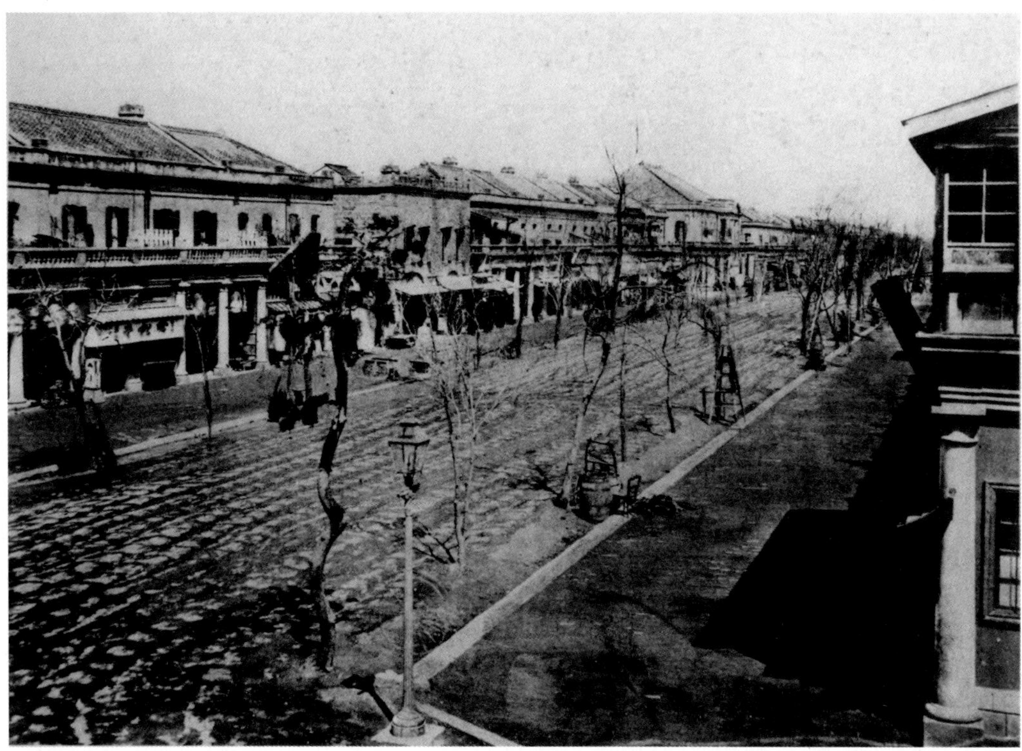

Although quite false in many ways, Europe, and certainly the USA, brought rhetorical notions of the fundamental equality of all people, which the Meiji authorities absorbed. The Edo social division of military (samurai) and commoner was thus abolished. A new Japanese peerage was imposed, which the USA did not have, but it was no more oppressive than the peerages of Europe after which its titles, costumes and leisure activities were modelled. For the mass of people, a kind of egalitarianism had indeed arrived. This was also imprinted on Tokyo. Nihon-bashi remained the city centre, and in due course, in 1911, it would be given another handsome bridge, which remains in place. The orientation of streets, however, changed. Edo had been accessed by palanquin, or often by water. Tokyo's iconic conveyance became the rickshaw. Though popularly thought of as Indian, the rickshaw was entirely Japanese, and its root, *jinrikisha*, 'man-powered vehicle', was

109 Unknown artist, *Ginza Bricktown with Trees*, photograph, c. 1890. The Ginza is still one of Tokyo's premier streets, but was first built to offer an experience of international shopping. It had the city's first public lighting. However, its architecture was unsuited to the Japanese climate.

a Meiji neologism. Horse-drawn trolleybuses were soon running too. After the status-bound world of Edo, in which even how and where one moved depended on heredity, the rickshaw, for general hire, and the collective omnibus were marks of the different age.

Tokyo acquired a purpose-built shopping street, not an old place in Edo but a new one, called the Ginza ('silver monopoly') (illus. 109). It was equipped with gaslights to emblematize – or actually to *be* – a place of enlightenment. The slang *gin-bura*, 'lingering on the Ginza', was coined, and Tokyo gained another quintessential feature of modern life, the any-age, any-class, any-gender *flâneur*. (*Bura-bura* and *flâner* mean to loiter, or hang about).

Edo did not disappear in an instant, but it dwindled and departed. Today it is gone. Meiji Tokyo is also gone, though some impressive structures have survived. In a few decades, there would be the horrific Great Kanto Earthquake of 1923, then the fire-bombing of the Second World War. Today the physical space of Tokyo has changed again for car use, with boulevards and raised highways. The city as it exists today is now almost entirely from the late twentieth and twenty-first centuries. But it had a deep, multi-layered past, and, no doubt, a multi-layered future too.

References

Introduction

1 For a comprehensive treatment of early Kyoto screens, see Matthew McKelway, *Capitalscapes: Folding Screens and Political Imagination in Late Medieval Kyoto* (Honolulu, HI, 2006).

2 Miyamoto Kenji, *Edo no onmyōshi: Tenkai no randosukeepu dezain* (Jinbun Shoin, 2001). More generally, see Suzuki Ikkei, *Onmyō-dō: jujitsu to mashin no sekai* (Kōdansha, 2002).

3 Matsudaira Sadanobu, *Taikan zakki* [1795–7], in *Zoku Nihon zuihitsu taisei*, vol. VI (Yoshikawa Kōbunkan, 1980), pp. 25–253: p. 43.

One The Ideal City

1 John E. Hill, *Through the Jade Gate to Rome: A Study of the Silk Routes during the Later Han Dynasty, 1st to 2nd Centuries CE* (Scotts Valley, CA, 2009), p. 27.

2 Prior to this was Aramashi-kyō (today known as Fujiwara-kyō), which was built on a grid but with the palace in the centre. It was built in 694 and abandoned in 710.

3 See Ronald Toby, 'Why Leave Nara? Kammu and the Transfer of the Capital', *Monumenta Nipponica*, XL/3 (Autumn 1985), pp. 331–471.

4 See George Elison, 'Hideyoshi, the Bountiful Minister', in *Warlords, Artists, and Commoners: Japan in the Sixteenth Century*, ed. George Elison and Bardwell Smith (Honolulu, HI, 1981), pp. 223–44.

5 For a study of this phenomenon, and the expression used here, see Constantine Vaporis, *Tour of Duty: Samurai, Military Service in Edo, and the Culture of Early Modern Japan* (Honolulu, HI, 2008).

6 This term is from Matthew McKelway, *Capitalscapes: Folding Screens and Political Imagination in Late Medieval Kyoto* (Honolulu, HI, 2006).

7 For this process see Eiko Ikegami, *The Taming of the Samurai: Honorific Individualism and the Making of Modern Japan* (Cambridge, 1997), and Ujiie Miko, *Bushidō to erosu* (Kōdansha, 1995).

8 Shiba Kōkan, letter of 1813, see Timon Screech, trans. and ed., 'Comparisons of Cities', in *An Edo Anthology: Literature from Japan's Mega-City, 1750–1850*, ed. Sumie Jones (Honolulu, HI, 2013), pp. 443–65: p. 453. The person referred to was probably the artist Aikawa Hidenari (studio name: Minwa).

9 Ibid., p. 542.

10 See for example Kusumi Shigetoki, *Naniwa no kaze* [c. 1855], translated by Gerald Groemer as 'Breezes of Osaka' in his *The Land we Saw, the Times we Knew* (Honolulu, HI, 2019), pp. 299–324: p. 299.

11 'Kyō nite mo kyō natsukashiki ya hototogisu', Matsuo Bashō [1680] quoted in Ogata Tsutomu, ed., *Shinpen: Bashō taisei* (Sanshōdō, 1999), pp. 77, 122. Ogata insists on the reading *kyō*, not *miyako*.

12 Kimuro Bōun, *Mita kyō monogatari* [1781], translated by Timon Screech as 'Tales of the Kyō I Have Seen' in *An Edo Anthology*, ed. Jones, pp. 454–65: p. 463. See also Gerald Groemer, trans., 'Kyoto Observed', in *The Land we Saw*, pp. 194–219.

Two The Centre of the Shogun's Realm

1 Quoted in Akisato Ritō, *Miyako meisho zue* [1780]. See Takemura Toshinori, ed., *Nihon meisho fūzoku zue*, vol. VIII (Kadokawa, 1981), p. 22.

2 For details see Michael Cooper, *The Japanese Mission to Europe, 1582–1590: The Journey of Four Samurai Boys through Portugal, Spain and Italy* (Tenterden, 2005), and Derek Massarella, ed., *Japanese Travellers in Sixteenth-century Europe: A Dialogue Concerning the Mission of the Japanese Ambassadors to the Roman Curia (1590)*, trans. J. F. Moran (Farnham, 2012).

3 Volume one appeared in 1572, and volume two in 1588. The eventual publication would have six volumes and be completed only in 1617.

4 The screen is now paired with a world map, both are in the collection
  of Sannomaru Shōzō-kan (Museum of the Imperial Collections),
  Tokyo.

5 For this phenomenon see Edward Kamens, *Utamakura, Allusion, and
  Intertextuality in Traditional Japanese Poetry* (New Haven, CT, 1997).

6 'Koma tomete sode uchiharau kage mo nashi Sano no watari no
  yuki no yūgure'. *Shin-kokinshū* (New Anthology of Verses Ancient
  and Modern), no. 671. All editions of the New Anthology follow the
  classical numbering of the verses.

7 *The Tale of the Heike* [c. 1325], trans. Helen McCullough (Stanford,
  CA, 1988), p. 154.

8 'Samushiro ya matsu ya no aki no kaze fukete tsuki wo katashiku uji
  no hashi hime'. *Shin-kokinshū*, no. 420.

9 John Kieschnick, *The Impact of Buddhism on Chinese Material Culture*
  (Princeton, NJ, 2003), pp. 201–11.

10 Nigita Yūgi, *Nagasaki meishō zue* [c. 1800], in Takemura Toshinori, ed.,
  Nihon meisho fūzoku zue, vol. xv (Kadokawa, 1983), pp. 33–240:
  pp. 36–7. Popularly known as the 'Spectacles Bridge' (*megane-bashi*),
  it was technically the Tenth Bridge.

11 Ibid.

12 Leonard Blussé and Cynthia Viallé, eds, *The Deshima Dagregisters*,
  12 vols (Leiden, 1986–2005), pp. 346 and 358.

13 Saitō Yukio et al., *Edo meisho zue* [1834], in *Nihon meisho fūzoku zue*,
  vol. iv, ed. Matsubara Hideaki (Kadokawa, 1981), p. 207.

14 This suggestion is not well attested, but see https://ja.wikipedia.org/
  wiki/太鼓橋_(目黒区), accessed 3 March 2019.

15 Eiko Ikegami, *Bonds of Civility: Aesthetic Networks and the Political
  Origins of Japanese Culture* (Cambridge, MA, 2005), pp. 307–8.

16 See Thomas F. Cleary, trans., *Entry into the Realm of Reality: The Text –
  The 'Gandavyuha', the Final Book of the 'Avatamsaka Sutra'* (Boston,
  MA, and Shaftesbury, 1987).

17 Ibid., p. 394.

18 See Yagi Kiyoharu, 'Keisei-ron no keifu', in *Nihon shisōshi kōza*, vol. iii
  (Perikansha, 2012), pp. 331–62.

19 Hamada Giichirō, ed., *Edo bungaku chimei jiten* (Tōkyōdō, 1973),
  p. 49.

20 Ibid.

21 Timon Screech, *The Shogun's Painted Culture: Fear and Creativity in the Japanese States, 1760–1829* (London, 2000), pp. 112–18, and Anne Walthall, 'Hiding the Shoguns: Secrecy and the Nature of Political Authority in Tokugawa Japan', in *The Culture of Secrecy in Japanese Religion*, ed. Bernard Scheid and Mark Teeuwen (London, 2006), pp. 331–56.

22 Nishiyama Matsunosuke et al., eds, *Edo-gaku jiten* (Kōbunsha, 1994), pp. 284–5.

23 The Ming coin issued by the Yongle Emperor (r. 1402–24), known as the *Yongle tongbao*, was used in Japan (pronounced *Eiraku tsūhō*); it was also minted locally, though highly debased. The ban of 1608 was not effective and was even revoked. The coin was only removed in 1670; sees Norman Jacobs and Cornelius Vermeule, *Japanese Coinage: A Monetary History of Japan* (New York, 1972), pp. 19, 27, and 'History of Japanese Coins' at www.mint.go.jp/eng/kids-eng/eng_kids_index.html, accessed 3 March 2019.

24 Tsunoyama Sakae, *Tokei no shakaishi* (Chūō Shinsho, 1984), p. 78.

25 Yosa Buson, *Mukashi o ima* [1774], in *Buson zenshū: Haishi bun*, vol. IV, ed. Ogata Tsutomu (Kōdansha, 1992–2009 [2001]), pp. 139–40. I am grateful to Minka Kulenovic for this reference.

26 Tsunoyama, *Tokei no shakaishi*, p. 78.

27 Ibid., pp. 78–9.

28 Illus. 36 suggests that this label was inscribed on the house.

29 Leonard Blussé and Cynthia Viallé, eds, *The Deshima Dagregisters*, vol. XI (Leiden, 2001), p. 54.

30 Timon Screech, ed., *Japan Extolled and Decried: Carl Peter Thunberg and the Shogun's Realm* (London, 2005), p. 149.

31 Ibid.

32 Leonard Blussé and Cynthia Viallé, eds, *The Deshima Dagregisters*, vol. XII (Leiden, 2005), pp. 294–8.

33 Ibid., p. 337.

34 Ibid., pp. 376, 408.

35 'Kapitan mo tsukabahasekeri kimi ga haru' [1778], quoted in Ogata, ed., *Shinpen: Bashō taisei*, vol. IV, p. 5.

36 'Oranda mo hana ni kinkeri uma no kura'. *Bashō kushū*, in *Nihon koten bungaku taikei*, vol. XLV, ed. Ōtani Tokuzō (Iwanami, 1962), p. 51.

37 Yanagisawa Kien, *Hitorine* [1724–5], in *Nihon koten bungaku taikei*, vol. XLVI (Iwanami, 1965), pp. 27–208: p. 169.

38 'Kore ni nomi tsūji wa irezu wakaruran kapitan no kiku kokuchō no kane'.

39 'Kokuchō no kane oranda o odorokashi'. *Haifū yanagidaru, kei*, 17.

40 Blussé and Viallé, eds, *Deshima Dagregisters*, vol. XII, p. 409.

41 Engelbert Kaempfer, *Kaempfer's Japan: Tokugawa Culture Observed*, trans. Beatrice Bodart-Bailey (Honolulu, HI, 1999), p. 350.

42 'Echigoya e iku uki-e no kazu no hairu'. For 'perspective pictures' showing the Echigo-ya, see Kishi Fumikazu, *Edo no enkinhō: uki-e no shikaku* (Keiso, 1994), pp. 33–5.

Three Edo as Sacred Space

1 See Nam-lin Hur, *Prayer and Play in Late Tokugawa Japan: Asakusa Sensoji and Edo Society* (Cambridge, MA, 2000).

2 See Terumi Toyama, 'The Significance of Copying: Replication of Kyoto's Sacred Spaces in Seventeenth Century Edo', unpublished PhD thesis, SOAS, University of London (2017), pp. 253–84.

3 Royall Tyler, trans. and ed., *Japanese Nō Dramas* (London, 1992), p. 66.

4 This is the account in *Heike monogatari* (early thirteenth century); see *The Tale of the Heike*, trans. Helen McCullough (Stanford, CA, 1988), p. 226. In this version, the goddess appears in the form of a dragon.

5 Andrew Watsky, *Chikubushima: Deploying the Sacred Arts in Momoyama Japan* (Seattle, WA, 2004), p. 208.

6 See Toyama, 'The Significance of Copying', pp. 188–222.

7 'Tobu ka to mieru kiyomizu no niwaka ame', *Haifu yanagidaru 86/20*.

8 Akisato Ritō, *Miyako meisho zue* [1780], in *Nihon meisho fūzoku zue*, vol. VIII, ed. Matsubara Hideaki (Kadokawa, 1981), p. 61.

9 Henry Smith, *Hiroshige's One Hundred Views of Edo* (New York, 1999), cat. 69.

10 The anonymous anthology is known as the *Haifū yanagidaru* (Comic Willow Tub), Okada Hajime, ed., *Haifū yanag darui zenshū* (Sanseido, 1999), 6 vols.

11 'Edo kenbutsu no yuitsu ha zeni to kane'. *Haifū yanagidaru, 36/17*.

12 'Kingin wa gyokuza de zeni wa ohizamoto'. *Haifū yanagidaru, 36/21*.

13 'Miyako no tera ryōgae shite edo e tatsu'. *Haifū yanagidaru, 32/9*.

14 The name can also be read Zonnō. As 'National Teacher' he was known as Fukō Kanchi Kokushi.

15 Sonehara Satoshi, *Shinkun ieyasu no tanjō* (Yoshikawa Kōbunkan, 2008), pp. 131–2.

16 William Coaldrake, 'The Mystery of the Meiji Model of the Shogun's Mausoleum', *Orientations*, XXXVII/4 (2006), pp. 34–40.

17 Sonehara, *Shinkun ieyasu*, pp. 123–4.

18 'Edo no zu ni ten o uttaru tsukuda-jima', quoted in *Edo bungaku chimei jiten*, ed. Hamada Giichirō (Tōkyōdō, 1973), p. 320.

19 Nishiyama Matsunosuke et al., eds, *Edo-gaku jiten* (Kōbunsha, 1994), p. 134.

20 Timon Screech, *The Lens within the Heart: The Western Scientific Gaze and Popular Imagery in Later Edo Japan*, 2nd edn (Honolulu, HI, 2002), pp. 244–7.

21 Hiruma Hisashi, *Edo no kaichō* (Yoshikawa Kōbunkan, 1980), pp. 43–8.

22 Leonard Blussé and Cynthia Viallé, eds, *The Deshima Dagregisters*, vol. X (Leiden, 1997), p. 88.

23 See Timon Screech, 'The Strangest Place in Edo: The Temple of the Five Hundred Arhats', *Monumenta Nipponica*, XLVIII/4 (Winter 1993), pp. 407–28.

24 Takahashi Ben, *Ikigaeru rakan-tachi: Tōkyō no Gohyaku rakan* (Ten'on-zan Gohyaku Rakanji, 1981), pp. 37–78.

25 'Bakuro-chō gohyaku no asu wa yonjūshichi'. *Haifū yanagidaru*, 8/104.

26 See Screech, 'Strangest Place', fig. 14.

27 Morishima Chūryō, *Kōmō zatsuwa* [1787], in *Edo kagaku koten sōsho*, vol. XXXI (Inawa, 1980), pp. 7–228: pp. 60–62, 68–77. Today the mythical Vulture Peak is associated with Gijjhakuta, near the Indian city of Rajgir, and not with the mountain in Sri Lanka.

28 Ibid., pp. 59–62.

29 N.H.N. Mody, *A Collection of Nagasaki Colour Prints and Paintings* (Rutland, VT, 1969), comments to plate 189.

Four Reading Edo Castle

1 This was an old expression and is perhaps apocryphally attributed to Ieyasu. It appears in his 'testament' (*Tōshōgū go-ikun*) and is often cited. See, *inter alia*, Sonehara Satoshi, *Shinkun ieyasu no tanjō*

(Yoshikawa Kōbunkan, 2008), p. 125. The full phrase is 'the tenka
is not the tenka of one person, but is the tenka of the tenka.' The
document is translated by A. L. Sadler as 'The Empire does not belong
to the Empire, neither does it belong to one man'; see his *The Maker of
Modern Japan: The Life of Shogun Tokugawa Ieyasu*, 2nd edn (Rutland,
VT, 1978), p. 387.

2 William Coaldrake, *Architecture and Authority in Japan* (London,
1996), pp. 129–37.

3 For a reproduction see www.digital.archives.go.jp/das/image-l/
M2010021217530946918, accessed 1 December 2018.

4 Herman Ooms, *Tokugawa Ideology: Early Constructs* (Ann Arbor, MI,
1998), pp. 65, 106.

5 Coaldrake, *Architecture and Authority*, pp. 193–207.

6 For two existing English-language appraisals of Nijō's extant rooms
see Karen M. Gerhart, *Eyes of Power: Art and Early Tokugawa Authority*
(Honolulu, HI, 1999), pp. 1–35, and Coaldrake, *Architecture and
Authority*, pp. 138–62.

7 Engelbert Kaempfer, *Kaempfer's Japan: Tokugawa Culture Observed*,
trans. Beatrice Bodart-Bailey (Honolulu, HI, 1999), pp. 364–5.

8 Leonard Blussé and Cynthia Viallé, eds, *The Deshima Dagregisters*,
vol. XIII (Leiden, 2010), p. 332.

9 Kano Yasunobu, *Gadō yōketsu*, in *Nihon garon taisei*, vol. IV, ed. Kōno
Motoaki et al. (Perikansha, 1997), pp. 7–110: p. 10.

10 Penelope Mason, 'Seisen'in and His Sketches: A Kanō Master and Edo
Castle', *Monumenta Nipponica*, XLIII/2 (Summer 1988), pp. 187–96:
p. 188.

Five The City's Poetic Presence

1 Robert Brower and Earl Miner, *Japanese Court Poetry* (Stanford, CA,
1961), pp. 14–15, 231–3 and *passim*.

2 'Yuku sue wa sora mo hitotsu no musashino ni, kusa no hara yori izuru
tsukikage'. *Shin-kokinshū*, no. 422.

3 'Musashino wa tsuki no irubeki mine mo nashi obana ga sue ni kakaru
shirakumo'. *Zoku-kokinshū*, no. 426. Minamoto no Michikata is also
known as Tsuchimikado Motochika.

4 For the link to Eitoku, see Joshua Mostow, *Courtly Visions: The Ise Stories
and the Politics of Cultural Appropriation* (Leiden, 2015), pp. 186–9.

5 See Laura Nenzi, *Excursions in Identity: Travel and the Intersection of Place, Gender, and Status in Edo Japan* (Honolulu, HI, 2008), p. 97.

6 Shiba Keiko, *Literary Creations of the Road: Women's Travel Diaries in Early Modern Japan*, trans. Motoko Ezaki (Lanham, MD, 2012), pp. 29–30.

7 The play has been translated by Susan Blackley Klein in Karen Brazell, ed., *Twelve Plays of the Noh and Kyogen Theatres* (Ithaca, NY, 1988), pp. 63–80.

8 This information is derived from www.mokuboji.com, accessed 23 December 2017.

9 Frank Feltens, 'Ogata Kōrin (1658–1716) and the Possibilities of Painting in Early Modern Japan', unpublished PhD dissertation, Columbia University, New York (2016), p. 103. My comments on Kōrin's biography are also from this source.

10 Letter to Ueshima Gennojō (1708 or 1709[?]), translated ibid., pp. 202–3.

Six A Trip to the Yoshiwara

1 The only previous treatments are Watanabe Shin'ichi, 'Yoshiwara e no michi', *Kokubungaku: Kaishaku to Kanshō*, 473 (1971), pp. 8–22, republished in Satō Yōjin, ed., *Senryū Yoshiwara fūzoku zue* (Chibunkaku, 1972). For a later period, see Robert Campbell, 'Poems on the Way to Yoshiwara', in *Imaging/Reading Eros: Proceedings for the Conference 'Sexuality and Edo Culture, 1750–1850'*, ed. Sumie Jones (Bloomington, IN, 1996), pp. 95–7. One contemporary text on the topic is Sobu Rokurō, *Yoshiwara fūzoku shiryō* (Tokyo: Bungei shiryō kenkyūkai, 1931), pp. 71–125, translated by Helen Nagata, 'Notes on a Guide to Love in the Yoshiwara', in *Seduction: Japan's Floating World: The John C. Weber Collection*, ed. Laura Allen (San Francisco, CA, 2015), pp. 219–38.

2 'Ni ka koku no mannaka o yuku sono hayasa'. *Haifū yanagidaru*, 31/31.

3 Henry Smith, *Hiroshige's One Hundred Views of Edo* (New York, 1988), calls it the 'Pine of Success' without noting the sense of inversion, cat. 61.

4 'Chokibune wa mina shiinoki e ya o hanasu nari'. Quoted in Hamada Giichirō, ed., *Edo bungaku chimei jiten* (Tōkyōdō, 1973), p. 205.

5 'Shiinoki wa tonosama yori mo na ga takaki' and 'Hidari yori migi ni miru shii omoshiroi'. Quoted in Hamada, ed., *Edo bungaku*, p. 205.

6 'Noborubeki tayori nakereba kinomoto ni shii o hiroite yo wo wataru ya'. See Shinpen kokka taikan, ed., *Shinpen kokka taikan*, vol. v (Kadokawa, 1989), p. 1168.

7 'Shiinoki wa ima mo kakurete yuku todoko'. Quoted in Watanabe, 'Yoshiwara', p. 17.

8 'Dote e torii ga merikonda yō ni mie'. *Haifū yanagidaru*, 36/32.

9 Anon., *Yoshiwara koi no michibiki*, in *Yoshiwara fūzoku shiryō*, ed. Sobu Rokurō (Tokyo: Bungei shiryō kenkyūkai, 1931), pp. 71–125; pp. 83 and 115. For a translation of the whole text, see Nagata, 'Notes on a Guide to Love in the Yoshiwara', pp. 219–38.

10 'Kimi ya koshi ware ya yukiken oboezu yume ka utsutsu ka nete ka samite ka'. *Shin-kokinshū*, 645.

11 'Kakikurezu kokoro no yume ni madoi ni ki yume utsutsu to ha yonobito sadamete'. *Shin-kokinshū*, 646.

12 'Kawara shi wa shitafuri suru miyakodori'. Quoted in Kubota Hiroshi, 'Shin-yoshiwara kaiwai', *Kokubungaku: Kaishaku to Kanshō*, 473 (1971), pp. 249–62: p. 260.

13 It was also claimed the name 'Japan' was applied because daimyo from across the country were required to fund the embankment; see anon., *Yoshiwara koi no michibiki* (1678), p. 85.

14 'Gokuraku to jigoku no michi wa san'ya-bashi'. *Haifū yanagidaru*, 76/9.

15 Sharaku-sai Manri, *Tōsei anabanashi*, quoted in Nakamura Yukihiko, 'Gesaku-ron', in *Nakamura Yukihiko chōbetsu-shū*, vol. VIII (Chūō Kōronsha, 1982), p. 124.

16 'Nakajuku no mae o genzoku o waratte'ku'. *Haifū yanagidaru*, 2/173.

17 'Hana no kumo kane wa ueno ka asakusa ka'. Quoted in *Bashō kushū*, in *Nihon koten bungaku taikei*, vol. XLV (Iwanami, 1962), p. 53.

18 'Dote o yuku isha wa ueno ka asakusa ka'. *Haifū yanagidaru*, 5/189 and 5/292.

19 Quoted in Nakamura, 'Gesaku-ron', p. 124.

20 'Shōtō-ji nani karetsuba to sugu tōri'. *Haifū yanagidaru*, 6/38.

21 See Hamada, ed., *Edo bungaku*, p. 371.

22 Moriyama Takamori, *Shizu no odamaki*, in *Nihon zuihitsu taisei*, series 3, vol. XXII (Yoshikawa Kōbunkan, 1974), pp. 225–67: p. 240.

23 'Toshidoshi saisai kyaku o yobu tame ni ue'. Quoted in Osaka Hōichi and Segawa Yoshio, 'Yoshiwara nenchū gyōji', *Kokubungaku: Kaishaku to Kanshō*, 473 (1971), pp. 78–107: p. 83.

24 Mitamura Engyō, 'Jikoku no hanashi', in *Mitamura Engyō zenshū*, vol. VII (Chūō Kōronsha, 1975), pp. 264–8.

25 Cecilia Seigle, *Yoshiwara: The Glittering World of the Japanese Courtesan* (Honolulu, HI, 1993), p. 23.

26 For an example see Nakano Mitsutoshi, 'Edo no yūri', in *Kyōden, Ikku, Shunsui*, Zusetsu: Nihon no koten vol. XVIII, ed. Kobayashi Tadashi et al. (Shūeisha, 1989), pp. 121–39: p. 132.

27 'Modoru choki daruma mo areba ne-jaka ari'. *Haifū yanagidaru*, 1/36.

28 'Yuku choki wa zazō kaeru choki ne-jaka'. *Haifū yanagidaru*, 160/38.

Selected Sources
and Further Reading

As the place of publication for all Japanese books is Tokyo, the publisher's name is given instead.

The following works were of particular value in preparing this book:

Hamada Giichirō, ed., *Edo bungaku chimei jiten* (Tōkyōdō, 1973)

Naitō Masatoshi, *Mato edo no toshi keikaku: Tokugawa shogun-ke no shirarezaru yabō* (Yōsensha, 1996)

Nishiyama Matsunosuke et al., eds, *Edo-gaku jiten* (Kōbunsha, 1994)

Okada Hajime et al., eds, *Haifū yanagidaru zenshū*, 13 vols (Sanseidō, 1999)

Ozawa Hiromu, *Toshi-zu keifu to edo* (Yoshikawa kōbun-kan, 2002)

Saitō Yukio et al., *Edo meisho zue* [1800], in *Nihon fūzoku meisho zue*, vol. IV, ed. Matsubara Hideaki (Kadokawa, 1981)

Toyama Terumi, 'The Significance of Copying: Replication of Kyoto's Sacred Spaces in Seventeenth Century Edo', unpublished PhD thesis, SOAS, University of London (2017)

The following works in English on the history of Edo and Tokyo are recommended for further reading:

Clements, Jonathan, *An Armchair Traveller's History of Tokyo* (London, 2018)

Enbutsu Sumiko, *Discover Shitamachi: A Walking Guide to the Other Tokyo*, 2nd edn (Shitamachi Times, 1986)

Groemer, Gerald, trans. and ed., *Portraits of Edo and Early Modern Japan: The Shogun's Capital in* Zuihitsu *Writings, 1657–1855* (Honolulu, HI, 2019)

Jinnai Hidenobu, 'The Spatial Structure of Edo', in *Tokugawa Japan: The Social and Economic Antecedents of Modern Japan*, ed. Chie Nakane and Shinzaburo Oishi (Tokyo University Press, 1992), pp. 124–46

Kinda, Akihiro, ed., *A Landscape History of Japan* (Kyoto, 2010)

Naito Akira et al., trans. and adapt. Mack Horton, *Edo, the City that Became Tokyo: An Illustrated History* (Kodansha International, 2003)

Nouët, Noël, *The Shogun's City* (London, 1990)

Rozman, Gilbert, *Urban Networks in Ch'ing China and Tokugawa Japan* (Princeton, NJ, 1973)

Seidensticker, Edward, *Low City, High City: Tokyo from Edo to the Earthquake* (Cambridge, MA, 1991)

Smith, Henry, *Hiroshige's One Hundred Views of Edo* (New York, 1988)

Sorensen, Andre, *The Making of Urban Japan: Cities and Planning from Edo to the Twenty-first Century* (Oxford, 2002)

Waley, Paul, *Tokyo: City of Stories* (New York, 1991)

——, and Nicolas Fiévé, eds, *Japanese Capitals in Historical Perspective: Place, Power and Memory in Kyoto, Edo and Tokyo* (Richmond, Surrey, 2000)

Yonemoto, Marcia, 'Nihonbashi: Edo's Contested Center', *East Asian History*, 17–18 (1999), pp. 49–71

The following works in English on the cultural history of the Edo period
are recommended for further reading:

Gerhart, Karen M., *Eyes of Power: Art and Early Tokugawa Authority*
(Honolulu, HI, 1999)
Guth, Christine, *Art of Edo Japan: The Artist and the City, 1615–1868*
(New Haven, CT, 2010)
Jones, Sumie, ed., *An Edo Anthology: Literature from Japan's Mega-City,
1750–1850* (Honolulu, HI, 2013)
Nakane, Chie, and Shinzaburo Oishi, eds, *Tokugawa Japan: The Social and
Economic Antecedents of Modern Japan* (Tokyo University Press, 1992)
Nishiyama Matsunosuke, *Edo Culture: Daily Life and Diversions in Urban
Japan, 1600–1868* (Honolulu, HI, 1997)
Screech, Timon, *Obtaining Images: Art Production and Display in Edo Japan*
(London, 2012)

General Bibliography

Akisato Ritō, *Miyako meisho zue* [1780], in *Nihon meisho fūzoku zue*, ed. Matsubara Hideaki, vol. VIII (Kadokawa, 1981)

Anonymous, *Tales of the Heike*, trans. Helen Craig McCullough (Stanford, CA, 1988)

Anonymous, *Yoshiwara koi no michibiki* (1678), in *Yoshiwara fūzoku shiryō*, ed. Sobu Rokurō (Bungei shiryō kenkyūkai, 1931), pp. 71–125

Asakura Haruhiko, ed., *Nihon meisho fūzoku zue* (Kadokawa, 1980)

Berry, Mary Elizabeth, *Hideyoshi* (Cambridge, 1982)

Blussé, Leonard, and Cynthia Viallé, eds, *The Deshima Dagregisters*, 13 vols (Leiden, 1986–2010)

Brazell, Karen, ed., *Twelve Plays of the Noh and Kyogen Theatres* (Ithaca, NY, 1988)

Brower, Robert, and Earl Miner, *Japanese Court Poetry* (Stanford, CA, 1961)

Campbell, Robert, 'Poems on the Way to Yoshiwara', in *Imaging/Reading Eros: Proceedings for the Conference 'Sexuality and Edo Culture, 1750–1850'*, ed. Sumie Jones (Bloomington, IN, 1996), pp. 95–7

Cleary, Thomas, trans., *Entry into the Realm of Reality: The Text – The 'Gandavyuha', The Final Book of the 'Avatamsaka Sutra'* (Boston, MA, and Shaftesbury, 1987)

Coaldrake, William, 'The Mystery of the Meiji Model of the Shogun's Mausoleum', *Orientations*, XXXVII/4 (2006), pp. 34–40

——, *Architecture and Authority in Japan* (London, 1996)

Cooper, Michael, *The Japanese Mission to Europe, 1582–1590* (Folkestone, 2005)

Elison, George, 'Hideyoshi, the Bountiful Minister', in *Warlords, Artists and Commoners: Japan in the Sixteenth Century*, ed. George Elison and Bardwell Smith (Honolulu, HI, 1981), pp. 223–44

Feltens, Frank, 'Ogata Kōrin (1658–1716) and the Possibilities of Painting in Early Modern Japan', unpublished PhD dissertation, Columbia University, New York (2016)

Groemer, Gerald, trans. and ed., *Portraits of Edo and Early Modern Japan: The Shogun's Capital in Zuihitsu Writings, 1657–1855* (Honolulu, HI, 2019)

Hill, John E., *Through the Jade Gate to Rome: A Study of the Silk Routes during the Later Han Dynasty, 1st to 2nd Centuries CE* (Scotts Valley, CA, 2009)

Hiruma Hisashi, *Edo no kaichō* (Yoshikawa Kōbunkan, 1980)

Hur, Nam-lin, *Prayer and Play in Late Tokugawa Japan: Asakusa Sensōji and Edo Culture* (Cambridge, MA, 2000)

Ikegami, Eiko, *Bonds of Civility: Aesthetic Networks and the Political Origins of Japanese Culture* (New York and Cambridge, 2005)

——, *The Taming of the Samurai: Honorific Individualism and the Making of Modern Japan* (Cambridge, MA, 1997)

Jacobs, Norman, and Cornelius Vermeule, *Japanese Coinage* (New York, 1972)

Kaempfer, Engelbert, *Kaempfer's Japan: Tokugawa Culture Observed*, trans. Beatrice Bodart-Bailey (Honolulu, HI, 1999)

Kamens, Edward, *Utamakura, Allusion, and Intertextuality in Traditional Japanese Poetry* (New Haven, CT, 1997)

Kano Yasunobu, *Gadō yōketsu*, in *Nihon garon taisei*, vol. IV, ed. Kōno Motoaki et al. (Perikansha, 1997), pp. 7–110

Kieschnick, John, *The Impact of Buddhism on Chinese Material Culture* (Princeton, NJ, 2003)

Kimuro Bōun, *Mita kyō monogatari* [1781], trans. by Timon Screech as 'Tales of the Kyō I Have Seen', in *An Edo Anthology: Literature from Japan's Mega-city, 1750–1850*, ed. Sumie Jones (Honolulu, HI, 2013), pp. 454–65

——, *Mita kyō monogatari* [1781], trans. by Gerald Groemer as 'Kyoto Observed', in Groemer, *The Land we Saw, the Times we Knew* (Honolulu, HI, 2019), pp. 194–229

Kishi Fumikazu, *Edo no enkinhō: uki-e no shikaku* (Keiso, 1994)

Kubota Hiroshi, 'Shin-yoshiwara kaiwai', *Kokubungaku: Kaishaku to Kanshō*, CCCVXXIII (1971), pp. 249–62

Kuroda Hideo, *Edo-zu byōbu no nazo o toku* (Kadokawa Gakugei, 2010)

Kusumi Shigetoki, *Naniwa no kaze* [*c.* 1855], trans. by Gerald Groemer as 'Breezes of Osaka', in Groemer, *The Land we Saw, the Times we Knew* (Honolulu, HI, 2019), pp. 299–324

Lippit, Yukio, *Painting of the Realm: The Kano House of Painters in 17th-century Japan* (Seattle, WA, 2012)

McClain, Ian, et al., eds, *Edo and Paris* (Ithaca, NY, 1995)

McKelway, Matthew, *Capitalscapes: Folding Screens and Political Imagination in Late Medieval Kyoto* (Honolulu, HI, 2006)

Mason, Penelope, 'Seisen'in and His Sketches: A Kanō Master and Edo Castle', *Monumenta Nipponica*, XLIII/2 (1988), pp. 187–96

Massarella, Derek, ed., *Japanese Travellers in Sixteenth-century Europe: A Dialogue Concerning the Mission of the Japanese Ambassadors to the Roman Curia (1590)*, trans. J. F. Moran (Farnham, 2012)

Matsudaira Sadanobu, *Taikan zakki* [1795–7], in *Zoku Nihon zuihitsu taisei*, vol. VI (Yoshikawa Kōbunkan, 1980), pp. 25–253

Mitamura Engyō, 'Jikoku no hanashi', in *Mitamura Engyō zenshū*, vol. VII (Chūō Kōronsha, 1975), pp. 264–8

Miyamoto Kenji, *Edo no onmyōshi: Tenkai no randosukeepu dezain* (Jinbun Shoin, 2001)

Mody, N.H.N., *A Collection of Nagasaki Colour Prints and Paintings* (Rutland, VT, 1969)

Morikawa Kenroku, ed., *Haibun haiku sen*, in *Nihon meichō zenshū* (Nihon meichō zenshū kankō-kai, 1928), vol. XXVII, pp. 235–6

Morishima Chūryō, *Kōmō zatsuwa*, in *Edo kagaku koten sōsho*, vol. XXXI (Inawa, 1980), pp. 7–228

Moriyama Takamori, *Shizu no odamaki*, in *Nihon zuihitsu taisei*, series 3, vol. XXII (Yoshikawa Kōbunkan, 1974), pp. 225–67

Mostow, Joshua, *Courtly Visions: The Ise Stories and the Politics of Cultural Appropriation* (Leiden, 2015)

Nagata, Helen, trans., 'Notes on a Guide to Love in the Yoshiwara', translation of anon., *Yoshiwara koi no michibiki* [1678], in *Seduction: Japan's Floating World: The John C. Weber Collection*, ed. Laura Allen (San Francisco, CA, 2015), pp. 219–38

Nakamura Yukihiko, 'Gesaku-ron', in *Nakamura Yukihiko chojutsu-shū*, vol. VIII (Chūō Kōronsha, 1982)

Nakano Mitsutoshi, 'Edo no yūri', in *Kyōden, Ikku, Shunsui, Zusetsu: Nihon no koten*, vol. XVIII, ed. Kobayashi Tadashi et al. (Shūei-sha, 1980), pp. 121–39

Nenzi, Laura, *Excursions in Identity: Travel and the Intersection of Place, Gender, and Status in Edo Japan* (Honolulu, HI, 2008)

Nigita Yūgi, *Nagasaki meishō zue* [c. 1800], in *Nihon meisho fūzoku zue*, vol. XV, ed. Ikeda Yosaburō et al. (Kadokawa, 1983), pp. 33–240

Ogata Tsutomu, ed., *Shinpen: Bashō taisei* (Sanshōdō, 1999)

Ooms, Herman, *Tokugawa Ideology: Early Constructs* (Ann Arbor, MI, 1998)

Ōsaka Hōichi and Segawa Yoshio, 'Yoshiwara nenchū gyōji', *Kokubungaku: Kaishaku to Kanshō*, CCCCVXXIII (1971), pp. 78–107

Rosenfield, John M., *Preserving the Dharma: Hōzan Tankai and Japanese Buddhist Art of the Early Modern Era* (Princeton, NJ, 2015)

Sadler, A. L., *The Maker of Modern Japan: The Life of Shogun Tokugawa Ieyasu*, 2nd edn (Rutland, VT, 1978)

Satō Yōjin, ed., *Senryū Yoshiwara fūzoku zue* (Chibunkaku, 1972)

Screech, Timon, 'Comparisons of Cities', in *An Edo Anthology: Literature from Japan's Mega-city, 1750–1850*, ed. Sumie Jones (Honolulu, HI, 2013), pp. 443–65

——, *Edo no ōbushin: Tokugawa toshi keikaku no shigaku*, trans. Morishita Masaaki (Kōdansha, 2007)

——, *The Lens within the Heart: The Western Scientific Gaze and Popular Imagery in Later Edo Japan*, 2nd edn (Honolulu, HI, 2002)

——, *The Shogun's Painted Culture: Fear and Creativity in the Japanese States, 1760–1829* (London, 2000)

——, 'The Strangest Place in Edo: The Temple of the Five Hundred Arhats', *Monumenta Nipponica*, XLVIII/4 (Winter 1993), pp. 407–28

——, ed. and intro., *Japan Extolled and Decried: Carl Peter Thunberg and the Shogun's Realm, 1775–1796* (London, 2005)

Seigle, Cecilia, *Yoshiwara: The Glittering World of the Japanese Courtesan* (Honolulu, HI, 1993)

Shiba Keiko, *Literary Creations of the Road: Women's Travel Diaries in Early Modern Japan*, trans. Motoko Ezaki (Lanham, MD, 2012)

Sonehara Satoshi, *Shinkun ieyasu no tanjō: tōshōgō to gongen-sama* (Yoshikawa Kōbunsha, 2008)

Suzuki Ikkei, *Onmyō-dō: jujitsu to mashin no sekai* (Kōdansha, 2002)

Suzuki Masao, *Edo no hashi* (Sanseidō, 2006)

Takahashi Ben, *Ikigaeru rakan-tachi: Tōkyō Gohyaku rakan* (Ten'on-zan Gohyaku Rakanji, 1981)

Toby, Ronald, 'Why Leave Nara: Kammu and the Transfer of the Capital', *Monumenta Nipponica*, XL/3 (Autumn 1985), pp. 331–471

Tsunoyama Sakae, *Tokei no shakaishi* (Chūō Kōronsha, 1984)

Tyler, Royall, trans., *Japanese Nō Dramas* (London, 1992)

Ujiie Miko, *Bushidō to erosu* (Kodansha, 1995)

Umehara Takeshi, *Kyōto hakken: chirei chinkon* (Shinchōsha, 1997)

Van Goethem, Ellen, *Nagaoka: Japan's Forgotten Capital* (Leiden, 2008)

Vaporis, Constantine, *Tour of Duty: Samurai, Military Service in Edo and the Culture of Early Modern Japan* (Honolulu, HI, 2008)

Walthall, Anne, 'Hiding the Shoguns: Secrecy and the Nature of Political Authority in Tokugawa Japan', in *The Culture of Secrecy in Japanese Religion*, ed. Bernard Scheid and Mark Teeuwen (London, 2006), pp. 331–56

Ward, Philip, *Japanese Capitals: A Cultural Historical and Artistic Guide to Nara, Kyoto and Tokyo, Successive Capitals of Japan* (Cambridge, 1985)

Watanabe Shin'ichi, 'Yoshiwara e no michi', *Kokubungaku: Kaishaku to Kanshō*, CCCCVXXIII (1971), pp. 8–22

Watsky, Andrew, *Chikubushima: Deploying the Sacred Arts in Momoyama Japan* (Seattle, WA, 2004)

Yagi Kiyoharu, 'Keisei-ron no keifu', in *Nihon shisō kōza*, vol. III (Perikansha, 2012), pp. 331–62

Yanagisawa Kien, *Hitorine* [1724–5], in *Nihon koten bungaku taikei*, vol. XLVI (Iwanami, 1965), pp. 27–208

Yosa Buson, *Mukashi o ima* [1774], in *Buson zenshū: Haishi bun*, vol. IV, ed. Ogata Tsutomu (Kōdansha, 2001), pp. 139–40

Acknowledgements

I would like to thank all the students at SOAS, University of London, to whom I have taught Edo town planning over many years, gaining from their insights and observations. Thanks are also due to James McMullen, who first introduced me to the *Shin-kokinshū*, and to Kasuya Hiroki, who did the same for the *Haifū-yanagidaru*. Citations from both anthologies enrich this book – and also my life. During the process of writing, stimulating colleagues have included Beth Berry, John Carpenter, Tim Clark, Alan Cummings, Julie Davis, Steve Dodd, Lucia Dolce, Drew Gerstle, Fabio Gygi, Enze Han, Katsuya Hirano, Adam Kern, Yukio Lippit, Shane McCausland, Melissa McCormick, Matthew McKelway, Doreen Mueller, Stephen Nelson, Jenny Preston, Matthew Stavros, Terumi Toyama, Melanie Trede, Keith Vincent and many more.

Exploring Edo would never have been possible without first having companions with whom to walk the streets of Tokyo. Special friends are Princess Akiko of Mikasa, Hanano Gōichi, Ken Kondō, Wil Lautenschlager, Masaru Nakao, Klaus Naumann, Gary Perlman and Tan'o Yasunori. Morishita Masaaki helped me at an early stage of this project, while Lucy North read and commented on several versions of the present manuscript. Matsushima Jin has taught me much about power and authority in the Edo period, while Matsuo Hōdō enlightened me about Buddhism. I am always happy to acknowledge my great debts to Kobayashi Tadashi, Takayama Hiroshi and Tanaka Yūko.

Publication support was offered by the Great Britain Sasakawa Foundation and the Japan Research Centre, SOAS, *Fuwaku* funds. Without both, this volume would not have looked as it does.

Photo Acknowledgements

The author and publishers wish to express their thanks to the below sources of illustrative material and/or permission to reproduce it. Every effort has been made to contact copyright holders; should there be any we have been unable to reach or to whom inaccurate acknowledgements have been made please contact the publishers, and full adjustments will be made to any subsequent printings. Some locations of artworks are also given below, in the interest of brevity:

From Enrin Akamatsu, *Hieizan shashinchō* (Sakamoto, 1912), courtesy National Diet Library, Tokyo: 39; Ansharphoto/Shutterstock.com: 17; from the Architectural Institute of Japan [Nihon Kenchiku Gakkai], *Meiji Taishō Kenchiku Shashin Shūran* (Tokyo, 1936), courtesy National Diet Library, Tokyo: 109; Art Gallery of South Australia, Adelaide: 87; Art Institute of Chicago: 52, 57, 58, 107; Asian Art Museum of San Francisco, The Avery Brundage Collection: 96 (B63D7.a-.b); Asian Art Museum of San Francisco, Gift of Edith Fried, photograph © Asian Art Museum of San Francisco: 97 (2005.59); photo Damiano Baschiera/Unsplash: 23; Boston Public Library: 2; Georg Braun and Franz Hogenberg, *Civitates orbis terrarium* (Cologne, 1572): 18, 24; The British Museum, London: 45, 46, 103; The Cleveland Museum of Art, OH: 86, 91; Edo-Tokyo Museum: 67; Eisei Bunko Museum, Tokyo: 95; Freer Gallery of Art, The Gerhard Pulverer Collection, Smithsonian Institution, Washington, DC: 30; Gohyaku Rakanji, Tokyo: 63; Idemitsu Museum of Arts, Tokyo: 4, 20; Jōkō-ji, Nara prefecture: 102; Jukō-in, Kyoto: 70; from Engelbert Kaempfer, J.G. Scheuchzer, trans., *The History of Japan:*

Giving an Account of the Ancient and Present State and Government of that Empire, vol. II (London, 1728): 84; Kimiko and John Powers Collection, Carbondale, CO: 36; Kobe City Museum: 7, 64; Los Angeles County Museum of Art (LACMA): 34; The Metropolitan Museum of Art, New York: 26, 28, 29, 31, 38, 65, 69, 98, 99, 100, 101, 105; MOA Museum of Art, Atami: 94; Museum of Fine Arts, Boston: 32, 43, 48, 51, 53, 59; Museum of the Imperial Collections [Sannomaru-Shōzōkan], Tokyo: 19, 22, 71; National Diet Library, Tokyo: 35, 37, 40, 41, 42, 55, 62, 88, 89, 90, 104; National Museum of Japanese History [Rekihaku], Sakura: 5, 21, 49; Ninomaru Palace, Nijō Castle, Kyoto: 73, 74, 75, 76, 77, 78, 79, 80, 81, 82; private collection: 3, 25, 54; Rijksmuseum, Amsterdam: 106; Royal Collection Trust/© Her Majesty Queen Elizabeth II 2019: 56; photo Timon Screech: 33; Sennyī-ji, Kyoto: 83; courtesy Matthew Stavros: 10, 12; Tokyo National Museum: 85, 92; photo John Tsantes and Neil Greentree, © Robert Feinberg: 44; University of Tokyo, Ono Hideo Collection: 16; Antonio Visentini, *Urbis Venetiarum Prospectus Celebriores* (Venice, 1742), photo Royal Collection Trust/© Her Majesty Queen Elizabeth II 2019: 6; Waseda University Library: 8, 61; courtesy Jan Wignall: 9; World Museum, Liverpool: 60; Yamatane Museum of Art, Tokyo: 93.

Index

Illustration numbers are indicated by *italics*

alternate attendance (*sankin kōtai*) 42
Asakusa Kannon 9, 37, 90–91, 94, 96, 107–9, 111, 122, 187, 195, 202, *95*, *196*
awe (*osore*) 46, 73, 139, 192

Bodhidarma (Daruma) 190, 191, 210, *190*
Braun, Georg, and Franz Hogenberg 54, 62, *55–7*, *62*, *64*

Canaletto 16, *17*
Central States (China) 25–6, 77
China *see* Central States; Ming Dynasty; Tang Dynasty
Chōbunsai Eishi 189, 207–8, *189*, *193*
Christianity 36, 53–4, 58, 130

Dutch 68, 79–84, 122, 125, 127, 156–7

earthquakes 9
Edo meisho zue (Illustrated Famous Places in Edo) 95, *86*, *95*, *114*, *123*
Edo screens (*Edo-zu byōbu*) 13, 46–7
Idemitsu Version 13, 15–16, 130, *13*, *60*
Rekihaku Version 14–16, 77, 105, 130, *14*, *61*, *104*

fengsui see geomancy
fires 22, 23, 68, 82–3, 85, 101
Great Fire of 1657 (*furisode* fire) 15, 46, 131, 186, *49*
Great Fire of Kyoto, 1788 (*tenmei* fire) 50, *50*
floating world (*ukiyo*) 22, 185–91, 196, 206, 207, 209
Fujiwara no Teika 64–5, 67, 162–4

geomancy 18–19, 29–31, 43–4, 89–92, 141
'iconography of absence' 76

Hidden Buddhas (*hibutsu*) 100, 101, 113, 122
hinin (untouchable class) 110, 187

kabuki 16, 110, 186, 203
Kaempfer, Engelbert 85, 156–7, 160, *157*
Kan'ei-ji 93–6, 100, 101, 107, 109, 111, 115, 202, 213, *93*, *95*
Kano Eitoku 135–7, 143, 146, 170, *136*, *137*
Kano Osanobu (Seisen-in), 159, 160, *194*
Kano Tan'yū 138–9, 146, 156–9, 181, 183, *147*, *149*, *150–51*, *182*
Kano Yasunobu 158

Katsushika Hokusai 72, 73–5, 77, 86–7, 102, 120, 126, 133–4, 151, *72–5, 81, 87, 103, 121, 126, 134, 174, 200–201*
Keian Disturbance 131–2
Kitagawa Utamaro 195, 209–10, *207, 209*
Kitao Yoshimasa 75, *76*
Korea 39, 156, *156*
Kurosawa Akira 28, 33, *33*

Matsudaira Sadanobu 22
Matsuo Bashō 48–9, 78, 83
Ming Dynasty 123–5, 135, 183
Mt Fuji 21, 72, 159, 161–3, 166, 168–72, *72,* 180, 183, *76, 86, 87, 126, 134, 166, 172, 180–82*

Nagasaki 32, 36, 41, 68, 79, 122–3, *68*
Nikkō 70–71, 76, 115, 169
nō (Noh) theatre 97, 99, 119–21, 172–3

Ogata Kōrin 176–9, *178*
Osaka 9, 22, 36–8, 41, 48, 51, 79, 99, 118–19

perspective 16, 72, 75–7, 83, 84, 87, 106
poetic pillows (*uta-makura*) 162–5
prostitution *see* sex work
puns and punning 59, 67, 72, 146–7, 152, 163, 169, 193, 199

Rakuchū rakugai zu see 'scenes in and around the *raku*'
Ryukyus, kingdom of the 148

Saga editions (*Saga-bon*) 170–71, *171*
Sakai Hōitsu (Tadanao) 178, *179*
'scenes in and around the *raku*' 44–5, *12*
Sensō-ji *see* Asakusa Kannon
Sesshū Tōyō 181, 183–4, *181*
sex work 21, 186–7, 203
Shrakusai Manri 202–3
Shiba Kōkan 83, 126, 128, *84, 126*
Shikitei Sanba 22, *23*
Shōei Hokuju *111*
Sumiyoshi Gokei *100*
Suzuki Harunobu 102, 118, 191, *103, 117, 190*
Suzuki Kiitsu 179–81, *64–5, 181*
Suzuki Shūitsu 98

Tales of the Heike (*Heike monogatari*) 65
Tales of Ise (*Ise monogatari*) 20, 167–72, 183–4, 196–8, *171, 178–80*
Tang Dynasty 26–7, 93, 119, 144, *24, 173*
Tani Bunchō 125–6, *125*
Tenkai (Nankōbō) 92, 96
Tōkaidō 54, 59, 70, 111, 120, 161, 172, 183
Toyotomi Hideyoshi 35–7, 40, 45, 51–4, 58, 99
Tsutaya Jūzaburō 206, 209

Uji 64–8, 123, 162, 165, *66*
Utagawa Hiroshige 67, 107, 118, 203, 205, *68, 82, 93, 97, 108, 116, 204*
Utagawa Toyoharu 16–18, 63, *17, 106*
Utagawa Toyohiro *118*
Utagawa Toyokuni 22, *23*

Venice 16, 43, 54, 62–3, 76, *62–3*

Yosa Buson 78–9

Zen Buddhism 111, 113–14, 120, 123, 181, 183, 190, 191, 209, 210